Autonomic Systems

The AUTONOMIC SYSTEMS book series provides a platform of communication between academia and industry by publishing research monographs, outstanding PhD theses, and peer-reviewed compiled contributions on the latest developments in the field of autonomic systems.

It covers a broad range of topics from the theory of autonomic systems that are researched by academia and industry. Hence, cutting-edge research, prototypical case studies, as well as industrial applications are in the focus of this book series. Fast reviewing provides a most convenient way to publish latest results in this rapid moving research area.

The topics covered by the series include (among others):

- self-* properties in autonomic systems (e.g. self-management, self-healing)
- architectures, models, and languages for building autonomic systems
- trust, negotiation, and risk management in autonomic systems
- theoretical foundations of autonomic systems
- applications and novel computing paradigms of autonomic systems

For further volumes:
www.springer.com/series/8123

Run-time Models for Self-managing Systems and Applications

Danilo Ardagna
Li Zhang

Editors

 Birkhäuser

Editors

Danilo Ardagna
Dipartimento di Elettronica e Informazione
Politecnico di Milano
Via Golgi 42
20133 Milan
Italy
ardagna@elet.polimi.it

Li Zhang
IBM
Thomas J. Watson Research Center
19 Skyline Drive
Hawthorne, NY 10532
USA
zhangli@us.ibm.com

1998 ACM Computing Classification: C.4 [Performance of Systems]: Fault tolerance; Modeling techniques; Performance attributes; Reliability, availability, and serviceability; D.2.8 [Metrics]: Performance measures; I.2.8 [Problem Solving, Control Methods, and Search]: Control theory

Mathematics Subject Classification (2000): 68-xx, 68M15, 68M20, 68N30, 68-Uxx, 93-04

ISBN 978-3-0346-0432-1   e-ISBN 978-3-0346-0433-8
DOI 10.1007/978-3-0346-0433-8

Cover design: deblik, Berlin

Printed on acid-free paper

Springer Basel AG is part of Springer Science+Business Media

www.birkhauser-science.com

Preface

The complexity of Information Technology (IT) systems has been steadily increasing in the past decades. In October 2001, IBM released the "Autonomic Computing Manifesto" observing that current applications have reached the size of millions of lines of code, while physical infrastructures include thousands of heterogeneous servers requiring skilled IT professionals to install, configure, tune, and maintain. System complexity has been recognized as the main obstacle to the further advancement of IT technology.

The basic idea of Autonomic Computing is to develop IT systems that are able to manage themselves, as the human autonomic nervous system governs basic body functions such as heart rate or body temperature, thus freeing the conscious brain—IT administrators—from the burden of dealing with low-level vital functions.

Autonomic Computing systems can be implemented by introducing autonomic controllers which continuously *monitor*, *analyze*, *plan*, and *execute* (the famous MAPE cycle) reconfiguration actions on the system components. Monitoring activities are deployed to measure the workload and performance metrics of each running component so as to identify system faults. The goal of the analysis activities is to determine the status of components from the monitoring data, and to forecast future conditions based on historical observations. Finally, plan and execute activities aim at deciding and actuating the next system configuration, for example, deciding whether to accept or reject new requests, determining the best application to servers assignment, in order to the achieve the *self-optimization* goals.

Performance models have been widely used for the design and implementation of computer systems and nowadays play a central role in the MAPE cycle. Performance models have been traditionally adopted for the design, capacity planning, and management of computing systems. At design time, performance models have been used to support capacity planning of the physical infrastructure, to analyze the effects and trade-offs of different architectural choices, and to discover potential bottlenecks which may degrade system performance. In addition, performance models can also be used at run-time to assess the compliance of the running system with respect to the design goals and to measure the real system performance parameters in order to fill the gap between the design goals and the run-time behaviors.

Models at run-time can also assess the compliance of service level agreements and trigger autonomic system re-configurations.

The aim of this book is to investigate concepts, models and tools for the run-time management of autonomic computing systems. These topics are of particular importance for complex systems operating in a highly dynamic environment. For example, power management of modern CPU and resource allocation techniques in virtualized autonomic service centers can be actuated at very fine grained time scales. In such situations, traditional performance modelling techniques for steady state analysis provide only a rough estimate of the system behavior. Additional techniques are required to effectively account for workload fluctuations and to support efficiently the monitor, analyze and plan activities of the MAPE cycle.

This book includes advanced techniques, frameworks and solutions for the run-time estimation of autonomic systems performance, the analysis of transient conditions and their applications in advanced prototype environments.

In particular, the first chapter by Mark Squillante provides an overview of recent stochastic models, methods and results for the performance analysis of multiserver systems. Significant progress have been made in the past for single server systems. Due to the complexity of current systems, stochastic analysis of multiserver systems is particular important both for the performance evaluation, as well as for the optimization of Autonomic Computing infrastructures.

The second chapter by Casolari and Colajanni focuses on the monitoring and analysis activities of the MAPE cycle, investigating the problem of prediction of incoming workload and system resource utilizations. In particular, this chapter shows that raw time series from a highly dynamic environment may have limited predictability due to measurements noise and system instability. It evaluates the impact of different choices of prediction models parameters on different time series, suggesting how to treat input data, and whether it is convenient to choose the parameters of a prediction model in a static or dynamic way.

The third chapter by Kumar et al. analyzes the adoption of the Extended Kalman Filter framework for the real-time estimation of the performance parameters of an open queueing network model with multiple classes of transactional workload in an adaptive software systems. This chapter reveals specific problems encountered for multiple classes of workload and proposes an effective solution.

While the first book chapters take a *white/gray-box* perspective to model an Autonomic Computing system, the fourth chapter by Poussot-Vassal et al. proposes *black-box* models based on the Linear Parametrically Varying framework. It presents a controller based on the Model Predictive Control theory to determine the optimal trade-off between the Quality of Service requirements and the energy saving objectives. The controller operates at very fine grained time scales (i.e., few seconds/one minute) to achieve an adequate level of control.

The fifth chapter by Calcavecchia et al. is devoted to an autonomic framework called *SelfLets*. This framework is able to host various prediction and run-time models that can be dynamically plugged and unplugged in the component nodes of a large scale distributed infrastructure. Furthermore, the use of prediction models for the design of run-time load-balancing policies is also analyzed.

The sixth chapter by Autili et al. describes the use of run-time models for the assessment of the dependability of autonomic software based systems. Dependability is of paramount importance for modern systems. Despite this, most of the research works in the Autonomic Computing literature focus on response time or throughput performance metrics with little emphasis on the infrastructure dependability, which has been demonstrated in many cases to be the weakest link in the chain. This Chapter describes the approach that two recent European funded projects (namely, PLASTIC and CONNECT) have undertaken to address the challenge of assessing the dependability of Autonomic Computing systems.

Finally, the seventh chapter by Castillo et al. introduces the main challenges and future research directions for the adoption of run-time models to support advanced data analytics applications in the cloud. The Chapter discusses many issues including workload characterization, application profiling, data usage pattern analysis, cloud resource allocation, data placement and dynamic migration, and cloud performance prediction.

Several chapters in this book are extended versions of the best papers presented in Pisa, Italy at the ROSSA 2009 workshop (1st International Workshop on Run-time mOdels for Self-managing Systems and Applications). The editors would like to express their sincere gratitude to the ROSSA program committee members who have reviewed both the initial and the extended versions of the ROSSA papers. Particular thanks are expressed to Marco Bergamasco, Giuliano Casale, Lucy Cherkasova, Ivica Crnkovic, Carlo Ghezzi, Heiko Koziolek, Samuel Kounev, Diwakar Krishnamurthy, Marco Lovera, Raffaela Mirandola, Giovanni Pacifici, Alma Riska, Jerry Rolia, Evgenia Smirni, Mark Squillante, Malgorzata Steinder, and Asser Tantawi.

Milan, Italy   Danilo Ardagna[1]
Hawthorne, USA   Li Zhang

[1]The work of Danilo Ardagna has been partially supported by the GAME-IT project funded by Politecnico di Milano, by the FP7 Q-ImPrESS research project, and by the IDEAS-ERC project SMScom.

Contents

Stochastic Analysis and Optimization of Multiserver Systems

Mark S. Squillante

Abstract Motivated by emerging trends and applications such as autonomic computing, this chapter presents an overview of some research in the stochastic analysis and optimization of multiserver systems. Our primary focus is on multiserver systems in general, since this research provides the mathematical methods and results that have been and will continue to be used for the stochastic analysis and/or optimization of existing and future multiserver systems arising in a wide variety of application domains including autonomic computing.

Keywords Stochastic analysis · Stochastic optimization/control · Multiserver systems · Multidimensional stochastic processes

Mathematics Subject Classification (2000) Primary 60G20 · 65K10 · 93E03 · Secondary 60K25 · 68M20 · 90B15 · 90B36 · 90C30

1 Introduction

In the beginning there was the single-server queue. And the queue was in its simplest form, and void of known results. And man studied the single-server queue to let there be light upon this darkness. And man derived its mathematical properties and applied these results to the design, analysis and optimization of computer systems and networks. And the derivations of these mathematical results and their applications proved to be fruitful and they multiplied. And the book of Cohen [16], from the family of Temple priests (kohanim), was the authoritative text on this subject, often referred to as the bible of the single-server queue, presenting and deriving some of the most fundamental results in the area. And man saw that the single-server queue was good, both in theory and in practice.

Those who know the author will not require any explanation that the above analogy is intended to make a serious point, and those who do not know the author

D. Ardagna, L. Zhang (eds.), *Run-time Models for Self-managing Systems and Applications*, 1–24,
Autonomic Systems, DOI 10.1007/978-3-0346-0433-8_1, © Springer Basel AG 2010

should understand that no disrespect is intended in *any* way. Our intention here is to highlight the important role that the single-server queue often played in the genesis of the stochastic analysis and optimization of multiserver systems in practice. As a specific example, from the earliest days of computing up until the last decade or so, there was a continual debate among computer architects about whether improved performance in computer designs should be achieved through increasing the speed of a single centralized processor or through the use of multiple processors, with the decision always being made in favor of the single-server design approach (with the exception, of course, that multiserver computer systems were indeed built, but they were in the vast minority and were built for other reasons) [77]. Many of the most important reasons for this consistent design choice were based (consciously or not) on the mathematical properties and optimization results obtained for the single-server and multiserver queueing systems under the type of scheduling policies (relatively simple timesharing) and workloads (not involving heavy-tailed service time distributions) found in the computer systems of the day. The more recent switch to multiserver computer designs by computer architects over the past decade or so, with multiple processors on each of the multiple chips comprising the computer, has been the result of constraints due to physics and power consumption and changes in the objective function rather than the fundamental properties established for single-server and multiserver systems [77].

On the other hand, the interest in and development of multiserver systems has moved far beyond its initial role as a natural alternative design to single-server systems. New and emerging trends in technology and a wide variety of applications have created a significant increase in both the level and breadth of interest in the stochastic analysis and optimization of multiserver systems. One particularly important recent and emerging trend in technology and applications, as well as the focus of the present book, is autonomic computing. An autonomic computing system is a complex computing environment comprised of many interconnected components that operate at different time scales in a largely independent fashion and that manage themselves to satisfy high-level system management and performance requirements. Autonomic computing systems are also dynamic environments in which optimal self-management decisions must be made continually over time and at multiple time scales. Fundamental problems involved in achieving the goals of autonomic computing concern a general mathematical framework that provides the underlying foundation and supports the design, architecture and algorithms of the decision making components employed throughout the autonomic computing system. At the most basic level, such autonomic computing environments are general multiserver systems of various forms which reflect the increasing complexity of current and future computing systems. Hence, a fundamental aspect of the desired mathematical framework is the stochastic analysis and optimization of multiserver systems in general, where autonomic computing as well as other emerging trends have created a significant increase in the complexity and diversity of the multiserver systems of interest with respect to the analysis and optimization of such stochastic systems.

We therefore consider in this chapter some fundamental approaches, methods and results comprising a mathematical framework for the general stochastic analysis and optimization of multiserver systems over time, including the complexities and difficulties at various time scales of autonomic computing and other emerging trends in technology. While stochastic analysis and optimization each play a predominant role, it can be difficult some times to separate these aspects of the desired mathematical framework to a great extent. In many cases, the stochastic optimization of a multiserver system can be based on a stochastic analysis of the multiserver system over which the optimization is performed. Similarly, once one derives a stochastic analysis of a multiserver system, it can be quite natural to then want to perform a stochastic optimization of the multiserver system upon gaining insights through this analysis.

The overwhelming breadth and depth of the relevant research literature on the stochastic analysis and optimization of multiserver systems prohibits an exhaustive exposition, and thus we do not even attempt to do so. We do attempt to consider a broad range of approaches, methods and results that have been and will continue to be used in the stochastic analysis and optimization of existing and future multiserver systems, as motivated by autonomic computing and other emerging applications. However, this chapter considers only a very small fraction of the relevant research on the stochastic analysis and optimization of multiserver systems. We focus on explicit mathematical models, and in particular stochastic models, of general multiserver systems. Even within this context, a number of important areas are not covered at all, such as the vast research on many server systems motivated by call centers and other service operations management systems; see, e.g., [35]. Once again, the subject matter is simply far too broad and deep for us to provide an exhaustive exposition. Finally, we refer the interested reader to two very nice survey papers [1, 12] and the references therein for additional research studies related to the stochastic analysis and optimization of multiserver systems.

The chapter is organized as follows. We first summarize the general multiserver model and some mathematical definitions and results used in the chapter. Instead of being spread throughout the chapter, we centralize this material in Sect. 2 for easier reference. The next two sections primarily consider exact methods and results, where Sects. 3 and 4 focus on boundary value problems and stability and throughput, respectively. Section 5 considers both exact and approximate approaches, whereas approximations based on limiting regimes are considered in Sect. 6. A few issues related to decentralized control and dynamics are briefly discussed in Sect. 7, followed by some concluding remarks.

2 Technical Preliminaries

2.1 Generic Model Description

We consider a generic multiserver system consisting of S servers in which customers arrive according to an exogenous stochastic process $A(t)$ with mean interarrival time $\lambda^{-1} = \mathbb{E}[A]$ and customer service times on server $s = 1, \ldots, S$ follow a stochastic process $B_s(t)$ with mean $\mu_s^{-1} = \mathbb{E}[B_s]$. In multiclass instances of this generic multiserver system, customers of class $c = 1, \ldots, C$ arrive according to an exogenous stochastic arrival process $A_c(t)$ with mean interarrival time $\lambda_c^{-1} = \mathbb{E}[A_c]$ and class c customer service times on server $s = 1, \ldots, S$ follow a stochastic process $B_{sc}(t)$ with mean $\mu_{sc}^{-1} = \mathbb{E}[B_{sc}]$. We allow $\mathbb{E}[A] = \infty$ and $\mathbb{E}[A_c] = \infty$, in which case the corresponding exogenous arrival process is not considered, and we allow $\mathbb{E}[B_s] = \infty$ and $\mathbb{E}[B_{sc}] = \infty$, in which case the corresponding service process is not considered. Let $Q_i(t)$ denote the number of type-i customers in the multiserver system at time t, and let $\mathbf{Q}(t) = (Q_i(t))_{i \in \mathcal{Q}}$ be the corresponding number in system vector (often the queue length vector process), where the index i can represent a server or customer class or combination of both with the set of such indices denoted by $\mathcal{Q}$. Define $\mathbf{Q} = \{\mathbf{Q}(t); t \geq 0\}$ to be the corresponding multidimensional stochastic number in system process for the multiserver system. Further assumptions can be, and typically are, imposed on the above stochastic processes, but we instead focus on a generic multiserver system and consider the stochastic analysis and optimization of these systems in general, leaving it to the references to provide the additional assumptions associated with any specific results.

A wide variety of structural organizations and topologies exist for such generic multiserver systems and this continues to grow. These organizations and topologies include a single queue of customers being served by a set of servers, through a single-tier of multiple servers that service multiple queues of different classes of customers, up to a network of single-server queues or multiserver queues in either of these forms under arbitrary organizations and topologies, as well as every possibility in between and any possible combination. The servers can be homogeneous or heterogeneous. Upon completing the service of a customer, the server follows a scheduling policy to determine which customer to serve next, including the possibility of remaining idle even when customers are waiting as the policy need not be work conserving. Upon completing its service at a server, the customer follows a routing policy to determine whether it leaves the system or moves to one of the system queues to receive service, possibly switching to another customer class. Once again, we make no specific assumptions about the scheduling or routing policies employed in the multiserver system, leaving it to the references to provide additional assumptions associated with any specific results. Our interests in this chapter span the entire spectrum of multiserver systems in general and most of the statements in the chapter will correspond to this entire spectrum of multiserver organizations and topologies. Any statements intended for a specific organization or topology should be clear from the context.

2.2 Mathematical Definitions and Results

In this section we briefly summarize some mathematical definitions and results used throughout the chapter. These mathematical methods and results can play an important role in the analysis and optimization of multiserver systems, as we shall see in subsequent sections; they can equally play an important role in the analysis and optimization of multidimensional stochastic models in general. Many technical details are omitted and we refer the interested reader to the references provided. Let $\mathbb{R}^+$ ($\mathbb{R}_+$) and $\mathbb{Z}^+$ ($\mathbb{Z}_+$) denote the set of positive (nonnegative) reals and integers, respectively, and define $\mathbf{e}$ to be a column vector of proper order containing all ones.

Consider a discrete-time Markov process $\mathbf{X}^{\circ} = \{\mathbf{X}^{\circ}(t); t \in \mathbb{Z}_+\}$ on a countable, multidimensional state space $\mathcal{X}$. The definition of a corresponding Lyapunov function can be stated as follows. A nonnegative function $\Phi : \mathcal{X} \to \mathbb{R}_+$ is a *Lyapunov function* if there exist some $\gamma > 0$ and $B \geq 0$ such that for any $t \in \mathbb{Z}^+$ and any $\mathbf{x} \in \mathcal{X}$, with $\Phi(\mathbf{x}) > B$,

$$\mathbb{E}[\Phi(\mathbf{X}^{\circ}(t+1)) \mid \mathbf{X}^{\circ}(t) = \mathbf{x}] \leq \Phi(\mathbf{x}) - \gamma.$$

Refer to, e.g., [29, 63] for additional technical details.

Consider a discrete-time Markov process $\mathbf{X}^{\circ} = \{\mathbf{X}^{\circ}(t); t \in \mathbb{Z}_+\}$ on a countable, multidimensional state space $\mathcal{X} = \bigcup_{i=1}^{L} \mathcal{X}_i$ with transition probability matrix $\mathbf{T}^{\circ}$ having the form

$$\mathbf{T}^{\circ} = \begin{pmatrix} \mathbf{P}^{\circ}_{11} & \mathbf{P}^{\circ}_{12} & \cdots & \mathbf{P}^{\circ}_{1L} \\ \mathbf{P}^{\circ}_{21} & \mathbf{P}^{\circ}_{22} & \cdots & \mathbf{P}^{\circ}_{2L} \\ \vdots & \vdots & \vdots & \vdots \\ \mathbf{P}^{\circ}_{L1} & \mathbf{P}^{\circ}_{L2} & \cdots & \mathbf{P}^{\circ}_{LL} \end{pmatrix}, \tag{2.1}$$

where $\mathbf{P}^{\circ}_{ik}$ has dimension $|\mathcal{X}_i| \times |\mathcal{X}_k|$, $i, k = 1, \dots, L$. The matrix $\mathbf{P}^{\circ}_{ik}$ defines the transitions from states in $\mathcal{X}_i$ to states in $\mathcal{X}_k$, $i, k = 1, \dots, L$, and L denotes the number of block partitions of $\mathbf{T}^{\circ}$. Define for $\mathbf{x}_{i,j} \in \mathcal{X}_i$, $j \in \{1, \dots, |\mathcal{X}_i|\}$, $i = 1, \dots, L$,

$$\pi(\mathbf{x}_{i,j}) \triangleq \lim_{t \to \infty} \mathbb{P}[\mathbf{X}^{\circ}(t) = \mathbf{x}_{i,j}],$$

$$\boldsymbol{\pi}_i \triangleq (\pi(\mathbf{x}_{i,1}), \pi(\mathbf{x}_{i,2}), \dots, \pi(\mathbf{x}_{i,|\mathcal{X}_i|})),$$

$$\boldsymbol{\pi} \triangleq (\boldsymbol{\pi}_1, \boldsymbol{\pi}_2, \dots, \boldsymbol{\pi}_L).$$

The limiting probability vector $\boldsymbol{\pi}$ is the stationary distribution of the stochastic process $\mathbf{X}^{\circ}$, which we assume to be irreducible and ergodic and thus the stationary distribution is uniquely determined by solving the global balance equations $\boldsymbol{\pi} \mathbf{T}^{\circ} = \boldsymbol{\pi}$ and the normalizing constraint $\boldsymbol{\pi} \mathbf{e} = 1$.

Consider a continuous-time Markov process $\mathbf{X} = \{\mathbf{X}(t); t \in \mathbb{R}_+\}$, on a countable, multidimensional state space $\mathcal{X} = \bigcup_{i=0}^{\infty} \mathcal{X}_i$ with infinitesimal generator matrix $\mathbf{T}$ having the form

$$\mathbf{T} = \begin{pmatrix} \mathbf{B}_{00} & \mathbf{B}_{01} & \mathbf{0} & \mathbf{0} & \mathbf{0} & \cdots \\ \mathbf{B}_{10} & \mathbf{B}_{11} & \mathbf{A}_0 & \mathbf{0} & \mathbf{0} & \cdots \\ \mathbf{0} & \mathbf{A}_2 & \mathbf{A}_1 & \mathbf{A}_0 & \mathbf{0} & \cdots \\ \mathbf{0} & \mathbf{0} & \mathbf{A}_2 & \mathbf{A}_1 & \mathbf{A}_0 & \cdots \\ \vdots & \vdots & \vdots & \vdots & \vdots & \ddots \end{pmatrix}, \tag{2.2}$$

where $\mathbf{B}_{00}, \mathbf{B}_{01}, \mathbf{B}_{10}, \mathbf{B}_{11}, \mathbf{A}_{k:k=0,1,2}$, have dimensions $|\mathcal{X}_B| \times |\mathcal{X}_B|, |\mathcal{X}_B| \times |\mathcal{X}_N|$, $|\mathcal{X}_N| \times |\mathcal{X}_B|, |\mathcal{X}_N| \times |\mathcal{X}_N|, |\mathcal{X}_N| \times |\mathcal{X}_N|$, respectively, with $\mathcal{X}_B = \bigcup_{i=0}^{N-1} \mathcal{X}_i$. The matrix $\mathbf{A}_2$ defines the transitions from states in $\mathcal{X}_i$ to states in $\mathcal{X}_{i-1}, i \in \{N+1, N+2, \ldots\}$, $\mathbf{A}_0$ defines the transitions from states in $\mathcal{X}_i$ to states in $\mathcal{X}_{i+1}, i \in \{N, N+1, \ldots\}$, and the off-diagonal elements of $\mathbf{A}_1$ define the transitions between states within $\mathcal{X}_i, i \in \{N+1, N+2, \ldots\}$. Define for $\mathbf{x}_{i,j} \in \mathcal{X}_i, j \in \{1, \ldots, |\mathcal{X}_i|\}, i \in \mathbb{Z}_+$,

$$\pi(\mathbf{x}_{i,j}) \triangleq \lim_{t \to \infty} \mathbb{P}[\mathbf{X}(t) = \mathbf{x}_{i,j}],$$

$$\boldsymbol{\pi}_i \triangleq (\pi(\mathbf{x}_{i,1}), \pi(\mathbf{x}_{i,2}), \ldots, \pi(\mathbf{x}_{i,|\mathcal{X}_i|})),$$

$$\boldsymbol{\pi} \triangleq (\boldsymbol{\pi}_0, \boldsymbol{\pi}_1, \boldsymbol{\pi}_2, \ldots).$$

The limiting probability vector $\boldsymbol{\pi}$ is the stationary distribution of the stochastic process $\mathbf{X}$, which we assume to be irreducible and ergodic and thus the stationary distribution is uniquely determined by solving the global balance equations $\boldsymbol{\pi}\mathbf{T} = \mathbf{0}$ and the normalizing constraint $\boldsymbol{\pi}\mathbf{e} = 1$. From standard matrix-analytic analysis, the stationary distribution $\boldsymbol{\pi}$ has a matrix-geometric form given by

$$\boldsymbol{\pi}_{N+n} = \boldsymbol{\pi}_N \mathbf{R}^n, \quad n \in \mathbb{Z}_+, \tag{2.3}$$

$$\mathbf{0} = (\boldsymbol{\pi}_0, \boldsymbol{\pi}_1, \ldots, \boldsymbol{\pi}_N) \begin{pmatrix} \mathbf{B}_{00} & \mathbf{B}_{01} \\ \mathbf{B}_{10} & \mathbf{B}_{11} + \mathbf{R}\mathbf{A}_2 \end{pmatrix}, \tag{2.4}$$

$$1 = (\boldsymbol{\pi}_0, \boldsymbol{\pi}_1, \ldots, \boldsymbol{\pi}_{N-1})\mathbf{e} + \boldsymbol{\pi}_N (\mathbf{I} - \mathbf{R})^{-1}\mathbf{e}, \tag{2.5}$$

where $\mathbf{R}$ is the minimal nonnegative matrix that satisfies $\mathbf{R}^2 \mathbf{A}_2 + \mathbf{R}\mathbf{A}_1 + \mathbf{A}_0 = \mathbf{0}$. Refer to, e.g., [56, 68, 69] for additional details.

Consider a continuous-time Markov process $\mathbf{X} = \{\mathbf{X}(t) ; t \in \mathbb{R}_+\}$, on a countable, multidimensional state space $\mathcal{X}$. The *fluid limit* of this process is associated with the almost sure convergence of the scaled process $\tilde{\mathbf{X}}^n(t) = \mathbf{X}^n(nt)/n$ as $n \to \infty$ such that

$$\tilde{\mathbf{X}}^n \to \tilde{\mathbf{X}}, \quad \text{u.o.c.,} \quad \text{as } n \to \infty.$$

Similarly, the *diffusion limit* of the stochastic process $\mathbf{X}$ is associated with the weak convergence of the scaled process $\widehat{\mathbf{X}}^n(t) = \mathbf{X}^n(nt)/\sqrt{n}$ as $n \to \infty$ such that

$$\widehat{\mathbf{X}}^n \xrightarrow{d} \widehat{\mathbf{X}}, \quad \text{as } n \to \infty.$$

Refer to, e.g., [15, 93] for additional technical details.

Consider a sequence of multiserver systems, indexed by $n = 1, 2, \ldots$, where the nth system operates under the control policy $\mathbb{K}^n$, in the heavy traffic limit (commensurate with diffusion scaling of the associated underlying stochastic processes) as $n \to \infty$. Let $J^n(\mathbb{K}^n)$ be the expected cost for the nth multiserver system under the control policy $\mathbb{K}^n$. Then a control policy $\mathbb{K}^{n,*}$ is called *asymptotically optimal* if for any feasible policy $\mathbb{K}^n$, we have

$$\liminf \frac{J^n(\mathbb{K}^n)}{J^n(\mathbb{K}^{n,*})} \geq 1, \quad \text{as } n \to \infty. \tag{2.6}$$

This definition indicates that the cost $J^* = \lim_{n \to \infty} J^n(\mathbb{K}^{n,*})$ is the best cost one can achieve asymptotically and that this asymptotically minimal cost is achieved by the sequence of control policies $\{\mathbb{K}^{n,*}\}$. Refer to, e.g., [7] for additional technical details.

3 Boundary Value Problems

The stochastic analysis and optimization of multiserver systems often involve the analysis of Markov processes defined on countable, multidimensional state spaces. This general class of multidimensional problems is notoriously difficult to solve exactly with analytic solution methods. In fact, these multidimensional aspects of the stochastic process underlying the multiserver system is one of the major sources of complexity and difficulty in the stochastic analysis and optimization of multiserver systems. On the other hand, a number of general approaches have been developed to solve certain instances of two-dimensional multiserver systems.

In one well-known example of the so-called two coupled processor model [27], it has been shown that the functional equations for the two-dimensional generating function of the joint queue length distribution can be reduced to a Riemann-Hilbert boundary value problem, making it possible to exploit results from the general theory of boundary value equations and singular integral equations. Systematic and detailed studies of this general approach and its use in the stochastic analysis and optimization of distinct multiserver systems can be found in [19, 28]. Some additional applications of this approach include shortest queue routing, fork-join queues, the so-called 2×2 switch, two-dimensional random walks, and the M/G/2 queue. We refer the interested reader to [1, 18, 19, 28] and the references cited therein, noting that other related general approaches are discussed in [1].

Another application of this approach is the classical longest queue model in which a single server always serves the longest of two queues with ties broken in a probabilistic manner. The relevant functional equation for a version of the longest queue model is reduced to a Riemann boundary value problem in [17], which also includes a derivation of the solution of this boundary value problem. Another version of the longest queue model is considered in [30] and [95], where the former determines the limiting probabilities for a corresponding Markov process by solving a functional equation for the generating function obtained from the relevant balance equations and the latter determines these limiting probabilities directly from the balance equations. More recently, an explicit solution for the stationary distribution of the longest queue model has been obtained in [57] based on a matrix-analytic analysis, in terms of versions of (2.3)–(2.5), where explicit expressions for the elements of the **R** matrix are determined through the solution of a corresponding lattice path counting problem derived using path decomposition, Bernoulli excursions and hypergeometric functions. The results in [57] also support the multi-server version of this longest queue model, and further provide explicit solutions for the stationary distribution of a general class of random walks in the quarter-plane (namely, $\mathbb{Z}_+^2$ [28]).

4 Stability and Throughput

The stability of multiserver systems represents important issues in the stochastic analysis and optimization of such systems. Stability is also directly related to the maximum throughput of multiserver systems, which is often an important performance objective for the design and optimization of these multiserver systems. Moreover, the rate at which the maximum throughput of a multiserver system scales with respect to the number of servers S as $S \to \infty$ is another important topic of both theoretical and practical interest for the analysis and optimization of multiserver systems.

The stability of multiserver systems has been a fundamental aspect of the stochastic analysis of these systems from the very beginning, with the stability conditions also providing the maximum throughput of the system. In recent years, the issue of stability has received a great deal of attention, especially with respect to single-class and multiclass queueing networks. This recent interest was piqued by several studies showing that the traditional stability condition, namely that the nominal load at each queue/server is less than unity, is not sufficient for a large class of multiserver systems under various scheduling policies. (For example, mutual blocking among the servers can cause such instabilities; see, e.g., [13, 53] and the references cited therein.) A wide variety of methods and results have been developed to address the stability of multiserver systems, and we refer the interested reader to [29, 63] and the references therein for a thorough treatment of much of this research. Of particular interest is the unified approach via fluid limits developed in [22], generalizing the related earlier work in [79], based on the key result that a queueing network is stable if the corresponding fluid limit network is stable in the sense that the fluid network eventually reaches zero and stays there regardless of the initial multiserver system configuration. This approach and related extensions have played an important role in determining the stability conditions of multiserver systems, and the design of optimal scheduling policies, especially since the analysis can focus on the fluid limit of the multiserver system rather than the more complex stochastic system.

Due to the explosive growth in wireless technology and applications, the asymptotic rate at which the maximum throughput of wireless networks scales with respect to the size of the network S has become an important theoretical and practical issue. A random multiserver model of static wireless networks was used in [37] to show that the maximum throughput per source-destination pair is $O(1/\sqrt{S})$ as $S \to \infty$. Also presented is a $\Theta(1/\sqrt{S \log S})$ throughput scheme, which has been generalized to a parametrized version that achieves the optimal throughput-delay tradeoff for maximum throughputs of $O(1/\sqrt{S \log S})$ [24–26]. See [48, 54, 58] for further extensions of the original model and their analyses. The focus has recently turned to the asymptotic scalability of wireless networks under constant-size buffers at each server of the multiserver system, for which it has been shown that there is no end-to-end protocol capable of achieving the maximum throughput of $O(1/\sqrt{S})$ as $S \to \infty$ [46, 47]. However, it is also shown that there exists a protocol which achieves the asymptotic maximum throughput of $O(1/\sqrt{S \log S})$ with constant-size per-server buffers and which has to employ a local buffer coordination scheduling scheme.

The methods and results used to determine the stability conditions, and in turn maximum throughput, of multiserver systems have also been extended to obtain a broader set of performance metrics through important connections between the stability and the stationary distribution π of multiserver systems. As a specific example, a general methodology is proposed in [9] based on Lyapunov functions to study the stationary distribution of infinite multidimensional Markov processes $\mathbf{Q}$, which model a general set of multiclass multiserver systems. This methodology is based on key results showing that if there exist linear or piecewise linear Lyapunov functions which establish the stability of multiserver systems, then these Lyapunov functions can also be used to determine upper and lower bounds on the stationary tail distribution, which in turn provide bounds on the expected queue lengths. These upper and lower bounds hold uniformly under any work conserving policy, and the lower bounds are further extended to priority policies. The results in [9] also represent the first explicit geometric upper and lower bounds on the tail probabilities of the multidimensional queue length process $\mathbf{Q}$ for such general multiserver systems.

In another example related to infinite multidimensional Markov processes [34], more specifically a stochastic online version of the classical bin packing scheduling problem, a stochastic analysis of the corresponding multiserver system is developed based on a combination of a Lyapunov function technique and matrix-analytic methods. These results include the stability conditions and the stationary distribution π of the joint queue length process $\mathbf{Q}$ for general stochastic multidimensional bin packing processes. The stability and stationary distribution results are both derived in a recursive manner by exploiting a priority structural property, where the stability condition for the current level of the partitioned queue length process is obtained using a Lyapunov function technique involving the stationary distribution for the previous level of the partitioned queue length process, and the stationary distribution for the current level is obtained from (discrete-time) versions of (2.3)–(2.5). In addition, various performance metrics are obtained including asymptotic decay rates and expected wasted space, and large deviations bounds are used to obtain an accurate level of truncation. The approach in [34] is also based on a form of stochastic decomposition, which is generally considered in more detail in the next section.

5 Stochastic Decomposition

The multidimensional aspects of stochastic processes underlying multiserver systems are one of the many sources of complexity in their stochastic analysis and optimization, which often involve various dependencies and dynamic interactions among the different dimensions of the multidimensional process. Hence, a considerable number of general approaches have been developed that essentially decompose the complex multidimensional stochastic process into a combination of various forms of simpler processes with reduced dimensionality.

One general class of stochastic decomposition approaches is based on the theory of nearly completely decomposable stochastic systems. Consider a discrete-time Markov process with transition probability matrix $\mathbf{T}^{\mathrm{o}} = [t^{\mathrm{o}}_{\mathbf{x}_{i,j} \mathbf{x}_{k,\ell}}]$ in the form of (2.1) and with state space $\mathcal{X}$. When $|\mathcal{X}|$ is very large, computing the stationary distribution (as well as functionals of the stationary distribution) directly from the transition probability matrix can be prohibitively expensive in both time and space. Suppose, however, that the block submatrices along the main diagonal (i.e., $\mathbf{P}^{\mathrm{o}}_{11}, \ldots, \mathbf{P}^{\mathrm{o}}_{LL}$) consist of relatively large probability mass, while the elements of the other block submatrices are very small in comparison (i.e., $\mathbf{P}^{\mathrm{o}}_{ik} \approx \mathbf{0}$, $i \neq k$). Matrices of this type are called nearly completely decomposable [20], in which case the matrix $\mathbf{T}^{\mathrm{o}}$ can be written in the form $\mathbf{T}^{\mathrm{o}} = \mathbf{W}^* + \epsilon \mathbf{D}$ where $\mathbf{W}^* = \mathrm{diag}(\mathbf{W}^*_1, \mathbf{W}^*_2, \ldots, \mathbf{W}^*_L)$, the matrices $\mathbf{W}^*_i$ are stochastic and completely decomposable, $i = 1, \ldots, L$, ϵ is small compared to the elements of $\mathbf{W}^*$, and the absolute value of each element of $\mathbf{D}$ is less than or equal to 1. The model solution is then based on extensions of the Simon-Ando approximations for the stationary distribution of the corresponding Markov process. More specifically, given a function $F(\mathbf{T}^{\mathrm{o}})$ of interest, which can include its stationary distribution $\boldsymbol{\pi}$, it follows from the theory of nearly completely decomposable matrices that the function can be approximated as $F(\mathbf{T}^{\mathrm{o}}) \approx \sum_{i=1}^{L} \widetilde{\pi}_i F(\mathbf{W}^*_i)$, the accuracy of which is known to be within $O(\epsilon)$ [20]. Here, $F(\mathbf{W}^*_i)$ is determined from the matrix $\mathbf{W}^*_i$ and its invariant probability vector $\widehat{\boldsymbol{\pi}}_i$, while $\widetilde{\pi}_i$ is determined as the invariant probability vector of the stochastic matrix of dimension $L \times L$ whose elements are given by $\widehat{t}^{\mathrm{o}}_{ik} = \sum_{j=1}^{|\mathcal{X}_i|} \sum_{\ell=1}^{|\mathcal{X}_k|} \widehat{\pi}_{ij} t^{\mathrm{o}}_{\mathbf{x}_{i,j} \mathbf{x}_{k,\ell}}$. Note that $\widehat{t}^{\mathrm{o}}_{ik} = \mathbb{P}[\mathbf{X}^{\mathrm{o}}(t+1) \in \mathcal{X}_k | \mathbf{X}^{\mathrm{o}}(t) \in \mathcal{X}_i]$, $i, k = 1, \ldots, L$. Error bounds can also be obtained within this framework; see, e.g., [21, 89]. As a specific example, refer to [4] for model instances where $F(\mathbf{T}^{\mathrm{o}})$ represents the stationary page fault probability for a computer program model $\mathbf{T}^{\mathrm{o}}$ and a finite storage capacity. A solution for instances of these computer storage models with $F(\mathbf{W}^*_i) = 0$, $i = 1, \ldots, L$, while $F(\mathbf{T}^{\mathrm{o}}) \neq 0$ is derived in [75, 84] based on first passage times, recurrence times, taboo probabilities and first entrance methods, whereas standard nearly completely decomposable models and analyses obviously break down and fail in such model instances. For additional details on nearly completely decomposable stochastic systems and their solutions, we refer the interested reader to [20] and the references therein.

Another general class of stochastic decomposition approaches is based on models of each dimension of the multidimensional process in isolation together with a fixed-point equation to capture the dependencies and dynamic interactions among the multiple dimensions. In order to consider one of the most well-known examples of this general approach, let us first recall that the classical Erlang loss model consists of J links, with each link j having capacity C_j, and a set of routes $\mathcal{R}$ defined as a collection of links. Calls for route r arrive with rate λ_r and require capacity $\mathbf{A}_{jr}$ from link j, $\mathbf{A}_{jr} \geq 0$. Such a call arrival is lost if the available capacity on any link j is less than $\mathbf{A}_{jr}$, $\forall j = 1, \ldots, J$, and otherwise the call reserves the available capacity $\mathbf{A}_{jr}$ on each link j for a duration having mean μ_r^{-1}, $\forall j = 1, \ldots, J$. The traffic intensity for route r is denoted by $\rho_r = \lambda_r / \mu_r$. It is well known that there exists a unique stationary distribution $\boldsymbol{\pi}$ for the number of active calls on all routes r and that $\boldsymbol{\pi}$ has a product-form solution in terms of the traffic intensities ρ_r. Then the stationary probability L_r that a call on route r is lost can be expressed in terms of this stationary distribution. However, the computational complexity of calculating the exact stationary distribution is known to be $\sharp P$ complete [59], thus causing such calculations to be computationally intractable even for moderate values of J and $|\mathcal{R}|$. We refer the interested reader to [52] and the references therein for additional details.

The well-known Erlang fixed-point approximation has been developed to address this computational complexity and it is based on a stochastic decomposition in which the multidimensional Erlang formula is replaced by a system of J nonlinear equations in terms of the one-dimensional Erlang formula. More specifically, the stationary loss probabilities L_r for routes r are given by

$$L_r = 1 - \prod_{j=1}^{J} (1 - B_j)^{\mathbf{A}_{jr}},$$

where the blocking probabilities B_j for links j satisfy the system of nonlinear equations

$$B_j = E\left((1 - B_j)^{-1} \sum_{r=1}^{|\mathcal{R}|} \mathbf{A}_{jr} \rho_r \prod_{i=1}^{J} (1 - B_i)^{\mathbf{A}_{ir}}, C_j \right), \tag{5.1}$$

with

$$E(\rho, C) = \frac{\rho^C}{C!} \left(\sum_{n=0}^{C} \frac{\rho^n}{n!} \right)^{-1}$$

being the Erlang formula for the loss probability of an isolated link of capacity C under traffic from an exogenous stream with intensity ρ. Furthermore, it is well-known that there exists a solution $\mathbf{B} \in [0, 1]^J$ of the Erlang fixed-point equations (5.1) and that this solution converges to the exact solution of the original Erlang loss model in the limit as the traffic intensity vector ρ and capacity vector $\mathbf{C}$ are increased together in fixed proportion; see [51, 52, 92]. The corresponding capacity planning optimization problem to maximize profit as a function of the loss probabilities L_r and capacities C_j has been considered within this context [52, 92]. The asymptotic exactness of the Erlang fixed-point approximation and optimization based on this approximation, which follows from an instance of the central limit theorem for conditional Poisson random variables, is an important aspect of this general decomposition approach for the stochastic analysis and optimization of complex multiserver systems, though establishing such results is not always possible. Various extensions of the Erlang loss model and Erlang fixed-point approximation are also possible, including recent results to support less restrictive call arrival processes [11] and on optimal capacity planning under time-varying multiclass workloads [10]. More accurate approximations for the Erlang loss model have also been recently developed; refer to [3, 49].

Another example of this general stochastic decomposition approach was developed in [65, 83] to obtain the stationary distribution π of a (symmetric) multiserver system in which a scheduling policy assigns customers to the server where they are served most efficiently and in which a threshold-based scheduling policy manages the tradeoff between balancing the workload among the servers and serving the customers in the most efficient manner. A matrix-analytic analysis of the stochastic processes modeling each server in isolation is derived to obtain the corresponding stationary probability vectors in terms of their arrival and departure processes which are modified to reflect the probabilistic behavior of the other servers. These probability vectors are given by versions of (2.3)–(2.5), where explicit solutions for the elements of the matrix $\mathbf{R}$ are obtained in several instances of the multiserver system. Then the modified arrival and departure processes of each server are expressed in terms of the corresponding stationary probability vector, and the final solution of the system of equations is obtained via a fixed-point iteration. This solution can be shown to be asymptotically exact, in terms of the number of servers S, under certain conditions. The results of this study illustrate and quantify the significant performance benefits of the dynamic threshold-based scheduling policy, particularly at moderate to relatively heavy traffic intensities, but also demonstrate the potential for unstable behavior where servers spend most of their time inefficiently serving customers when thresholds are selected inappropriately. The stochastic analysis in [65, 83] can be used to determine the optimal threshold values for the multiserver system as a function of its parameters. Related (non-symmetric) instances of this multiserver system and this dynamic threshold-based scheduling policy have also been considered within the context of diffusion limiting regimes; refer to Sect. 6.

Yet another general class of stochastic decomposition approaches is based on exploiting various priority structural properties to reduce the dimensionality of the multiserver system in a recursive manner. Although this general approach was originally developed for single-server systems with multiple queues under a priority scheduling discipline (see, e.g., [36, 45]), it has been extended and generalized in many different ways for the stochastic analysis and optimization of multiserver systems. The basic idea consists of a recursive mathematical procedure starting with the two highest priority dimensions of the process that involves: (i) analyzing the probabilistic behavior of the so-called completion-time process, which characterizes the intervals between consecutive points when customers of the lower priority dimension begin service within a busy period; (ii) obtaining the distributional characteristics of related busy-period processes through an analysis of associated stochastic processes and modified service time distributions in isolation; and (iii) determining the solution of the two-dimensional priority process from a combination of these results. These steps are repeated to obtain the solution for the $(c + 1)$-dimensional priority process using the results for the c-dimensional priority process, until reaching the final solution for the original multidimensional stochastic process. Refer to, e.g., [36, 45], and the references cited therein.

One example of this general approach for the stochastic analysis of multiserver systems was discussed at the end of Sect. 4. Several related extensions of this general approach have been developed for the stochastic analysis and optimization of various multiserver systems, as parallel computing systems under a multiclass gang scheduling policy [86], a (single-class) combination of spacesharing and timesharing policies [82], and different (single-class) dynamic coscheduling policies

[87, 88]. These approaches generally exploit distinct priority structures in the underlying multidimensional stochastic process together with the probabilistic behavior of dependence structures and dynamics resulting from the multiserver workloads and policies. More specifically, these approaches investigate each dimension of the stochastic process in isolation based on an analysis of the probabilistic behavior of a set of stochastic processes analogous to the completion-time process together with an analysis of related busy-period processes and modified service time distributions. In [86], this involves deriving expressions for the conditional distributions of the per-class timeplexing-cycle processes (which characterize the intervals between consecutive quanta for a class) given the queue length vectors in terms of the stationary distributions for the other classes. (In a limiting regime, the exact stationary distribution for the queue length process of each class can be obtained in isolation as an alternating service process with vacations representing periods when other classes receive service.) In [82], this involves deriving a first-passage time analysis of the probabilistic behavior of the departure processes associated with the set of timeplexing-cycle processes (which characterize the intervals between consecutive quanta for a customer) to obtain a set of modified service time distributions that incorporate the effects of timesharing. In [87, 88], this involves deriving an analysis of the probabilistic behavior of a set of overall service processes at each server (characterizing the various states that every parallel application can be in) and expressing this probabilistic behavior in terms of the corresponding stationary distributions for the other servers. A fixed-point iteration is used in all of these cases to solve the resulting system of equations and obtain the stationary distribution of the corresponding multidimensional stochastic process in the form of (2.3)–(2.5). The probability distributions obtained from each stochastic analysis in isolation are either used directly or replaced with more compact (approximate) forms that are constructed by fitting phase-type distributions to match as many moments (and/or other associated probabilistic functionals) of the original distributions as are of interest using any of the best known methods. In particular, classical busy-period results (refer to, e.g., [67, 69]) can be exploited to obtain a more compact (approximate) form for any busy-period distribution. See also [23].

A similar approach was subsequently taken in [39, 40] for the stochastic analysis of customer assignment with cycle stealing in multiserver systems under a central queue or immediate dispatch. The workload consists of two classes denoted by C_1 and C_2. At any given time, a single server is associated with each class and the cycle stealing mechanism allows the server associated with C_2 to serve customers of C_1. In the immediate dispatch case, the stationary distribution for the C_2 process can be determined in isolation using matrix-analytic methods with the solution given by versions of (2.3)–(2.5); the sojourn time moments can be directly obtained using virtual waiting time analysis for the case of Poisson arrivals. Since the servicing of C_1 customers depends upon the C_2 process, the first three moments of the busy and idle periods of the C_2 process are obtained and used to construct corresponding two-stage Coxian distributions with matching moments. The C_1 process is augmented with the approximate busy and idle period distributions of the C_2 process and analyzed in isolation using matrix-analytic methods to obtain the corresponding stationary distribution in the form of (2.3)–(2.5). This analysis of the multiserver system under immediate dispatch is also extended to the case of multiple C_1 servers. Turning to the analysis for the central queue case, there are some differences in the details of the analysis as one would expect, but the basic approach is quite similar. The stationary distribution for the C_2 process can be determined in isolation using matrix-analytic methods where the first C_2 arrival of a busy period either starts service immediately or must wait for the completion of a C_1 customer already in service; the mean sojourn time can be directly obtained, in the case of Poisson arrivals, using known results for the M/G/1 queue with setup times [90]. A stochastic process is formulated to represent the C_1 process together with the probabilistic behavior of various busy periods associated with C_2, where the first three moments of each of the latter random processes are obtained and used to construct corresponding two-stage Coxian distributions with matching moments. The stationary distribution of this process for C_1 customers can be determined using matrix-analytic methods with the solution given by versions of (2.3)–(2.5). The results of these studies demonstrate that cycle stealing can significantly improve the performance of C_1 customers, while the penalty incurred by C_2 customers is relatively small. Performance improvements are found to be greater for both C_1 and C_2 under a central queue than under immediate dispatch.

This approach was subsequently used in the so-called method of dimensionality reduction that applies to a class of recursive foreground-background stochastic processes, which includes cycle stealing under immediate dispatch, and a class of generalized foreground-background stochastic processes, which includes cycle stealing under a central queue [71]. Two approximations of dimensionality reduction are also proposed in [71], each attempting to reduce the computational complexity of the recursive use of dimensionality reduction by ignoring dependencies to varying degrees (namely, partial and complete independence assumptions) while maintaining reasonable accuracy. The method of dimensionality reduction has been applied to a number of different multiserver systems, including multiserver systems with multiple priority classes [41], threshold-based policies for reducing switching costs in cycle stealing [72, 73], and threshold-based policies for the so-called Beneficiary-Donor model [74].

6 Stochastic Process Limits

The many sources of complexity and difficulty in the stochastic analysis and optimization of multiserver systems often make an exact analysis intractable for numerous instances of multiserver systems. Hence, a considerable number of general approaches have been developed based on an investigation of the underlying stochastic process and associated control problem in some limiting regime.

The analysis of fluid limits of multiserver systems is one important example of this general approach in which the asymptotic behavior of the underlying stochastic process is typically characterized via a functional strong law of large numbers. As such, the stochastic system is approximated by a deterministic system comprised of dynamic continuous flows of fluid to be drained in a manner analogous to the servicing of discrete customers in the original stochastic system. In addition to the methods and results presented in Sect. 4, this approach and related extensions have played an important role in the analysis and optimization of multiserver systems. One example is developed in [14, 15] to study the optimal dynamic control and scheduling of multiclass fluid networks. An algorithmic procedure is presented that systematically solves the dynamic scheduling problem by solving a sequence of linear programs. Several important properties of this procedure are established, including an example that a globally optimal solution (namely one rendering optimality of the objective function over every point of time) may not exist, and thus the solution procedure is myopic in this respect. The solution procedure generates within a bounded number of iterations a policy, in the form of dynamic capacity allocation among all fluid classes at each node in the network, that consists of a finite set of linear intervals over the entire time horizon and that is guaranteed to yield a stable fluid network.

In another example associated with the dynamic scheduling of multiclass fluid queueing networks [5], an optimal control approach to the optimization of fluid relaxations of multiclass stochastic networks is developed based on the Pontryagin maximum principle and related theory [76, 80]. The maximum principle is used to derive the exact optimal control policies in the fluid limiting regime for several canonical examples of multiserver systems. A numerical method is proposed, based on the structure of the optimal policy, to compute exact solutions for the fluid network optimal control problem using a discrete approximation that is continually refined until the solution no longer improves. Due to the dimensionality difficulties of this exact approach, an efficient approximate algorithm is also developed to compute the fluid optimal control based on a heuristic that learns from the exact solution of special cases. Numerical experiments illustrate that a pairwise interaction heuristic yields near-optimal policies. More recently, efficient approximation algorithms have been developed for the class of separated continuous linear programming problems that arise as fluid relaxations of multiclass stochastic networks. For example, in [32], a proposed polynomial-time algorithm is shown to provide a solution that, for given constants $\epsilon > 0$ and $\delta > 0$, drains the fluid network with total cost at most $(1 + \epsilon)\text{OPT} + \delta$, where OPT is the minimum cost drainage.

Many optimal control problems in multiserver systems can be studied as Markov decision processes. However, the well known difficulty with this approach for some multiserver systems is the so-called curse of dimensionality. In [60, 61], a form of unification is established between the dynamic programming equations of the Markov decision process of a stochastic network control problem and a related total-cost optimal control problem for the corresponding linear fluid network. This and related results in [60, 61] form the basis of a general framework for constructing control algorithms for multiclass queueing networks, with network sequencing and routing problems considered as special cases. Numerical examples are presented showing close similarity between the optimal policy from the proposed framework and the average-cost optimal policy. In [62], the connections between multidimensional Markov decision processes associated with the optimal control of stochastic networks and the corresponding optimal fluid limit control processes are further studied within the context of the control of stochastic networks using state-dependent safety-stocks. For a few canonical examples, it is shown that the proposed policy is fluid-scale asymptotically optimal and approximately average-cost optimal, leading to a new technique to obtain fluid-scale asymptotic optimality for general networks modeled in discrete time. These results are based on the construction of an approximate solution to the average-cost dynamic programming equations using a perturbation of the value function for an associated fluid model.

The analysis of diffusion limits of multiserver systems is another important example of the general approach of this section in which the asymptotic behavior of the underlying stochastic process is typically characterized via a functional central limit theorem. As such, the stochastic processes underlying the multiserver system are approximated by various Brownian motions that describe the heavy-traffic system behavior. A wide variety of methods and results for this diffusion approximation approach have been developed to address the general stochastic analysis and optimization of multiserver systems, and we refer the interested reader to, e.g., [42, 93] and the references therein. Of particular interest is the well-known Halfin-Whitt regime [38, 93], for which certain heavy-traffic limits have been established as the traffic intensity goes to unity and $S \to \infty$ in an S-server queueing system. This framework and related extensions have played an important role in the stochastic analysis and optimization of multiserver systems, with applications in various areas such as large call center environments where resource (agent) capacity planning and scheduling problems have received considerable attention. In one example associated with the dynamic scheduling of multiclass queueing systems in the Halfin-Whitt heavy-traffic regime [44], the Hamilton-Jacobi-Bellman equation associated with the limiting diffusion control problem is shown to have a smooth solution with an optimal policy having a so-called bang-bang control. Several qualitative insights are also derived from the stochastic analysis, including a square root rule for the capacity planning of large multiserver systems.

Another general class of diffusion approximation approaches have played an important role in the stochastic analysis and optimization of multiserver systems based on solving the corresponding Brownian control problem. As a representative example having received considerable attention, consider a multiserver system in which each class of customers can be served at any one of a (per-class) subset of the servers, with specific class-server service rates. The Brownian control problem associated with the dynamic scheduling of customers in this multiclass parallel-server system to minimize the cumulative holding costs of customers is studied in [43] where, assuming a so-called complete resource pooling condition, a particular discretization method is proposed to find discrete-review policy solutions. (A symmetric version of the general problem, discussed in Sect. 5, is studied in [65, 83].) Under the same heavy-traffic complete resource pooling assumption, a candidate for an asymptotically optimal control policy in the form of a dynamic threshold policy is proposed in [94] for the original multiserver system. It is then established that this dynamic threshold scheduling policy is asymptotically optimal in the heavy traffic limit under the complete resource pooling condition and that the limiting cost is the same as the optimal cost in the Brownian control problem [7, 8]. Also, for numerical solutions of such control problems in general, refer to [55].

Another example of this general approach consists of first determining derivatives of the performance function of interest at $\rho = 0$, using a Taylor expansion of the function near $\rho = 0$, then determining the diffusion limit of the underlying stochastic process, and finally obtaining a closed-form approximation for the performance function (e.g., the expected sojourn time in the multiserver system) by interpolating between these light-traffic and heavy-traffic limits. This approach was originally proposed in [78] where the 0th through $n - 1$st order light-traffic derivatives are combined with the heavy-traffic limit to obtain an nth degree polynomial in ρ as an approximation to the normalized performance function, which in turn is used to produce the desired closed-form approximation. Several instances of this general approach have been developed for the stochastic analysis and optimization of various multiserver systems, including symmetric fork-join queueing systems (see below) [91] and optimal resource allocation in parallel-server systems [85].

Several other multiserver systems have been studied in various limiting regimes. One example is shortest queue routing systems in which each of the S servers has its own dedicated queue and customers join the queue with the shortest length at the instant of their arrival. An analysis of the shortest queue system based on a diffusion limit approximation is presented in [33], whereas an exact analysis for the two-server case [2] and mean sojourn time approximations [64] have also been obtained. A related optimal multiclass scheduling problem is studied in [81] together with the associated sequencing problem at each of the S servers. Another example is fork-join queueing systems in which each server has its own dedicated queue and each customer arrival forks into S tasks, with the ith task assigned to the ith server, such that the customer departs the system only after all of its tasks have received service. An analysis of the fork-join queueing system using an interpolation approximation based on light and heavy traffic limits is presented in [91], whereas an analysis for the two-server case [31] and bounds on various performance metrics [6, 66] have also been obtained.

7 Decentralized Control and Dynamics

Another important source of complexity and difficulty in the stochastic analysis and optimization of multiserver systems often arises as a result of the decentralized management of (large-scale) environments comprised of a collection of multiserver systems. Hence, an additional number of fundamental issues need to be taken into account in the stochastic analysis and optimization of such multiserver systems over time.

One particularly important issue concerns the quality of a decentralized optimization of the entire collection of multiserver systems in comparison with a globally optimal solution of a centrally managed instance of this entire system; see, e.g., [70]. More specifically, consider a hierarchical system where the first level of the hierarchy consists of n multiserver systems, each of which in turn is the root of a subhierarchy of multiserver systems. A utility function $f_i(x_i, r_i, u_i)$ is associated with the ith multiserver system of the first level, where x_i is the set of variables (including policies) that can be changed or affected in multiserver system i, r_i is the set of resources allocated to multiserver system i, and u_i is the set of external variables (including workloads) that impact multiserver system i. The total utility function for the entire hierarchical system is given by $h(f_1(x_1, r_1, u_1), \ldots, f_n(x_n, r_n, u_n))$, such that h aggregates the utility of each multiserver system of the first level into a single total utility. Then the overall goal of the collection of multiserver systems is to globally optimize the total utility function h among all feasible resource allocations $r_1, \ldots, r_n$ and all feasible sets of variables (policies) $x_1, \ldots, x_n$, yielding total utility h_c. Namely, we have

$$h_c = \min_{x_i, r_i} h(f_1(x_1, r_1, u_1), \ldots, f_n(x_n, r_n, u_n)).$$

On the other hand, the decentralized optimization of this hierarchy of multiserver systems involves each of the n multiserver systems optimizing its local utility function

$$g_i(r_i, u_i) = \min_{x_i} f_i(x_i, r_i, u_i)$$

among all feasible sets of variables (policies) x_i given the set of resources r_i allocated by the central manager to multiserver system i. In turn, the central manager optimizes the total utility function $h(g_1(r_1, u_1), \ldots, g_n(r_n, u_n))$ among all feasible resource allocations $r_1, \ldots, r_n$ for the collection of multiserver systems, yielding total utility h_d. Namely, we have

$$h_d = \min_{r_i} h(g_1(r_1, u_1), \ldots, g_n(r_n, u_n)).$$

Then it can be easily shown [70] that as long as the aggregation function h is order preserving (in the sense that $h(x) \geq h(y)$ whenever $x \geq y$ where $x \geq y$ if $x_k \geq y_k$ for all k and $h : \mathbb{R}^n \to \mathbb{R}^m$), the decentralized optimal solution is as good as the centralized optimal solution, i.e., $h_c = h_d$. The same arguments can be applied recursively at each level of the hierarchy with respect to the decentralized optimization of the entire subcollection of multiserver systems. We refer the interested reader to [70] for additional details.

Another fundamental issue that needs to be addressed in the stochastic analysis and optimization of multiserver systems concerns the dynamics of the system over time and at multiple time scales. Various aspects of each multiserver system (e.g., the external variables u_i) can vary over time, and thus the above decentralized optimization decisions may occur on a periodic basis. The time scales at which these decisions are made at each level of the hierarchical collection of multiserver systems depend upon several factors, including the delays, overheads and constraints involved in making changes to decision variables, the service-level agreements and performance guarantees of each multiserver system, and the properties of the underlying (nonstationary) stochastic processes. In such circumstances, it is well known that even very simple (e.g., linear) models, which are only piecewise continuous or contain a feedback element, may exhibit chaotic behavior (in the sense of difficult to predict and qualitatively very sensitive to initial or control conditions) [50]. As an elementary instance in which adding time delay can produce locally unstable behavior (and hence can produce chaos on the larger scale), consider a linear dynamical system $y_{n+1} = (s - d)y_n + D$ with constant parameters, where the new system state depends only on the closest previous state. This system is stable when $|\xi| \leq 1$ and asymptotically stable when $|\xi| < 1$, where $\xi = s - d$ denotes the eigenvalue of the dynamical system. On the other hand, if the balance of $s - d$ is spread over time, we have a system $y_{n+1} = sy_n - dy_{n-1} + D$ in which now the stability condition is that both solutions of $\xi^2 - s\xi + d$ (the characteristic polynomial of the new system) satisfy $|\xi| \leq 1$. Here the growth rate s corresponds to the rate of growth in the backlog of customers in the multiserver systems and the decay rate d corresponds to the resource allocation in the multiserver systems. In the first dynamical system equation, the growth rate and the decay rate cancel each other within the same time interval, and thus we focus on the net effect which, by assumption, is such that the backlog remains bounded. In the presence of time delay as in the second dynamical system equation, the decay rate (or the resource allocation) corresponds to a different time interval than the growth rate (or the customer backlog), which in some cases produces instabilities. When the dynamical system is near such a fix point and it is globally bounded (by some non-linear dependencies) in such a way that the trajectories return to this fix point, then the instability of the fix point produces very chaotic behavior due to the irregular number of iterates involved in returns to this fix point. Chaos can be controllable in special cases, for example many stochastically stable systems exhibit individual chaotic trajectories, but with very well behaved distributions or moments. The transitions from a deterministic regime, where all trajectories are predictable at all times, to a stochastic regime, where most of the trajectories are predictable over long intervals of time, may go through all kinds of uncontrollable evolutions. It is therefore essential for the stochastic analysis and (decentralized) optimization of multiserver systems to determine the types of possible asymptotic behavior and the stability of such behavior under small perturbations of the system, and to conceive of mechanisms exposing the type of behavior in which the system currently resides. For additional details, we refer the interested reader to [70].

8 Conclusions

The genesis of multiserver systems may have been as straightforward extensions and alternatives to single-server systems, but new and emerging trends such as autonomic computing have been driving a significant growth of interest in multiserver systems. This growth has resulted in new formulations and even greater complexities in the multiserver systems in general from both theoretical and practical perspectives. The stochastic analysis and optimization of multiserver systems must address these complexities and difficulties. This will require extensions of existing solution methods and results, including some of the general approaches considered in this chapter, but will also require the development of new solutions methods and the derivation of new results in the stochastic analysis and optimization of multiserver systems.

Acknowledgements The author especially thanks Danilo Ardagna and Li Zhang for their kind invitation to write this chapter. He also thanks Alan Hoffman, Yingdong Lu, Baruch Schieber, Mayank Sharma and Shmuel Winograd for helpful comments on an earlier version of the chapter, as well as Dan Prener for fruitful discussions regarding some of the computer architecture points in the introduction.

References

[1] Adan, I.J., Boxma, O.J., Resing, J.: Queueing models with multiple waiting lines. Queueing Syst. Theory Appl. **37**, 65–98 (2001)

[2] Adan, I.J., Wessels, J., Zijm, W.: Analysis of the asymmetric shortest queue problem. Queueing Syst. Theory Appl. **8**, 1–58 (1989)

[3] Anselmi, J., Lu, Y., Sharma, M., Squillante, M.S.: Improved approximations for the Erlang loss model. Queueing Syst. Theory Appl. **63**, 217–239 (2009)

[4] Aven, O.I., Coffman, E.G. Jr., Kogan, Y.A.: Stochastic Analysis of Computer Storage. Dordrecht, Reidel (1987)

[5] Avram, F., Bertsimas, D., Ricard, M.: Fluid models of sequencing problems in open queueing networks: An optimal control approach. In: F. Kelly, R. Williams (eds.) Stochastic Networks. IMA, vol. 71, pp. 199–234 (1995)

[6] Baccelli, F., Makowski, A.M., Shwartz, A.: The fork-join queue and related systems with synchronization constraints: Stochastic ordering and computable bounds. Adv. Appl. Probab. **21**, 629–660 (1989)

[7] Bell, S.L., Williams, R.J.: Dynamic scheduling of a system with two parallel servers in heavy traffic with resource pooling: Asymptotic optimality of a threshold policy. Ann. Appl. Probab. **11**, 608–649 (2001)

[8] Bell, S.L., Williams, R.J.: Dynamic scheduling of a parallel server system in heavy traffic with complete resource pooling: Asymptotic optimality of a threshold policy. Electron. J. Probab. **10**, 1044–1115 (2005)

[9] Bertsimas, D., Gamarnik, D., Tsitsiklis, J.: Performance of multiclass Markovian queueing networks via piecewise linear Lyapunov functions. Ann. Appl. Probab. **11**(4), 1384–1428 (2001)

[10] Bhadra, S., Lu, Y., Squillante, M.S.: Optimal capacity planning in stochastic loss networks with time-varying workloads. In: Proceedings of ACM SIGMETRICS Conference on Measurement and Modeling of Computer Systems, pp. 227–238. ACM, New York (2007)

[11] Bonald, T.: The Erlang model with non-Poisson call arrivals. In: Proceedings of Joint SIGMETRICS/Performance Conference on Measurement and Modeling of Computer Systems, pp. 276–286. ACM, New York (2006)

[12] Boxma, O.J., Koole, G.M., Liu, Z.: Queueing-theoretic solution methods for models of parallel and distributed systems. In: O.J. Boxma, G.M. Koole (eds.) Performance Evaluation of Parallel and Distributed Systems, pp. 1–24. CWI Tract 105, Amsterdam (1994)

[13] Bramson, M.: Instability of FIFO queueing networks. Ann. Appl. Probab. **4**, 414–431 (1994)

[14] Chen, H., Yao, D.D.: Dynamic scheduling of a multiclass fluid network. Oper. Res. **41**(6), 1104–1115 (1993)

[15] Chen, H., Yao, D.D.: Fundamentals of Queueing Networks: Performance, Asymptotics, and Optimization. Springer, Berlin (2001)

[16] Cohen, J.W.: The Single Server Queue, 1st edn., North-Holland, Amsterdam (1969). Second edition, 1982

[17] Cohen, J.W.: A two-queue, one-server model with priority for the longer queue. Queueing Syst. Theory Appl. **2**(3), 261–283 (1987)

[18] Cohen, J.W.: Boundary value problems in queueing theory. Queueing Syst. Theory Appl. **3**, 97–128 (1988)

[19] Cohen, J.W., Boxma, O.J.: Boundary Value Problems in Queueing System Analysis. North-Holland, Amsterdam (1983)
[20] Courtois, P.J.: Decomposability. Academic Press, San Diego (1977)
[21] Courtois, P.J., Semal, P.: Error bounds for the analysis by decomposition of non-negative matrices. In: Proceedings of International Workshop on Applied Mathematics and Performance/Reliability Models of Computer/Communication Systems, pp. 253–268 (1983)
[22] Dai, J.G.: On positive Harris recurrence of multiclass queueing networks: A unified approach via fluid limit models. Ann. Appl. Probab. **5**, 49–77 (1995)
[23] Dallery, Y., Frein, Y.: On decomposition methods for tandem queueing networks with blocking. Oper. Res. **41**, 386–399 (1993)
[24] El Gamal, A., Mammen, J., Prabhakar, B., Shah, D.: Throughput-delay trade-off in wireless networks. In: Proc. IEEE Infocom, March 2004
[25] El Gamal, A., Mammen, J., Prabhakar, B., Shah, D.: Optimal throughput-delay scaling in wireless networks—Part I: The fluid model. IEEE Trans. Inf. Theory **52**(6), 2568–2592 (2006)
[26] El Gamal, A., Mammen, J., Prabhakar, B., Shah, D.: Optimal throughput-delay scaling in wireless networks—Part II: Constant-size packets. IEEE Trans. Inf. Theory **52**(11), 5111–5116 (2006)
[27] Fayolle, G., Iasnogorodski, R.: Two coupled processors: The reduction to a Reimann-Hilbert problem. Z. Wahrscheinlichkeitstheor. Verw. Geb. **47**, 325–351 (1979)
[28] Fayolle, G., Iasnogorodski, R., Malyshev, V.: Random Walks in the Quarter-Plane: Algebraic Methods, Boundary Value Problems and Applications. Springer, Berlin (1999)
[29] Fayolle, G., Malyshev, V.A., Menshikov, M.V.: Topics in the Constructive Theory of Countable Markov Chains. Cambridge University Press, Cambridge (1995)
[30] Flatto, L.: The longer queue model. Probab. Eng. Inf. Sci. **3**, 537–559 (1989)
[31] Flatto, L., Hahn, S.: Two parallel queues created by arrivals with two demands. SIAM J. Appl. Math. **44**, 1041–1053 (1984)
[32] Fleischer, L.K., Sethuraman, J.: Efficient algorithms for separated continuous linear programs: The multicommodity flow problem with holding costs and extensions. Math. Oper. Res. **30**(4), 916–938 (2005)
[33] Foschini, G.J., Salz, J.: A basic dynamic routing problem and diffusion. IEEE Trans. Commun. **26**(3), 320–327 (1978)
[34] Gamarnik, D., Squillante, M.S.: Analysis of stochastic online bin packing processes. Stoch. Models **21**, 401–425 (2005)
[35] Gans, N., Koole, G., Mandelbaum, A.: Telephone call centers: Tutorial, review, and research prospects. Manuf. Serv. Oper. Manag. **5**, 79–141 (2003)
[36] Gaver, D.P., Jr.: A waiting line with interrupted service, including priorities. J. R. Stat. Soc., Ser. B **24**, 73–90 (1962)
[37] Gupta, P., Kumar, P.R.: The capacity of wireless networks. IEEE Trans. Inf. Theory **46**(2), 388–404 (2000)
[38] Halfin, S., Whitt, W.: Heavy-traffic limits for queues with many exponential servers. Oper. Res. **29**, 567–588 (1981)
[39] Harchol-Balter, M., Li, C., Osogami, T., Scheller-Wolf, A., Squillante, M.S.: Cycle stealing under immediate dispatch task assignment. In: Proceedings of Annual ACM Symposium on Parallel Algorithms and Architectures, pp. 274–285, June 2003
[40] Harchol-Balter, M., Li, C., Osogami, T., Scheller-Wolf, A., Squillante, M.S.: Task assignment with cycle stealing under central queue. In: Proceedings of International Conference on Distributed Computing Systems, pp. 628–637, May 2003
[41] Harchol-Balter, M., Osogami, T., Scheller-Wolf, A., Wierman, A.: Multi-server queueing systems with multiple priority classes. Queueing Syst. Theory Appl. **51**, 331–360 (2005)
[42] Harrison, J.M.: Brownian Motion and Stochastic Flow Systems. Wiley, New York (1985)
[43] Harrison, J.M., Lopez, M.J.: Heavy traffic resource pooling in parallel-server systems. Queueing Syst. Theory Appl. **33**, 339–368 (1989)
[44] Harrison, J.M., Zeevi, A.: Dynamic scheduling of a multiclass queue in the Halfin and Whitt heavy traffic regime. Oper. Res. **52**, 243–257 (2004)

[45] Jaiswal, N.K.: Priority Queues. Academic Press, San Diego (1968)
[46] Jelenković, P., Momčilović, P., Squillante, M.S.: Buffer scalability of wireless networks. In: Proc. IEEE Infocom, April 2006
[47] Jelenković, P., Momčilović, P., Squillante, M.S.: Scalability of wireless networks. IEEE/ACM Trans. Netw. **15**(2) (2007)
[48] Jovičić, A., Viswanath, P., Kulkarni, S.: Upper bounds to transport capacity of wireless networks. IEEE Trans. Inf. Theory **50**(11), 2555–2565 (2004)
[49] Jung, K., Lu, Y., Shah, D., Sharma, M., Squillante, M.S.: Revisiting stochastic loss networks: Structures and algorithms. In: Proceedings of ACM SIGMETRICS Conference on Measurement and Modeling of Computer Systems, pp. 407–418. ACM, New York (2008)
[50] Katok, A., Hasselblatt, B.: Introduction to the Modern Theory of Dynamical Systems. Cambridge University Press, Cambridge (1995)
[51] Kelly, F.P.: Blocking probabilities in large circuit-switched networks. Adv. Appl. Probab. **18**(2), 473–505 (1986)
[52] Kelly, F.P.: Loss networks. Ann. Appl. Probab. **1**(3), 319–378 (1991)
[53] Kumar, P.R.: Re-entrant lines. Queueing Syst. Theory Appl. **13**, 87–110 (1993)
[54] Kumar, P.R., Xie, L.-L.: A network information theory for wireless communications: Scaling laws and optimal operation. IEEE Trans. Inf. Theory **50**(5), 748–767 (2004)
[55] Kushner, H.J., Dupuis, P.: Numerical Methods for Stochastic Control Problems in Continuous Time. Springer, Berlin (1992)
[56] Latouche, G., Ramaswami, V.: Introduction to Matrix Analytic Methods in Stochastic Modeling. ASA-SIAM, Philadelphia (1999)
[57] van Leeuwaarden, J.S., Squillante, M.S., Winands, E.M.: Quasi-birth-and-death processes, lattice path counting, and hypergeometric functions. J. Appl. Probab. **46**(2), 507–520 (2009)
[58] Leveque, O., Telatar, E.: Information theoretic upper bounds on the capacity of ad hoc networks. IEEE Trans. Inf. Theory **51**(3), 858–865 (2005)
[59] Louth, G., Mitzenmacher, M., Kelly, F.: Computational complexity of loss networks. Theor. Comput. Sci. **125**(1), 45–59 (1994)
[60] Meyn, S.P.: Sequencing and routing in multiclass queueing networks. Part I: Feedback regulation. SIAM J. Control Optim. **40**, 741–776 (2001)
[61] Meyn, S.P.: Sequencing and routing in multiclass queueing networks. Part II: Workload relaxations. SIAM J. Control Optim. **42**, 178–217 (2003)
[62] Meyn, S.P.: Dynamic safety-stocks for asymptotic optimality in stochastic networks. Queueing Syst. Theory Appl. **50**, 255–297 (2005)
[63] Meyn, S.P., Tweedie, R.L.: Markov Chains and Stochastic Stability. Springer, Berlin (1993). Available at probability.ca/MT
[64] Nelson, R.D., Philips, T.K.: An approximation for the mean response time for shortest queue routing with general interarrival and service times. Perform. Eval. **17**, 123–139 (1993)
[65] Nelson, R.D., Squillante, M.S.: Parallel-server stochastic systems with dynamic affinity scheduling and load balancing. Preprint (2006)
[66] Nelson, R.D., Tantawi, A.N.: Approximate analysis of fork/join synchronization in parallel queues. IEEE Trans. Comput. **37**(6), 739–743 (1988)
[67] Neuts, M.F.: Moment formulas for the Markov renewal branching process. Adv. Appl. Probab. **8**, 690–711 (1978)
[68] Neuts, M.F.: Matrix-Geometric Solutions in Stochastic Models: An Algorithmic Approach. Johns Hopkins University Press, Baltimore (1981)
[69] Neuts, M.F.: Structured Stochastic Matrices of M/G/1 Type and Their Applications. Dekker, New York (1989)
[70] Nowicki, T., Squillante, M.S., Wu, C.W.: Fundamentals of dynamic decentralized optimization in autonomic computing systems. In: Babaoglu, O., Jelasity, M., Montresor, A., Fetzer, C., Leonardi, S., van Moorsel, A., van Steen, M. (eds.) Self-star Properties in Complex Information Systems: Conceptual and Practical Foundations. Lecture Notes in Computer Science, vol. 3460, pp. 204–218. Springer, Berlin (2005)
[71] Osogami, T.: Analysis of Multi-server Systems via Dimensionality Reduction of Markov Chains. PhD thesis, Carnegie Mellon University (2005)

[72] Osogami, T., Harchol-Balter, M., Scheller-Wolf, A.: Analysis of cycle stealing with switching times and thresholds. In: Proceedings of ACM SIGMETRICS Conference on Measurement and Modeling of Computer Systems, pp. 184–195. ACM, New York (2003)

[73] Osogami, T., Harchol-Balter, M., Scheller-Wolf, A.: Analysis of cycle stealing with switching times and thresholds. Perform. Eval. **61**, 347–369 (2005)

[74] Osogami, T., Harchol-Balter, M., Scheller-Wolf, A., Zhang, L.: Exploring threshold-based policies for load sharing. In: Proceedings of the 42nd Annual Allerton Conference on Communication, Control, and Computing (2004)

[75] Peris, V.G., Squillante, M.S., Naik, V.K.: Analysis of the impact of memory in distributed parallel processing systems. In: Proceedings of ACM SIGMETRICS Conference on Measurement and Modeling of Computer Systems, pp. 5–18. ACM, New York (1994)

[76] Pontryagin, L., Boltyanskii, V., Gamkrelidze, R., Mishchenko, E.: The Mathematical Theory of Optimal Processes. Interscience, New York (1962)

[77] Prener, D.: Personal communication (2007)

[78] Reiman, M.I., Simon, B.: An interpolation approximation for queueing systems with Poisson input. Oper. Res. **36**(3), 454–469 (1988)

[79] Rybko, A.N., Stolyar, A.L.: Ergodicity of stochastic processes describing the operations of open queueing networks. Probl. Inf. Transm. **28**, 199–220 (1992)

[80] Seierstad, A., Sydsieter, K.: Sufficient conditions in optimal control theory. Int. Econ. Rev. **18**(2), 367–391 (1977)

[81] Sethuraman, J., Squillante, M.S.: Optimal stochastic scheduling in multiclass parallel queues. In: Proceedings of ACM SIGMETRICS Conference on Measurement and Modeling of Computer Systems, pp. 93–102. ACM, New York (1999)

[82] Sethuraman, J., Squillante, M.S.: Analysis of parallel-server queues under spacesharing and timesharing disciplines. In: Latouche, G., Taylor, P. (eds.) Matrix-Analytic Methods: Theory and Applications, pp. 357–380. World Scientific, Singapore (2002)

[83] Squillante, M.S.: Issues in Shared-Memory Multiprocessor Scheduling: A Performance Analysis. PhD thesis, Department of Computer Science, University of Washington, September 1990

[84] Squillante, M.S.: Stochastic analysis of resource allocation in parallel processing systems. In: Gelenbe, E. (ed.) Computer System Performance Modeling in Perspective: A Tribute to the Work of Prof. K.C. Sevcik, pp. 227–256. Imperial College Press, London (2005)

[85] Squillante, M.S., Tsoukatos, K.P.: Analysis of optimal scheduling in distributed parallel queueing systems. In: Proceedings of International Conference on Computer Communication, August 1995

[86] Squillante, M.S., Wang, F., Papaefthymiou, M.: Stochastic analysis of gang scheduling in parallel and distributed systems. Perform. Eval. **27&28**, 273–296 (1996)

[87] Squillante, M.S., Zhang, Y., Sivasubramaniam, A., Gautam, N.: Generalized parallel-server fork-join queues with dynamic task scheduling. Ann. Oper. Res. **160**, 227–255 (2008)

[88] Squillante, M.S., Zhang, Y., Sivasubramaniam, A., Gautam, N., Franke, H., Moreira, J.: Modeling and analysis of dynamic coscheduling in parallel and distributed environments. In: Proceedings of ACM SIGMETRICS Conference on Measurement and Modeling of Computer Systems, pp. 43–54. ACM, New York (2002)

[89] Stewart, G.W.: Computable error bounds for aggregated Markov chains. J. ACM **30**, 271–285 (1983)

[90] Takagi, H.: Queueing Analysis—A Foundation of Performance Evaluation, vol. 1. North-Holland, New York (1991)

[91] Varma, S., Makowski, A.M.: Interpolation approximations for symmetric fork-join queues. Perform. Eval. **20**, 245–265 (1994)

[92] Whitt, W.: Blocking when service is required from several facilities simultaneously. AT&T Bell Lab. Techn. J. **64**(8), 1807–1856 (1985)

[93] Whitt, W.: Stochastic-Process Limits. Springer, New York (2002)

[94] Williams, R.J.: On dynamic scheduling of a parallel server system with complete resource pooling. Fields Inst. Commun. **28**, 49–71 (2000)

[95] Zheng, Y., Zipkin, P.H.: A queueing model to analyze the value of centralized inventory information. Oper. Res. **38**, 296–307 (1990)

M.S. Squillante (✉)
Mathematical Sciences Department, IBM Thomas J. Watson Research Center, P.O. Box 218, Yorktown Heights, NY 10598, USA
e-mail: mss@watson.ibm.com

On the Selection of Models for Runtime Prediction of System Resources

Sara Casolari and Michele Colajanni

Abstract Applications and services delivered through large Internet Data Centers are now feasible thanks to network and server improvement, but also to virtualization, dynamic allocation of resources and dynamic migrations. The large number of servers and resources involved in these systems requires autonomic management strategies because no amount of human administrators would be capable of cloning and migrating virtual machines in time, as well as re-distributing or re-mapping the underlying hardware. At the basis of most autonomic management decisions, there is the need of evaluating own global behavior and change it when the evaluation indicates that they are not accomplishing what they were intended to do or some relevant anomalies are occurring. Decisions algorithms have to satisfy different time scales constraints. In this chapter we are interested to short-term contexts where runtime prediction models work on the basis of time series coming from samples of monitored system resources, such as disk, CPU and network utilization. In similar environments, we have to address two main issues. First, original time series are affected by limited predictability because measurements are characterized by noises due to system instability, variable offered load, heavy-tailed distributions, hardware and software interactions. Moreover, there is no existing criteria that can help us to choose a suitable prediction model and related parameters with the purpose of guaranteeing an adequate prediction quality. In this chapter, we evaluate the impact that different choices on prediction models have on different time series, and we suggest how to treat input data and whether it is convenient to choose the parameters of a prediction model in a static or dynamic way. Our conclusions are supported by a large set of analyses on realistic and synthetic data traces.

Keywords On-line prediction model · Internet-based system · Stochastic model

1 Introduction

The management of modern Internet Data Centers requires several autonomic management decisions that take real-time decisions on the basis of information related

D. Ardagna, L. Zhang (eds.), *Run-time Models for Self-managing Systems and Applications*, 25–44,
Autonomic Systems, DOI 10.1007/978-3-0346-0433-8_2, © Springer Basel AG 2010

to the current and future state of internal system components. Runtime prediction models that forecast the future behavior of system resources receiving as their input monitored samples play a crucial role in these autonomic algorithms. On the basis of samples frequency and time scale requirements of the decisions, we distinguish three main application contexts: *short-*, *medium-* and *long-term* [34]. In this chapter we focus on short-term management algorithms, such as overload and admission control, load dispatching and intra-host reconfigurations, that require autonomic decisions in the order of few seconds. The literature proposes many models for predicting the load of internal resources [5, 10, 11, 17, 20, 27–29]. Each of them is characterized by different types of input data and many parameters [14], but they provide no methodology for choosing which model is preferable in a specific context, how to set the model parameters, and whether it is necessary or not to treat the input data sets.

In this chapter, we propose some criteria for the choice of the most suitable prediction models to be used in different short-term autonomic contexts by considering that each model must satisfy the time constraints of the application context and achieve a required prediction quality. To this purpose it is possible to leverage several different implementations of the same prediction model. In this chapter we focus on two main features: the implementation of algorithms for input data treatment, and the static or dynamic estimation of the model parameters. We analyze the quality of the prediction models for different statistical properties of the monitored samples and different time requirements.

In this chapter we propose two main contributes. The first important result is that the noise component of a time series influences the quality of the prediction both in terms of reliability and in terms of accuracy. For this reason, the proposed criteria to choose the prediction models take into account the statistical properties of the input time series and the time constraints of the application context. We demonstrate that the models that use on-line filtering of the monitored samples and a dynamic estimation of the model parameters achieve the best prediction quality, but at the price of a high computational complexity. For this reason, they may be inadequate when adopted in short-term application contexts with strong time constraints. As a second contribution, we propose some criteria to choose among the several alternatives concerning any prediction model with the goal of satisfying the desired prediction quality and the time constraints imposed by the autonomic decision context. For example, runtime prediction models will be adopted in the sixth chapter for the design of an autonomic framework. Here, our main conclusions are supported by experiments on a large set of realistic and synthetic time series.

The rest of the chapter is organized as follows. Section 2 defines the runtime prediction problem and the performance metrics to evaluate the prediction quality in an autonomic context. Section 3 analyzes the statistical properties of the time series that may influence the prediction quality and presents the main features characterizing a runtime prediction model. Section 4 presents the criteria for choosing among the various alternatives existing in a prediction mechanism. Section 5 discusses the main experimental results for different characteristics of the time series that are related to system resources of Internet Data Centers. Section 6 concludes this chapter with some final remarks.

2 Background

The runtime prediction model of interest for this chapter consider samples related to system resources of Internet Data Centers adopting some autonomic management algorithm. These samples flow directly from system monitors or can pass also through on-line filters that denoise the raw data. Let S be the set of monitored samples and Y the set of filtered samples.

At sample j, the runtime prediction model takes as its input a subset of R time ordered samples referring to one system resource. This set is denoted by the time series $X[R]_j = (x_j, \ldots, x_{j-(R-1)})$.

If k is the *prediction window*, then a prediction model is a function $P()$ forecasting the value of the time series $X[R]_j$ at the sample $j + k$ that is,

$$\hat{x}_{j+k} = P(X[R]_j) \tag{2.1}$$

As we are interested to short-term forecasting models where samples are in the order of seconds and servers belong to Internet Data Centers, we must address the issue that the time series X is characterized by a chaotic behavior caused by a noise component that tends to deform the real view of a resource behavior [1, 10]. For prediction purposes, we can represent the time series X through a noise component e^* and an off-line filtered time series Y^* that is composed by denoised samples of X:

$$X = Y^* + e^* \tag{2.2}$$

When Y^* is denoised through off-line filtering methods, we can achieve an optimal representation of the time series. We use it as a term of reference when we have to evaluate the quality of the predicted results. A runtime prediction model operating in a time scale in the order of seconds can be evaluated through three factors: it must satisfy the time constraints imposed by the application context; it must achieve a prediction quality that is *accurate* and *reliable* as defined in [4, 18, 31].

Let $\hat{X}[N]$ denote a set of N predicted values. The *accuracy* corresponds to the degree of closeness of the predicted time series $\hat{X}$ to the optimal representation that in our case corresponds to the off-line filtered time series Y^*. If $\hat{X}[N] = (\hat{x}_1, \ldots, \hat{x}_N)$ is the predicted time series of N values and $Y^*[N] = (y_1^*, \ldots, y_N^*)$ is the corresponding off-line filtered time series, a popular metric for measuring the accuracy of $\hat{X}[N]$ is the Mean Square Error (MSE) [33], that is defined as follows:

$$MSE = \frac{\sum_{i=1}^{N}(\hat{x}_i - y_i^*)^2}{N} \tag{2.3}$$

where $\hat{x}_i$ and y_i^* are the values of the predicted time series and of the off-line filtered time series at sample i, respectively. The smaller the values of this difference, the greater is the accuracy of the prediction model.

The *reliability* measures the consistency of the prediction. It is typically associated to the width of the prediction interval that is the range of values, above and below the predicted time series, in which the samples of the time series X will fall with a certain probability [3]. The probabilities typically used to estimate the prediction interval are in the range 0.95–0.99 as in [16]. For example, by choosing a probability of 0.95, the lower limit l_{j+k} and the upper limit u_{j+k} of the prediction interval at sample $j + k$ are given by:

$$l_{j+k} = \hat{x}_{j+k} - 1.96\frac{\sigma_{\hat{x}}}{\sqrt{N}} \qquad u_{j+k} = \hat{x}_{j+k} + 1.96\frac{\sigma_{\hat{x}}}{\sqrt{N}} \qquad (2.4)$$

where $\sigma_{\hat{x}}$ is the standard deviation of the predicted time series $\hat{X}[R]_j$, and the coefficient 1.96 is obtained by the normal distribution table for a probability value 0.95 [16]. The difference $u_{j+k} - l_{j+k}$ determines the prediction interval width. Let $L[N] = (l_1, \ldots, l_N)$ be the set of the lower limit values and $U[N] = (u_1, \ldots, u_N)$ be the set of upper limit values in an observation period of N predictions. The reliability of the predicted time series $\hat{X}[N]$ in this observation period is the mean of the prediction intervals width [3], that is:

$$PI = \frac{\sum_{i=1}^{N}(u_i - l_i)}{N} \qquad (2.5)$$

Higher PI values are associated to less reliable predictions.

The quality of the prediction depends on the nature of the time series X and on the choice of the prediction mechanism, that will be described in Sect. 4. We should observe that the accuracy and reliability are independent attributes and a trade-off between their values does not exist. Simple strategies are able to pursue just an accurate or a reliable prediction. On the other hand, more complex solutions are able to improve both accuracy and reliability at the price of a higher computational cost.

3 Prediction in Noisy Contexts

Prediction in a noisy context related to autonomic decisions does not require just the application of one suitable model, but a complex mechanism with several alternatives. The presence of dozen of models, each with many parameters, disorients the choice because, to the best of our knowledge, there is no criteria for choosing which model is better in a certain context, how to set the model parameters, whether input data treatment is really necessary. For example, several models were proposed to forecast the resource state of servers that can be extended to Internet Data Center contexts. For example, the Linear Regression (LR) model was applied to Web-based systems [5], the Exponential Smoothing (ES) to the running time of jobs [11, 28], the Holt's methods (Holt's) to the throughput of large TCP transfers [17], the Autoregressive (AR) and Autoregressive Integrated Moving Average (ARIMA) to the load [10, 29] and network traffic [27]; the tendency based predictors, such as the Cubic Spline (CS), to the CPU load [20]. We outline the most important characteristics that all these prediction models have in common, and suggest the criteria that should drive the choice of the best alternatives during the different steps of the prediction mechanism. Moreover, we evaluate the impact of each choice on the quality of the prediction.

As it may be expected, any prediction model should consider the statistical characteristics of the input time series X where, as evidenced in [12], the most important features for prediction are:

- the *dispersion* of the noise component e^* of the time series, as defined in (2.2);
- the *correlation* between the noise component e^* and the off-line filtered time series Y^*, as defined in (2.2).

The second set of alternatives characterizing any model are related to the choices about how to use a prediction model. Indeed, once guaranteed that the time constraints imposed by the application context are satisfied, then we have the following choices to achieve an accurate and/or reliable prediction:

- the data passed to the prediction model may be a subset of the samples S or a subset of filtered samples Y;
- the parameters can be chosen once (static choice) or periodically (dynamic choice).

In Sect. 3.1 we describe the statistical properties that must be considered in a short-term prediction and we evaluate the relationship between the statistical properties and the prediction quality. Section 3.2 presents the possible alternatives obtained by combining the main features that characterize a prediction model.

3.1 Statistical Properties of Time Series

The dispersion of the noise component and the correlation between the noise component and the off-line filtered time series are the main statistical properties that influence the prediction quality. By referring to (2.2), the dispersion of the noise component e^* in a time series of N elements is denoted by its *standard deviation*, that is equal to:

$$\sigma_{e^*} = \sqrt{\frac{1}{N} \sum_{i=1}^{N} (e_i^* - \mu_{e^*})^2}. \tag{3.1}$$

where e_i^* is the noise component at sample i, and μ_{e^*} is the mean value of e^*. By increasing the value of σ_{e^*}, the dispersion of the time series augments thus complicating the possibility of achieving a reliable prediction [2].

The correlation between e^* and Y^* denotes that the noise component e_i^* at sample i can vary from one sample to another on the basis of the value of the off-line filtered sample y_i^*. At each sample i, we have a correlation between y_i^* and e_i^*, which is measured through the *correlation index* ρ [4]:

$$\rho = \frac{\sigma_{e^* y^*}}{\sigma_{e^*} \sigma_{y^*}} \tag{3.2}$$

where $\sigma_{e^*y^*}$ is the covariance of the time series Y^* and e^*, while σ_{y^*} and σ_{e^*} are their standard deviations, respectively. The correlation index measures the dependence of the noise component on the behavior of the off-line filtered time series Y^* that is the best representation of the time series X. If the correlation index is null, then the noise component e^* does not change as a function of the variations of Y^*. If the correlation index is not null, then the noise component is time variable and its behavior changes on the basis of the off-line filtered time series Y^*. The correlation of the noise component influences the accuracy of the prediction model as demonstrated in [14].

We offer a qualitative evaluation of the impact of these two statistical properties on the prediction accuracy and reliability.

Let us initially focus on the noise dispersion, by considering two time series composed by $N = 1000$ samples that have the same data profile and null correlation of the noise component, but that are characterized by different values of σ_{e^*}. Figures 1(a) and 1(b) show two time series with a $\rho = 0$ and σ_{e^*} equal to 0.05 and 0.2, respectively. If we apply a linear prediction model to these two time series, we get the results in Fig. 2. The continuous line is the off-line filtered time series Y^* that is the best representation of the time series X; the two dotted lines denote the lower and upper limit of the prediction interval evaluated with a 95% probability.

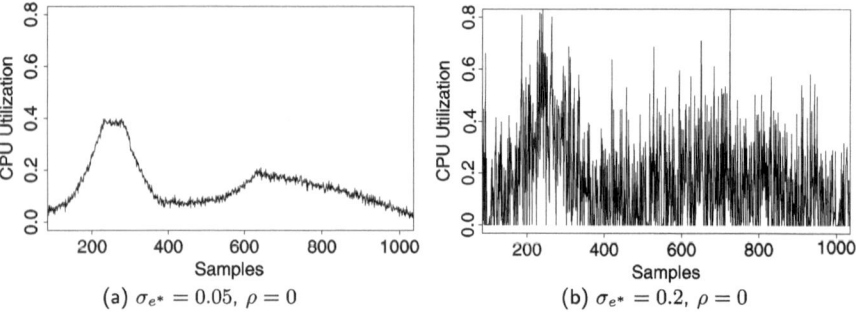

(a) $\sigma_{e^*} = 0.05,\ \rho = 0$ (b) $\sigma_{e^*} = 0.2,\ \rho = 0$

Fig. 1 Time series profiles

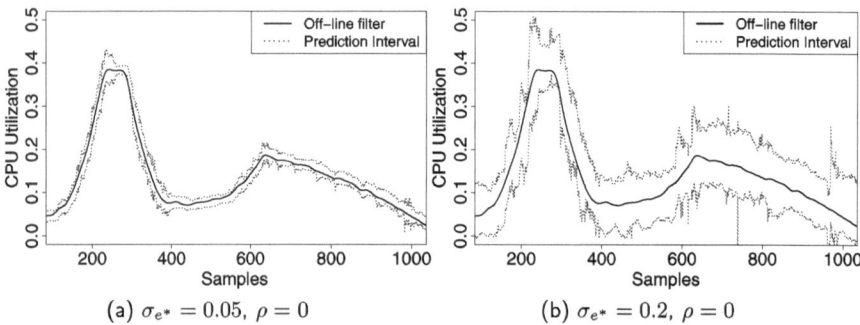

(a) $\sigma_{e^*} = 0.05,\ \rho = 0$ (b) $\sigma_{e^*} = 0.2,\ \rho = 0$

Fig. 2 Results of the prediction model (reliability)

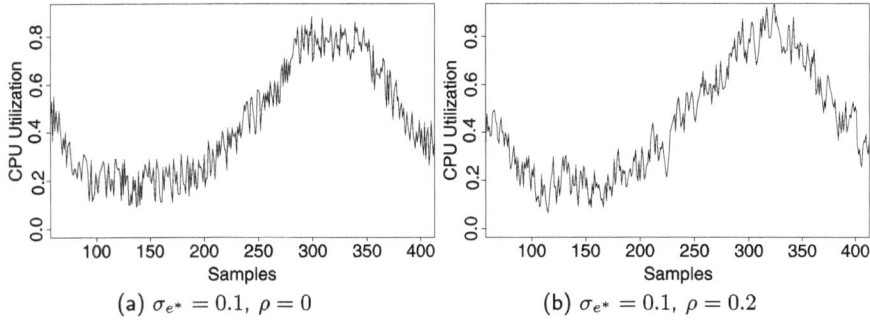

Fig. 3 Time series profiles

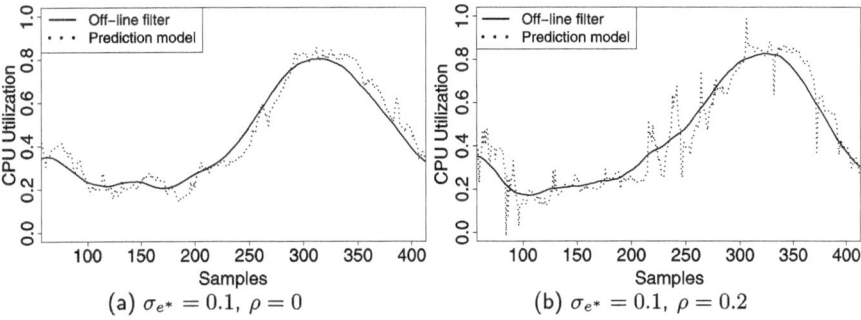

Fig. 4 Results of the prediction model (accuracy)

We recall that a prediction is reliable when this interval is narrow. Figure 2(a) shows that the upper and the lower limits of the prediction interval on the times series characterized by $\sigma_{e*} = 0.05$ are very close. When the time series is more scattered, as shown in Fig. 2(b), the reliability of the prediction decreases as evidenced by the much larger prediction interval. As the reliability is high when the prediction interval is narrow, we can give a qualitative confirmation that the noise dispersion σ_{e*} has a strong impact on the prediction reliability.

To evaluate the impact of the statistical properties on the accuracy, we consider two time series that have the same profile, same σ_{e*} and that are characterized by a correlation index equal to 0 (Fig. 3(a)) and 0.2 (Fig. 3(b)). These time series seem to have similar behavior but the prediction results shown in Fig. 4 evidence that their behavior is different. In these figures, the continuous line still denotes the off-line filtered time series Y^* of the time series X, and the dotted line represents the predicted time series $\hat{X}$. The deviation between the continuous line and the dotted line offers a qualitative view of the prediction accuracy: accurate models are able to forecast the behavior of X through a representation that is very close to the optimal representation. If we compare Figs. 4(a) and 4(b), we can observe that, when the time series is perturbed by a correlated noise component, the prediction results show a much higher distance between the line of the prediction model and the line of the off-line filtered representation.

3.2 Alternatives Choices for a Prediction Model

We have seen that the dispersion of the noise component e^* limits the prediction reliability, while the correlation between e^* and the time series Y^* influences the prediction accuracy. When we consider a prediction model and we want to achieve a reliable and accurate prediction, we can work on two directions: choosing raw samples S or on-line filtered samples Y; choosing static parameters or dynamic parameters.

On-line filtering is useful when monitored samples are embedded into a noisy signal and are perturbed by outliers [1, 10], while it is useless in a time series with low dispersion of the noise component. The static or dynamic choice of the parameters can impact not only on the prediction quality but also on the computational cost of the prediction models. Hence, in a context of short-term runtime predictions, this choice should be carefully pursued.

A *static* choice of parameters means that in the considered context of N predicted values, the prediction model works with the same set of parameters values. This solution has the lowest computational cost and, for this reason, it is typically used when the time constraints are strong.

A *dynamic* choice of the parameters means that the model parameters are re-evaluated at each prediction step. This should improve the prediction quality at the price of a higher computational cost.

Combining the choices on the input data with the static or dynamic estimation of parameters, we can identify several alternatives for the same prediction model. Choosing the best combination is not immediate even because each driver can be used to achieve better accuracy or better reliability. We can expect that the most computational expensive alternative (filtered input data and dynamic choice of the parameters) can achieve the best results. However, we have also to take into account the time constraints of the application context. In short-term forecasting in Internet Data Centers composed by hundreds or thousands of servers, where the state of each server may be represented by 6–7 time series corresponding to its most important internal resources, data filtering and adaptive estimation of parameters risk to be unfeasible.

In this chapter we want to define some basic criteria for choosing the most important features characterizing a prediction model: the characteristics of the input data (Sect. 4.1) and the static or dynamic estimation of parameters (Sect. 4.2).

4 Alternatives in a Prediction Mechanism

Each prediction mechanism is characterized by several alternative implementations, where the choice about filtering or not filtering input data, and choosing the best parameters of the prediction model in a static or dynamic way are the two most important. These alternatives characterize every prediction models and are especially important when they are used in an autonomic context without the possibility of human intervention and interpretation. In order to evaluate the consequences of each of these alternatives we initially take into account simple well known models. The motivation is that they are able to better evidence the impact on the prediction quality obtained by the different implementation choices and because they do not influence the quality through the usage of sophisticated prediction techniques. Our choice for simple models is also motivated by the application context characterized by short-time predictions suitable to autonomic decisions subject to real-time constraints in Internet Data Centers.

4.1 Monitored and Filtered Time Series

We propose some criteria to decide whether a runtime prediction model needs filtered samples Y or can work directly on monitored samples S to reach the objectives of accuracy and reliability while satisfying the time constraint imposed by the application context.

There are several interesting models for data treatment of time series (e.g., [15, 21]) that can be classified in two main groups: *smoothing* [7, 19, 25] and *interpolation* [8, 26, 32] techniques. However, we are not interested to decide which on-line filter is the best to denoise the monitored samples, but to evidence the impact of the different choices. For this reason, we consider a simple model, such as the Exponential Weighted Moving Average (EWMA), that is used in many fields: from signal processing, to telecommunications and control theory. It is useful in the application contexts characterized by runtime constraints and when data show some non-deterministic behaviors [19]. EWMA is the weighted mean of the R monitored samples of the time series $S[R]_j$, where the weights decrease exponentially. A filtered sample based on the EWMA, at sample j, is equal to:

$$y_j = \alpha s_j + (1 - \alpha)s_{j-1} \tag{4.1}$$

where the parameter $\alpha = \frac{2}{(R+1)}$ is the *smoothing factor* [22]. The initial value y_R is typically initialized to the arithmetic mean of the first R samples:

$$y_R = \frac{\sum_{1 \leq i \leq R} x_i}{R} \tag{4.2}$$

In Fig. 5, we give a visual interpretation of the impact of data filtering on two times series characterized by different noise components. Figure 5(a) shows monitored samples $S[R]$ (dots) referring to the CPU utilization of a server that has a low noise dispersion, and their filtered representation $Y[R]$ (continuous line). Here, filtering may be unnecessary because monitored samples already exhibit a clear trend component. On the other hand, when samples are characterized by a high noise dispersion, as in Fig. 5(b), an on-line filtering model is mandatory, because it reduces the chaotic view of samples by avoiding undesired noises and outliers.

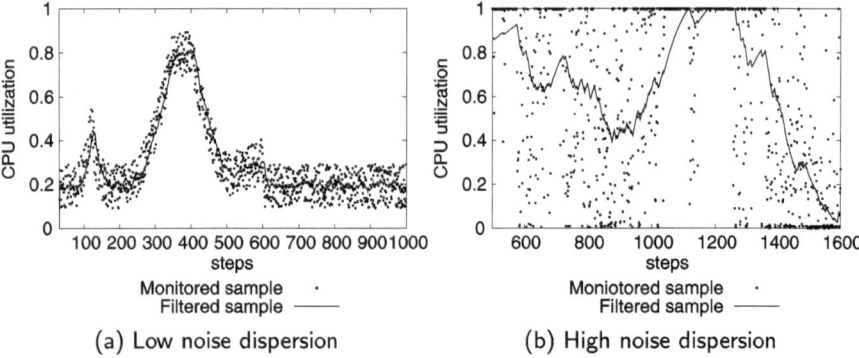

(a) Low noise dispersion   (b) High noise dispersion

Fig. 5 Monitored samples vs. Filtered samples

4.2 Static and Dynamic Parameters

Each prediction model can use different methodologies to estimate its parameters. In
a runtime application context, the choice of the parameters is even more important,
because it impacts not only the prediction quality but also the computational cost.

In this chapter we are interested to define a criteria to choose how estimating
the model parameters once the objectives of quality and the time constraints of the
application context have been settled. Again, we are not interested to consider and
compare several runtime prediction models, but to assess how different choices of
parameters in a simple forecasting model impact the accuracy and reliability of prediction. As an example of prediction model, we consider the Exponential Smoothing (ES) that is an intuitive forecasting method that unequally weights the samples
of the input time series $X[R]_j$ [13]. Non-uniform weighting is achieved through
smoothing parameters which determine how much weight is assigned to each sample. ES models have been adopted in many fields for decades [1, 6] and are suitable
to runtime applications.

Following the results of the previous section, we have to consider two versions
of ES, where parameters are statically or dynamically chosen: static Exponential
Smoothing (sES) and dynamic Exponential Smoothing (dES). The sES model predicts the value of $X[R]_j$ at k steps ahead as a weighted average of the last sample
x_j and of previously predicted samples $\hat{x}_j$:

$$\hat{x}_{j+k} = \gamma \hat{x}_j + (1 - \gamma)x_j \qquad (4.3)$$

where $0 < \gamma < 1$ is the *smoothing factor* that determines how much weight is given
to each sample. The more the behavior of the time series $X[R]_j$ changes, the more
the new sample x_i should influence the predicted sample $\hat{x}_{i+k}$, and thus, the higher
the smoothing parameter γ should be. The sES model is a simple linear algorithm
that is characterized by a very low prediction cost, but its accuracy depends on the
time series characteristics. When the time series changes slowly, it exhibits a good
prediction quality. When the time series is unstable, the prediction quality of the

sES decreases as well. Moreover, the sES tends to introduce a delay in the data prediction that is proportional to the size of the past time series $X[R]_j$. The delay in the prediction can limit the applicability of the model as it risks to be unsuitable in contexts that require reactive predictions.

We obtain a dynamic Exponential Smoothing model (dES) by re-evaluating the smoothing factor γ_j at each prediction sample j. There are different proposals for the dynamic estimation of γ_j (e.g., [9, 13, 30, 31]). Although there is no consensus, a widely used procedure is proposed by Trigg and Leach [30]. They define the smoothing parameter as the absolute value of the ratio of the smoothed error, A_j, to the absolute error, M_j:

$$\gamma_j = \frac{A_j}{M_j} \tag{4.4}$$

The smoothed and absolute errors are equal to:

$$A_j = \phi\epsilon_j + (1-\phi)A_{j-1} \qquad M_j = \phi|\epsilon_j| + (1-\phi)M_{j-1} \tag{4.5}$$

where $\epsilon_j = x_j - \hat{x}_j$ is the forecast error at sample j and ϕ is set arbitrary with 0.2 being a common choice [30]. This dynamical choice of γ_j should improve the prediction quality and should limit the delay problem related to sES.

The dES model is expected to be useful in contexts characterized by time series with a variable noise component. However, we should consider that the computational cost of the dES model is higher than that of the sES and this cost may limit the applicability of dES in contexts characterized by many monitored system resources. This limit is evident when we consider prediction models characterized by a high number of parameters, such as the ARIMA and the Bayesian models.

By combining the alternatives on input data and on parameters estimation, we identify four main alternatives for any prediction model:

- **M-sES**: the input time series is based on monitored samples S, and the prediction model uses a static estimation of parameters (e.g., sES).
- **F-sES**: the time series consists of filtered samples Y (e.g., through the EWMA model); the prediction model adopts a static evaluation of the parameters (e.g., sES).
- **M-dES**: the time series is composed by monitored samples S, and the prediction model updates dynamically its parameters on the basis of the statistical properties of monitored samples (e.g., dES).
- **F-dES**: the time series consists of on-line filtered samples (e.g., through the EWMA model), and the prediction model (e.g., dES) uses a dynamic estimation of the model parameters.

In the next section we evaluate the best combinations of different input samples and data manipulation that can improve accuracy and/or reliability. As anticipated at the end of Sect. 2, these attributes are not in opposition. Some alternatives may favor accuracy, other reliability, others both of them.

5 Results

We evaluate the accuracy and the reliability of the four combinations characterizing a prediction mechanism through the Mean Square Error (MSE) and the mean of Prediction Interval (PI), introduced in (2.3) and in (2.5), respectively. We recall that the Discrete Wavelet Transform (DWT) is chosen as the off-line filter that gives the most representative estimation of the input times series [23] and that is used as a reference term for assessing the accuracy and reliability of the predictions.

We evaluate the models for a wide range of time series that represent the CPU utilization sampled from servers of an Internet Data Center [1, 24]. We consider a profile of a denoised time series characterized by two increments of its values and followed by similar decreases. We generate several synthetic time series of the monitored samples by combining a denoised signal with several noise components characterized by different values of σ_{e*} and ρ. We evaluate the impact of each combination on the accuracy and reliability of the considered prediction models by considering:

- the intensity of the noise dispersion σ_e^* of the monitored time series;
- the size of the prediction window k;
- the level of the noise correlation ρ.

5.1 Sensitivity to the Noise Component

We evaluate how the accuracy and reliability of the prediction models are affected by a noise dispersion σ_{e*} ranging in $\{0.05, 0.1, 0.15, 0.2, 0.25, 0.3\}$. In this first set of experiments, ρ is set to 0. Figure 6 shows two time series characterized by $\rho = 0$ and σ_{e*} equal to 0.05 and 0.3, that point out how much the variability of a time series increases as a function of σ_{e*}.

Tables 1 and 2 show the results of the MSE and the PI, respectively, for every value of σ_{e*} and for a prediction window $k = 10$. The results of Table 1 highlights the ability of dynamic models, M-dES and F-dES, to obtain more accurate predictions (i.e., lower values of MSE) for any σ_{e*}. The dynamic models can better track

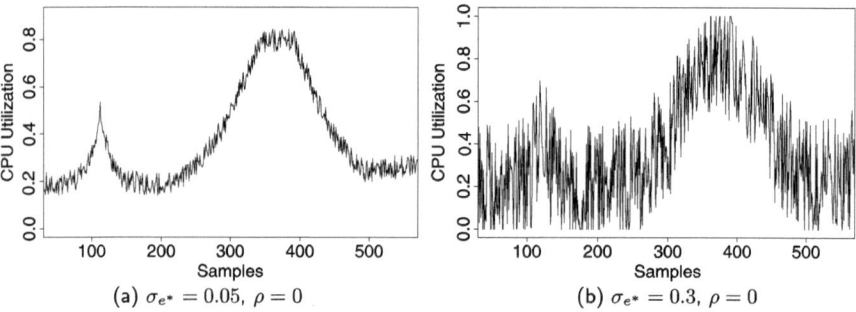

(a) $\sigma_{e*} = 0.05$, $\rho = 0$ (b) $\sigma_{e*} = 0.3$, $\rho = 0$

Fig. 6 Time series profiles

Table 1 MSE—$k = 10$, $\rho = 0$

	0.05	0.1	0.15	0.2	0.25	0.3
M-sES	0.040	0.072	0.100	0.115	0.146	0.152
F-sES	0.027	0.041	0.070	0.074	0.094	0.101
M-dES	0.020	0.027	0.030	0.033	0.049	0.057
F-dES	0.016	0.024	0.027	0.031	0.040	0.042

Table 2 PI—$k = 10$, $\rho = 0$

	0.05	0.1	0.15	0.2	0.25	0.3
M-sES	0.105	0.189	0.269	0.367	0.446	0.509
F-sES	0.046	0.071	0.106	0.164	0.198	0.231
M-dES	0.083	0.159	0.246	0.332	0.403	0.457
F-dES	0.026	0.052	0.087	0.122	0.136	0.165

changes in the behavior of the time series, as they evaluate dynamically their parameters. This characteristic seems necessary in non-stationary time series related to short-term application contexts.

The results of Table 2 show the PI values. The models based on an online filtered representation, F-sES and F-dES, are always characterized by lower prediction interval than the M-sES and M-dES models. In particular, the PI value of F-sES and F-dES are contained in range 2.67 and 23.12 while the values of the M-sES and M-dES are between 8.32 an 50.91. These results confirm that, by reducing the noise dispersion, on-line filtering limits the indeterminacy of time series and improves the prediction reliability. The prediction models using unfiltered monitored samples are too much sensitive to the variations of the noise dispersion. Moreover, in contexts characterized by high values of σ_{e*}, all prediction models are characterized by higher PI values thus confirming the impact of σ_{e*} on the reduction of the prediction reliability.

Figure 7 gives a qualitative representation of the behavior of the prediction models on time series with a low noise dispersion ($\sigma_{e*} = 0.05$). These graphs report for all prediction models the curve of the off-line filtered time series based on the DWT (continuous gray line), the curve of the predicted time series at $k = 10$ steps ahead (continuous black line) and the curves of prediction interval (dotted lines). The closeness between the curve of the filtered time series with the predicted curve represents the prediction accuracy, while the width of the prediction interval shows the prediction reliability. The results of Fig. 7 show that on a time series characterized by a low dispersion of the noise component, all models obtain similar prediction qualities both in terms of accuracy and of reliability. The M-sES and M-dES are subjected to some spikes that reduce their reliability (for example, near the sample 300 in Fig. 7(a) or from sample 300 to sample 400 in Fig. 7(c)). On the other hand, the prediction intervals of F-sES and F-dES models (Figs. 7(b) and 7(d)) are smaller with fewer spikes during the entire observation period.

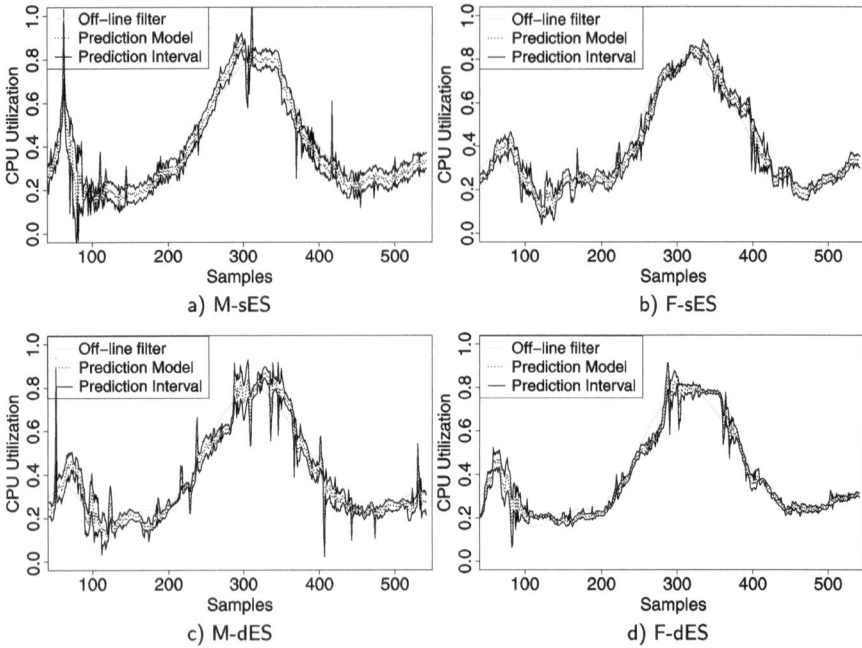

Fig. 7 Qualitative evaluation—$\sigma_{e^*} = 0.05$, $\rho = 0$

We pass now to consider a time series characterized by higher dispersions of the noise component ($\sigma_{e^*} = 0.3$). In this context the prediction qualities differ significantly as evidenced by Figs. 8 and 9 reporting accuracy and reliability of the models, respectively. In Fig. 8, the continuous line denotes the off-line filtered time series and the dotted lines represent the predicted time series. The predicted curves achieved by models with a static estimation of the parameters (Figs. 8(a) and 8(b)) are characterized by a high deviation from the best representation (continuous line), while models characterized by a dynamic estimation of the parameters are more accurate (see Figs. 8(c) and 8(d)). Since in a short-term application context the time series are not stationary and change their behavior over time, the static estimations of the parameters may be inappropriate.

We pass now to estimate the prediction reliability by considering the best representation of the time series (i.e., the off-line filtered time series represented as a continuous curve) and the prediction interval evaluated with a probability of 0.95 (dotted curves) by assuming the same statistical conditions for the input time series. We show that prediction models operating on unfiltered time series are characterized by large prediction intervals independently of a static (Fig. 9(a)) or dynamic (Fig. 9(c)) estimation of the parameters. On the other hand, the prediction models using filtered time series are much more reliable as shown by the narrow intervals in Figs. 9(b) and 9(d). We can conclude that for reliability purposes, data filtering is more important than a dynamic estimation of the parameters of the prediction model.

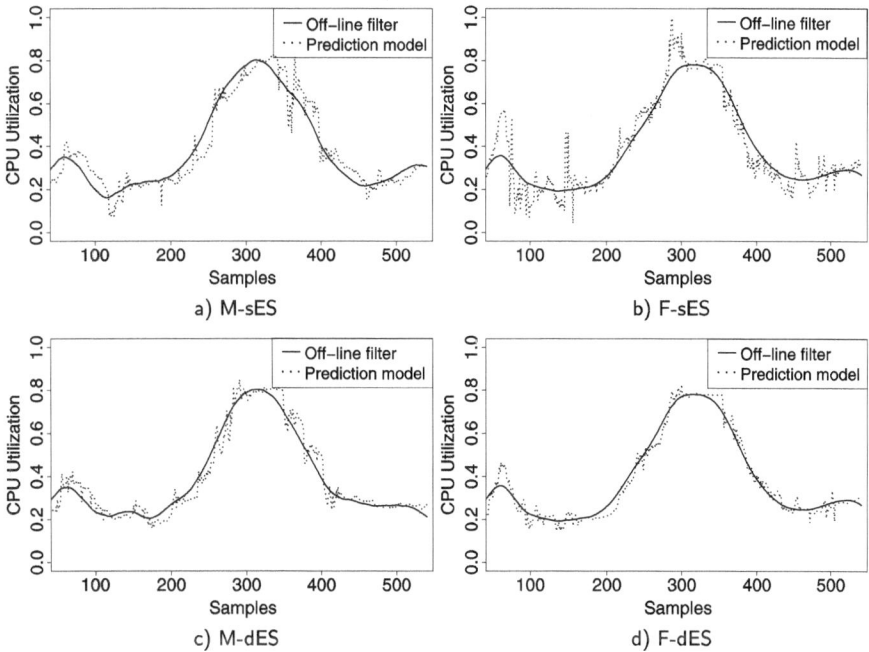

Fig. 8 Accuracy—$\sigma_{e^*} = 0.3$, $\rho = 0$

In application contexts characterized by a variable dispersion of the noise component, a real-time management system requiring reliable predictions must use a prediction mechanism that filters time series. If accuracy is more important, it is necessary to choose prediction models that use a dynamic estimation of the parameters. When both accuracy and reliability are important, the best prediction mechanism uses online filtering and dynamic estimation of model parameters, but these choices may result computationally too much expensive for some short-term application contexts.

5.2 Sensitivity Analysis

To demonstrate the robustness of criteria for the choice of the most adequate prediction model, we present the results of a sensitivity analysis to the prediction window (k) and to the correlation index (ρ).

We evaluate the accuracy and the reliability of the considered prediction models for $k = (1, 5, 10, 20)$ steps ahead and for two time series profiles characterized by a low noise dispersion ($\sigma_{e^*} = 0.1$), and high noise dispersion ($\sigma_{e^*} = 0.3$). The histograms in Fig. 10 and in Fig. 11 report the MSE and the PI, respectively. These figures confirm the main results of Sect. 5.1: the F-dES model has the lowest values of MSE and PI for both time series and for any prediction window. The prediction

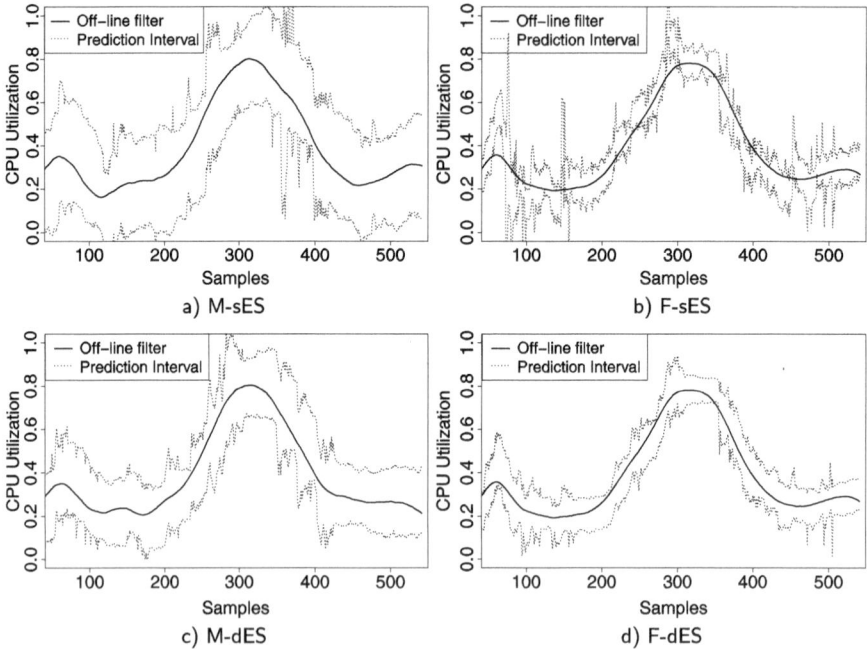

Fig. 9 Reliability—$\sigma_{e^*} = 0.3$, $\rho = 0$

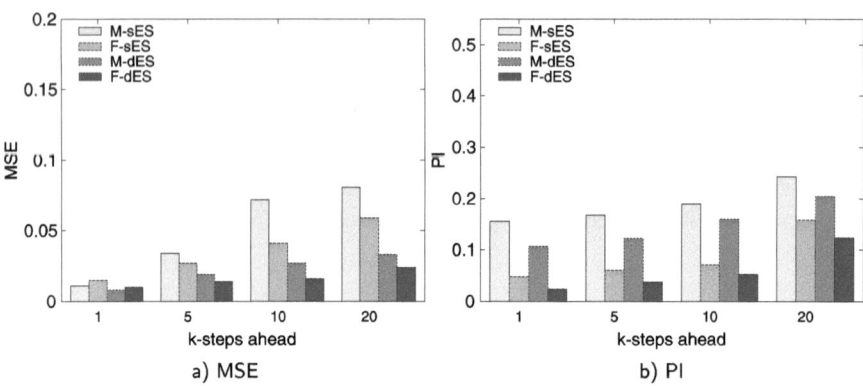

Fig. 10 Prediction quality as function of the k steps ahead—$\sigma_{e^*} = 0.1$, $\rho = 0$

accuracy and reliability of the other models confirm that, for all values of the prediction window, the dynamic models have lower values of the MSE while the prediction models based on an on-line filtered representation of input data have always smaller values of PI. However, it is important to observe that in contexts characterized by a low dispersion of the noise component, the models show similar MSE and PI values for every prediction window, as shown in Fig. 10. When the input time series are characterized by high values of the noise dispersion, then the performance metrics

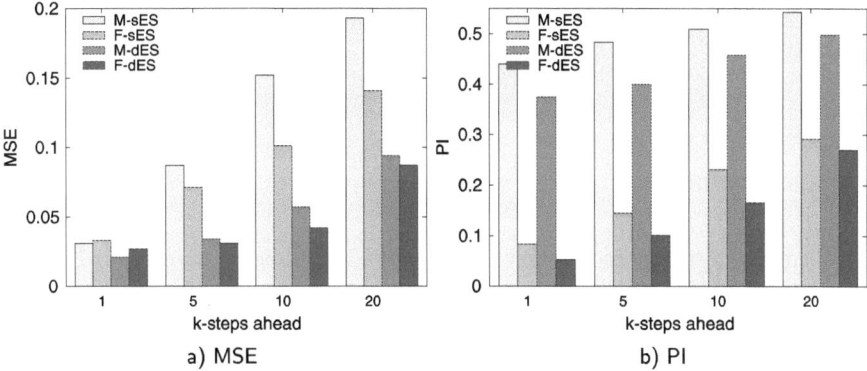

Fig. 11 Prediction quality as function of the k steps ahead—$\sigma_{e^*} = 0.3$, $\rho = 0$

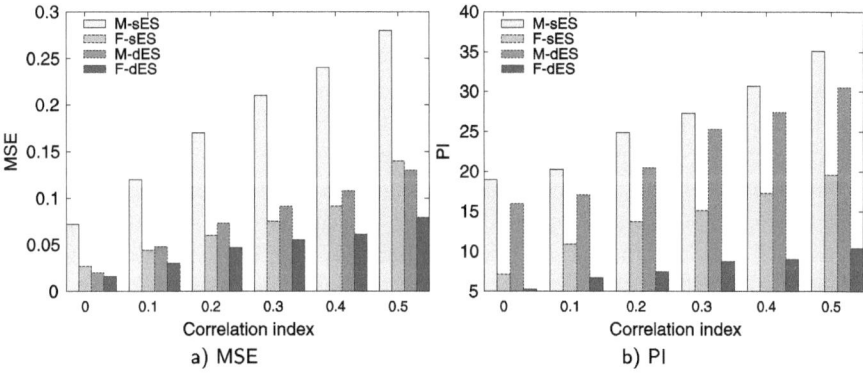

Fig. 12 Prediction quality as function of the ρ—$\sigma_{e^*} = 0.1$, $k = 10$

MSE and PI vary significantly on the basis of the prediction model. These results confirm that the proposed criteria to choose the adequate prediction model remain valid for different sizes of the prediction window. Moreover, they confirm that to obtain reliable predictions, the forecasting model has to work on on-line filtered samples while to improve the accuracy the prediction model has to estimate its parameters dynamically.

We are now interested to examine the effects of the correlation of the noise component ρ on the prediction quality by considering six representative examples of correlation indexes $\rho = \{0, 0.1, 0.2, 0.3, 0.4, 0.5\}$. As shown in Fig. 12, the accuracy and reliability of the considered models change significantly as a function of ρ. The histograms confirm that the MSE and PI augment as a function of increasing ρ values. When the input time series are characterized by a not null correlation index, a dynamic estimation of the parameters is insufficient to achieve accurate predictions, as well the on-line filtering of the monitored samples does not guarantee reliable predictions. In these contexts, both considered drivers (i.e., filtering and dynamic choice of parameters) are mandatory as shown in Fig. 12 where just the

F-dES model is able to achieve good accuracy (low MSE) and acceptable reliability (low PI).

6 Conclusions

In a context characterized by very large numbers of system resources, such as modern Internet Data Centers, decisions for access control, dynamic allocation of resources and dynamic migrations require autonomic management strategies because no amount of human administrators would be capable of cloning and migrating virtual machines in time, as well as re-distributing or re-mapping underlying resources. In this chapter we consider short-term prediction models that can support runtime management decisions, as we will see in the sixth chapter. Literature contains dozens of runtime prediction models, however there is no criteria for choosing which model is better in a certain context and how to set the model parameters in order to guarantee accurate and reliable predictions in a context characterized by no human intervention. We confirm that to forecast the future behavior of a system resource we have to take into account the statistical properties of the input data set coming from monitored measures and characterized by different noises. Then, we consider that any prediction model can work on two drivers: to treat or not its input data, to choose its parameters in a static or dynamic way. When the noise dispersion of the monitored measures is high, reliable predictions can be achieved only if prediction models work on filtered representations of input data. Moreover, a dynamic estimation of the model parameters is a key point to obtain accurate predictions when the time series are characterized by some correlation of the noise component. We have verified the proposed criteria for several conditions, one online filter and a simple prediction model, but it is worth to observe that main conclusions have general validity.

References

[1] Andreolini, M., Casolari, S., Colajanni, M.: Models and framework for supporting run-time decisions in web-based systems. ACM Trans. Web 2(3) (2008)
[2] Belsley, D.A.: Modelling and forecasting reliability. Int. J. Forecast. 4(3), 427–447 (1988)
[3] Bonett, D.: Approximate confidence interval for standard deviation of nonnormal distributions. Comput. Stat. Data Anal. 50(3), 775–882 (2006)
[4] Brockwell, P.J., Davis, R.A.: Introduction to Time Series and Forecasting. Springer, Berlin (2001)
[5] Casolari, S., Colajanni, M.: Short-term prediction models for server management in internet-based contexts. Decis. Support Syst. 48 (2009)
[6] Cherkasova, L., Phaal, P.: Session-based admission control: a mechanism for peak load management of commercial web sites. IEEE Trans. Comput. 51(6), 669–685 (2002)

[7] Crosby, S.A., Wallach, D.S., Riedi, R.H.: Opportunities and limits of remote timing attacks. ACM Trans. Inf. Syst. Secur. **12**(3), 1–29 (2009)

[8] De Boor, C., Swartz, B.: Piecewise monotone interpolation. J. Approx. Theory **21** (1977)

[9] Dennis, J.: A performance test of a run-based adaptive exponential smoothing. Prod. Invent. Manage. **19** (1978)

[10] Dinda, P., O'Hallaron, D.: Host load prediction using linear models. Cluster Comput. **3**(4) (2000)

[11] Dobber, M., Koole, G., Van det Mei, R.: Dynamic load balancing experiments in a grid. In: Proc. of the 5th IEEE International Symposium on Cluster Computing and on the Grid, May 2005

[12] Dobber, M., Van det Mei, R., Koole, G.: A prediction method for job runtimes in shared processors: Survey, statistical analysis and new avenues. Perform. Eval. (2007)

[13] Everette, S., Gardner, J.: Exponential smoothing: State of the art. J. Forecast. **4** (1985)

[14] Fildes, R.: Quantitative forecasting—the state of art-extrapolative models. J. Oper. Res. Soc. **30** (1979)

[15] Gaffney, P., Powell, M.: Optimal interpolation. Numer. Anal. **506** (1976)

[16] Goodwin, P., Önkal, D., Thomson, M.: Do forecasts expressed as prediction intervals improve production planning decisions? Eur. J. Oper. Res. **205**(1), 195–201 (2010)

[17] He, Q., Dovrolis, C., Ammar, M.: On the predictability of large transfer TCP throughput. In: Proc. of ACM SIGCOMM 2005, Aug. 2005

[18] Hyndman, R., Koehler, A., Snyder, R., Grose, S.: A state space framework for automatic forecasting using exponential smoothing methods. Int. J. Forecast. **18**(3)

[19] Lilja, D.J.: Measuring Computer Performance. A Practitioner's Guide. Cambridge University Press, Cambridge (2000)

[20] Lingyun, Y., Foster, I., Schopf, J.M.: Homeostatic and tendency-based CPU load predictions. In: Proc. of the 17th Parallel and Distributed Processing Symp., Nice, FR (2003)

[21] Mallat, S.: A theory of multiresolution signal decomposition, the wavelet representation. IEEE Trans. Pattern Anal. Mach. Intell. **11** (1989)

[22] Montgomery, D.C.: Introduction to Statistical Quality Control. Wiley, New York (2008)

[23] Nounou, M.N., Bakshi, B.R.: On-line multiscale filtering of random and gross errors without process models. AIChE J. **45** (1999)

[24] Pacifici, G., Segmuller, W., Spreitzer, M., Tantawi, A.: CPU demand for web serving: Measurement analysis and dynamic estimation. Perform. Eval. (2007)

[25] Percival, D.B., Walden, A.T.: Wavelet Methods for Time Series Analysis. Cambridge University Press, Cambridge (2000)

[26] Poirier, D.J.: Piecewise regression using cubic spline. J. Am. Stat. Assoc. **68**(343), 515–524 (1973)

[27] Qiao, Y., Dinda, P., Qiao, Y., Dinda, P.: Network traffic analysis, classification, and prediction. Technical report (2003)

[28] Shum, K.: Adaptive distributed computing through competition. In: Proc. of the 3th IEEE International Conference on Configurable Distributed System, May 1996

[29] Tran, N., Reed, D.: Automatic ARIMA time series modeling for adaptive I/O prefetching. IEEE Trans. Parallel Distrib. Syst. **15**(4), 362–377 (2004)

[30] Trigg, D., Leach, A.: Exponential smoothing with an adaptive response rate. Oper. Res. Q. **18** (1967)

[31] Whybark, D.C.: Comparison of adaptive forecasting techniques. Logist. Transp. Rev. **8**

[32] Wolber, G., Alfy, I.: Monotonic cubic spline interpolation. In: Computer Graphics International, Canmore, CA, July 1999

[33] Wolski, R.: Experiences with predicting resource performance on-line in computational grid settings. SIGMETRICS Perform. Eval. Rev. **30**(4), 41–49 (2003)

[34] Zhu, X., Young, D., Watson, B.J., Wang, Z., Rolia, J., Singhal, S., McKee, B., Hyser, C., Gmach, D., Gardner, R., Christian, T., Cherkasova, L.: 1000 islands: an integrated approach to resource management for virtualized data centers. Cluster Comput. **1**(1) (2009)

S. Casolari (✉)
Department of Information Engineering, University of Modena and Reggio Emilia, Modena, Italy
e-mail: sara.casolari@unimore.it

M. Colajanni
Department of Information Engineering, University of Modena and Reggio Emilia, Modena, Italy
e-mail: michele.colajanni@unimore.it

Estimating Model Parameters of Adaptive Software Systems in Real-Time

Dinesh Kumar, Asser Tantawi, and Li Zhang

Abstract Adaptive software systems have the ability to adapt to changes in workload and execution environment. In order to perform resource management through model based control in such systems, an accurate mechanism for estimating the software system's model parameters is required. This paper deals with real-time estimation of a performance model for adaptive software systems that process *multiple* classes of transactional workload. First, insights in to the static performance model estimation problem are provided. Then an Extended Kalman Filter (EKF) design is combined with an open queueing network model to dynamically estimate the model parameters in real-time. Specific problems that are encountered in the case of multiple classes of workload are analyzed. These problems arise mainly due to the under-deterministic nature of the estimation problem. This motivates us to propose a modified design of the filter. Insights for choosing tuning parameters of the modified design, i.e., number of constraints and sampling intervals are provided. The modified filter design is shown to effectively tackle problems with multiple classes of workload through experiments.

Keywords Performance modeling · Filtering · Queuing theory

1 Introduction

Today's software systems must continuously self-reconfigure their components to adapt to run-time changes in the host and network environments [1]. This is especially the case for Internet based online applications that operate in a highly dynamic environment with fast changing user workloads and browsing patterns. Changes may also occur in the virtualized system platform that runs the software application [2]. This paper considers such *Adaptive Software* (AS) systems [3–5] that process transactional user workload of request/ response type such as HTTP workload. Each transaction in an AS system that uses the server's resources differently can be

D. Ardagna, L. Zhang (eds.), *Run-time Models for Self-managing Systems and Applications*, 45–71, Autonomic Systems, DOI 10.1007/978-3-0346-0433-8_3, © Springer Basel AG 2010

classified into different classes. The quality of a software system is often measured in terms of its performance which can be for example, end to end response time from a user's point of view. A performance model of a system can be used for predictive analysis of the system, e.g., for response time prediction at hypothetical workloads. Performance model of an AS system can be useful for autonomic control, if it is updated in real-time to reflect the changes in the software system parameters [1]. However, performance modeling of an AS system is a challenging task. Classical queueing theory based performance models require the knowledge of parameters such as *service times* and *network queueing delays* for different classes of transactions. These parameters are used to compute and predict performance metrics such as average transaction response time, average number of jobs/transactions waiting to be processed, etc. There are existing techniques that make use of simulations and manual calibrations to compute similar performance metrics [6]. However, none of these techniques can be practically applied if the service times and network queueing delays are unknown. Instrumenting software applications with probes in order to actually measure the service time and delay parameters can be intrusive, requires extensive manual coding [7] and is time consuming. In fact, the source code of a standard, commercialized e-commerce software system may not even be accessible. Moreover, instrumentation is an iterative procedure and is difficult to pursue in a dynamically changing environment [7]. This is often the case for an AS system that undergoes continuous changes that can lead to *time-varying* service times and delays. These system parameters must therefore be estimated using only readily available measurement data. AMBIENCE [8, 9] which is a research prototype tool developed at IBM Research, makes use of a powerful Inferencing algorithm to estimate a service time and network queueing delay based performance model. Inferencing allows one to compute the service time and delay parameters from readily available measurement data on end-to-end response times, CPU utilizations and workload arrival rates. It however models service time and delay using *stationary* model parameters and cannot be used for AS systems with time-varying parameters.

Performance models can play an important role in accurately driving the necessary dynamic changes in an AS system. For instance, at runtime, software systems can better adapt to the changes in execution environment if an underlying performance model of the system is known. A performance model updated in *real-time* can be combined with model predictive control [10] to achieve autonomic control of a software system. Figure 1 shows the architecture of an example AS system studied in this paper. Reliable control of a software system in order to achieve the desired objective is critically dependent on the service time and queueing delay parameters that characterize the system. While study of optimal control strategies is a separate research area in itself, robust control can only be achieved if the system model parameters accurately reflect changes in the software system at runtime. Since autonomic control of a software system may lead to reconfiguration of its architecture at run-time, the underlying model parameters may not remain constant and can vary with time. It is thus important to accurately track the time-varying parameters of an AS system in real-time. Note that we *do not* study any kind of control mechanism in this work and focus only on model parameter estimation.

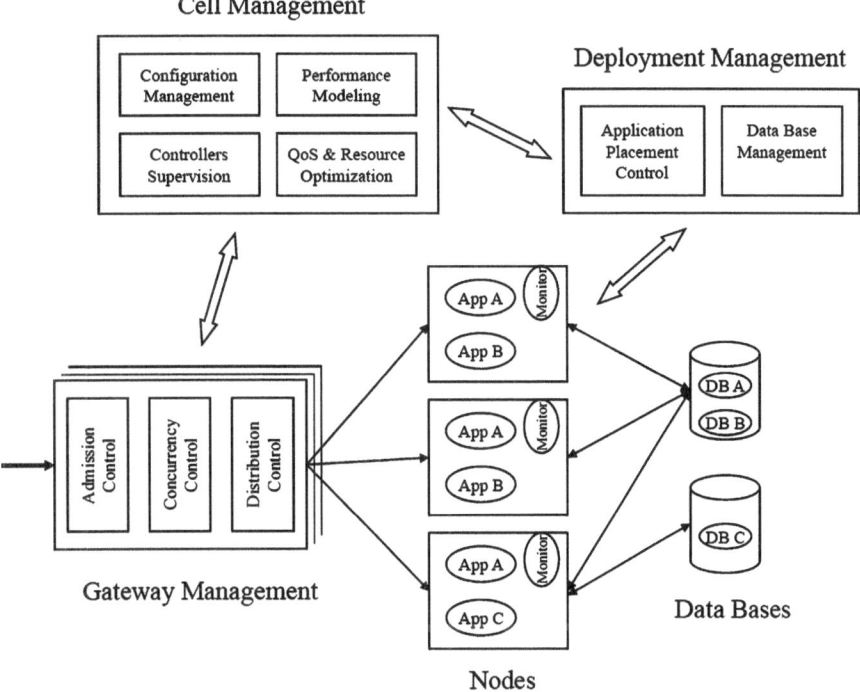

Fig. 1 Architecture of Adaptive Software System

1.1 Related Work

A prototype implementation of a performance management system for multi-tiered web applications deployed on clustered web servers is described in [11]. The management system allocates server resources dynamically in order to optimize the expected value of a system-wide utility function. Authors there use a closed queueing network model to predict the response time of requests for different resource allocations. However, the model parameters (number of clients and think time) are estimated by solving independent, *static* optimization problems at each measurement point. Urgaonkar et al. [12] develop another closed queueing network model of a multi-tiered system. Estimates of the model parameters, such as visit ratios and load-dependent service times, are obtained *off-line* through analyzing various measurement logs in the system. Their methodology lacks a sound analytical model for parameter estimation. Pacifici et al. [13] consider the problem of dynamically estimating CPU demands of applications using CPU utilization and throughput measurements. Using a linear model, they formulate the problem as a multivariate linear regression problem and analyze measurement data. However, their experimental results demonstrate that the approach is viable only for a *rough* estimation of the dynamically changing CPU demands.

Real-time performance modeling using Kalman filters [14] is an emerging area of research and only few related papers can be found in literature. To the best of our knowledge, only Zheng et al. [15–17] have demonstrated the effective use of an Extended Kalman Filter (EKF) [14] for tracking time-varying parameters of an AS system, for the purpose of real-time performance modeling. Though they provide theoretical insights for system models based on both closed and open multiclass queueing networks, their experimental results are only for the *single* class case. Colleagues of Zheng in [1] have studied real-time adaptive control of an autonomic computing environment. Two types of controllers are studied: threshold controller and feed-forward controller based on a Kalman filter model. The later is again based on the EKF design for performance modeling proposed in [15, 16, 18]. Once again only a single class of workload traffic is considered for the experimental results in [1]. Other colleagues of Zheng in [2] have studied model based autonomic server virtualization, but use system identification techniques instead of a Kalman filter. To summarize, none of the existing related work has investigated performance of Kalman filters in a *multi-class* workload environment.

1.2 Main Results and Contribution

The contributions of this work are *twofold*. First, we demonstrate that straightforward application of EKF is inadequate in a multi-class setting. We present experiments to show that for an open queueing network model of the software system, an EKF design in the lines of the work in [15–17] performs poorly for two important scenarios: 1) the model parameter estimates converge to the actual value very slowly when the variation in incoming workload is very low, 2) the estimates fail to converge quickly to the new value when there is a step-change in software parameters caused by adaptive reconfiguration of the software architecture. We argue that these anomalies occur due to the under-determined nature of the estimation problem for multiple classes of workloads. We therefore address this issue by modifying the EKF design by augmenting the measurement equation with a set of constraints based on past measurement values. Experiment results demonstrate that use of this modified EKF leads to significant improvement in convergence in the two cases. This is thus the second main contribution of our work.

2 System Description

A high level description of a three-tiered AS system and its management is depicted in Fig. 1. The first tier hosts gateway management components, the second tier hosts a web server and the adaptive software applications and the third tier comprises database services. The second tier consists of several server nodes that host the various applications. An adaptive software is deployed as an application in an application server that provides the necessary runtime environment. Several application servers may run on a given node and several instances of a given application may coexist at the same time. Incoming requests (workload) from users arrive at the first tier where they are routed to an appropriate node in the second tier. Servicing these requests by an application may trigger further requests to the database tier. The completion of a request triggers a response back to the user.

Two important performance concerns in such an AS system are resource utilization and quality of service in terms of response time. Several mechanisms are usually in place to alleviate such concerns. Let us focus on two broad categories of mechanisms that we call *Cell Management* and *Deployment Management*. The latter is concerned with placement of application instances in nodes, as well as database partitioning and replication. Cell management is concerned with the overall operation of the multi-tier system cell. Efficient cell and deployment management requires knowledge of performance models in order to predict performance and ensure optimal resource utilization through control. Control mechanisms such as configuration management, QoS and resource optimization, application placement control and database management are integral components of the cell and deployment managers. Other control mechanisms such as admission control, concurrency control and distribution control (or load balancing) are components of the first tier gateway manager. Monitoring agents running on various server nodes collect measurements that are fed to the cell and deployment management components. These measurements can be used to update the performance model of the system, which can in turn be employed by the various controller components.

The 'performance modeling' component is a key aspect of the cell manager since most of the control operations and resource optimization settings are based on a representative model of the system. Such models need to be dynamically updated in real-time to reflect the changing cell characteristics, be it resources, applications or user demand. In other words, real-time control of an AS system requires a real-time update of the performance model.

3 Static Performance Model Estimation

When performance characteristics of a software system are stationary in nature, its model parameters are easier to estimate as compared to adaptive software systems that exhibit non-stationary and changing behavior over time. Assuming that performance indicators and measurements of an adaptive software system can be split into stationary regimes over time, the AMBIENCE [8, 9, 19] tool can be used to estimate model parameters. As discussed earlier, AMBIENCE makes use of the powerful Inferencing engine for static performance model estimation of a software system. Figure 2 gives a block diagram overview of the Inferencing methodology that has been implemented with in AMBIENCE tool. In the left block a generic queuing network model is shown. This model depicts a generic 'task' or 'job' queuing network with in an arbitrary component of a software system. The queuing network model along with an optimization theory based formulation of the model parameter estimation

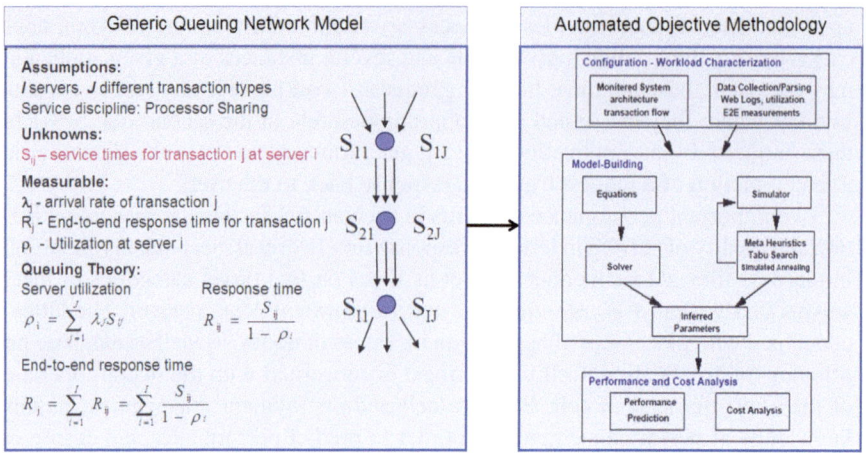

Fig. 2 AMBIENCE Inferencing engine for static performance model estimation

problem is the key component of the Inferencing engine. The 'Model-Building' box
in the right block presents the workflow involved in the Inferencing engine. Workload characterization, measurement and analysis proceed the model building and
inferencing phase. Once the model has been inferred performance analysis and prediction can be performed for answering various what-if questions. AMBIENCE tool
will be used for estimating expected values of parameters later in the chapter. These
expected values serve as a guideline as to how good are the real-time estimates both
qualitatively and quantitatively. Detailed description about the Inferencing methodology, procedure and best practices to be followed can be found in [8, 9, 19, 20]

4 Extended Kalman Filter Design

We present here an EKF design in the lines of the work in [15–17]. It is assumed that
the reader is aware of the general theory of Kalman filtering. The reader is referred
to [14] for the same. Kalman filter provides the required framework for estimating
model parameters in a real-time fashion by representing them as the state of an AS
system. Kalman filter is a minimum mean square error (MMSE) estimator that estimates the state from a series of incomplete and noisy measurements. It minimizes
the covariance of estimation error and operates by propagating both the mean and
covariance of state estimates through time. We propose an open queueing model
based EKF design for estimating service time and network queueing delay parameters of a single node, running a single application and processing three different
classes of traffic. It is sufficient to consider a single node and three traffic classes
to demonstrate the problems that are encountered in the AS system of Fig. 1 with
multiple classes of workload. Such a single node system is shown in Fig. 3.

The system in Fig. 3 is treated as a dynamical system. Measurements on workload arrival rate and transactional response times for each of the three user classes

Fig. 3 AS system with single
server node and three
workload classes

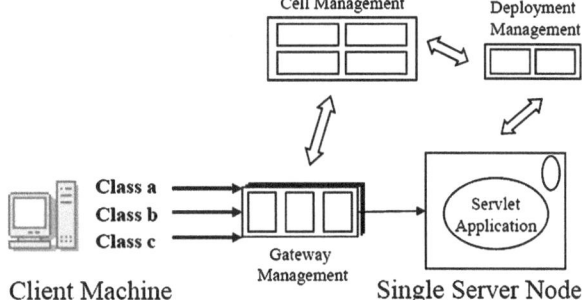

Client Machine   Single Server Node

and CPU utilization of the node are gathered at a sampling interval of T seconds.
These time series data are the input to the filter. Workload arriving at the software
system may be fast changing and non-stationary. Assume that T is small enough
(few seconds) so that the arriving workload can be considered stationary during this
sampling interval. Then the stationary, queueing theory based performance models
hold during this sampling interval. If we consider the state of the system to comprise
service time and network delay, then an EKF can be used to compute a time series
estimate of this state.

For three classes indexed as class a, b and c and a single node, we define the
system state x as,

$$x = \begin{bmatrix} s^a & s^b & s^c & d^a & d^b & d^c \end{bmatrix}^T, \tag{4.1}$$

where, s^a, s^b and s^c are service times at the server node for classes a, b and c,
respectively, and d^a, d^b and d^c are network delays for the three classes. Based
on an $M/G/1$ open queueing network model with processor sharing (PS) service
discipline [21], the measurement model [14] $z = h(x)$ is defined as,

$$\begin{bmatrix} R^a \\ R^b \\ R^c \\ u \end{bmatrix} = \begin{bmatrix} \frac{s^a}{1-u} + d^a \\ \frac{s^b}{1-u} + d^b \\ \frac{s^c}{1-u} + d^c \\ \frac{1}{P}(\lambda^a s^a + \lambda^b s^b + \lambda^c s^c) \end{bmatrix} \tag{4.2}$$

where, R^a, R^b and R^c are response times of the three classes, u is the CPU utilization averaged over all CPUs of the only node and P is the number of CPUs. If each
sampling interval is denoted by k then we may assume the following dynamics for
state evolution,

$$x_k = F_k x_{k-1} + w_k,$$

where, F_k is the state transition model which is applied to the previous state x_{k-1}
and w_k is the process noise which is assumed to be drawn from a zero mean, multivariate normal distribution with covariance Q_k, i.e., $w_k \sim \mathcal{N}(0, Q_k)$. The iterative
measurement equation [14] for Kalman filter is taken to be,

$$z_k = H_k x_k + v_k,$$

where, H_k is the observation model which maps the true state space into the observed space and v_k is the observation noise which is assumed to be zero mean, Gaussian white noise with covariance R_k, i.e., $v_k \sim \mathcal{N}(0, R_k)$. Since the measurement model in (4.2) is non-linear in terms of the system state parameters (due to utilization u in the denominator), we must use the 'Extended' version of the Kalman filter [14]. The corresponding Jacobian matrix of the measurement model is given by,

$$
H = \frac{\partial h}{\partial x} =
\begin{bmatrix}
\frac{1-u+\frac{\lambda^a s^a}{P}}{(1-u)^2} & \frac{\lambda^b s^a}{P(1-u)^2} & \frac{\lambda^c s^a}{P(1-u)^2} & 1 & 0 & 0 \\
\frac{\lambda^a s^b}{P(1-u)^2} & \frac{1-u+\frac{\lambda^b s^b}{P}}{(1-u)^2} & \frac{\lambda^c s^b}{P(1-u)^2} & 0 & 1 & 0 \\
\frac{\lambda^a s^c}{P(1-u)^2} & \frac{\lambda^b s^c}{P(1-u)^2} & \frac{1-u+\frac{\lambda^c s^c}{P}}{(1-u)^2} & 0 & 0 & 1 \\
\frac{\lambda^a}{P} & \frac{\lambda^b}{P} & \frac{\lambda^c}{P} & 0 & 0 & 0
\end{bmatrix}
$$

and H_k can be computed as,

$$
H_k = \left[\frac{\partial h}{\partial x} \right]_{\hat{x}_{k|k-1}}.
$$

We may now use the standard EKF theory [14] to track the system state over time. One of the major advantages of Kalman filter is that it is a recursive estimator. This means that only the estimated state from the previous time step and the current measurements are needed to compute the estimate for the current state. In the following EKF algorithm, the notation $\hat{x}_{n|m}$ represents the estimate of x at time n given observations up to and including time m. The state of the filter itself is represented by two variables:

1. $\hat{x}_{k|k}$ is the estimate of state at time k given observations up to and including time k.
2. $P_{k|k}$ is the error covariance matrix (a quantitative measure of estimated accuracy of the state estimate).

The Kalman filter algorithm has two distinct phases: *Predict* and *Update*. The predict phase uses state estimate from the previous time interval to produce an estimate of the state at current time interval. In the update phase, measurement information at the current time interval is used to refine this prediction to arrive at a new, more accurate state estimate, again for the current time interval. These two phases are given as,

Predict:

$$
\hat{x}_{k|k-1} = F_k \hat{x}_{k-1|k-1}
$$
$$
P_{k|k-1} = F_k P_{k-1|k-1} F_k^T + Q_k
$$

Update:

$$
\tilde{y}_k = z_k - h(\hat{x}_{k|k-1})
$$
$$
S_k = H_k P_{k|k-1} H_k^T + R_k
$$

$$K_k = P_{k|k-1} H_k^T S_k^{-1}$$

$$\hat{x}_{k|k} = \hat{x}_{k|k-1} + K_k \tilde{y}_k$$

$$P_{k|k} = (I - K_k H_k) P_{k|k-1}$$

A more detailed description of the two phases and notation can be found in [14]. The filter design proposed above was implemented as a stand-alone Java application. Measurements gathered during experiments were fed in to this application to obtain service time and delay estimates. The experimental results are presented later in Sect. 6.

5 Experimental Setup

In this section, we describe the experimental setup that was used to conduct the experiments. Figure 3 shows the single-node AS system with three user workload classes considered for our experimental setup. It consists of a web-based environment including a synthetic HTTP traffic generator at the client machine and an IBM WebSphere Virtual Enterprise cell [22] with a single server node. The architecture of an IBM WebSphere cell is similar to that shown in Figure 1. The actual application under consideration is a micro-benchmarking servlet that simulates an adaptive software application.

5.1 Simulated Adaptive Software

Details of how the servlet simulates an adaptive software are as follows. Each HTTP request/transaction is served by the micro-benchmarking servlet that alternates between *computing* and *sleeping*. Servlet parameters controlling the behavior of the execution of a request are: the total amount of computation (specified in terms of the number of loops over some arithmetic computation), duration of computation between sleeps and the duration of sleep. These parameters may be fixed or drawn from some probability distribution. The parameters can be provided in the HTTP request and are configurable through the synthetic traffic generator tool. Given values of these servlet parameters translate into values of service time and delay parameters. The actual translation function is not of importance as it may vary for different software systems. Adaptivity of a software system was simulated by manually changing the servlet parameters through an HTTP request, that resulted in modified values for the service time and delay parameters.

The actual expected values of service time and delay parameters can not be directly computed since the translation function is unknown. Moreover, the values are software and operating system environment dependent and may vary from one software system to another. We employ the AMBIENCE [8, 9] tool to estimate the expected values of service time and delay parameters. Then the EKF will be used for estimating their real values.

5.2 Estimating Expected Values of Parameters

The Inferencing technique implemented in the AMBIENCE tool [8, 9, 19] and discussed in Sect. 3 was used to estimate the expected values of the parameters. The response time and CPU utilization measurements gathered from different experiments were segmented in to stationary set of measurements for each experiment separately based on a-priori knowledge about the behavior of the system. Note that this may not be possible in real-world operating conditions since non-stationary behaviors and trends of software systems are very hard to predict in real-time. That is exactly when AMBIENCE can not be used and we need the filtering technique as discussed in the beginning. However, for experimental purposes non-stationary behavior of the system is known a-priori and this knowledge is used to split the measurement data in to stationary segments. The average values of the segmented response time and CPU utilization data are then input to the AMBIENCE tool to estimate the service time and delay parameters. Referring to Sect. 2.3 in [19], we may introduce an additional parameter called CPU overhead to be estimated as well. In that case, if there are K classes and M machines in the AS system then the number of experiments, r, required to estimate the parameters uniquely is given by,

$$r = \left\lceil \frac{KM}{K+M} + 1 \right\rceil. \tag{5.1}$$

Since in our case we have a single server machine this formula will simplify to,

$$r = \left\lceil \frac{K}{K+1} + 1 \right\rceil. \tag{5.2}$$

5.3 Traffic Generator

The traffic generator is written in Java and generates HTTP requests of different types. A configurable number of parallel threads simulate the web clients. The think time, defined as interval between the receipt of a response from server node and submission of a subsequent request, is specified by a probability distribution. We used the sum of a fixed bias (125 msec) and an exponentially distributed time with mean 125 msec. Load on the system can by altered by varying the number of clients. Changing the parameters may be performed manually or programmatically. In the LVW experiment of Sect. 6.1, the parameters were not changed and kept fixed, resulting in a stationary workload. In the SSP experiment of Sect. 6.2, an additional component of the traffic generator was activated that resulted in sinusoidal waves in the workload. This additional component took as input the amplitude (maximum number of clients), the phase in degrees (allowing different request flows to have different phases) and the periodic length (for the time duration of a sinusoidal cycle).

5.4 System Architecture and Hardware

The micro-benchmarking servlet was deployed as an application in the IBM Web-Sphere cell (see Fig. 1) that consisted of a single server node and additional management nodes: Cell, Deployment and Gateway manager. Monitoring agents ran on the server node for collecting statistical measures in a non-intrusive manner, without the need to instrument the application. In our experiments we measured workload arrival rates, response times of requests and CPU utilization of the server node. Once the micro-benchmarking servlet is deployed, the server node ceases to interact with the Deployment Manager. This ensures that management nodes do not interfere with request/transaction processing activity at the server node. IBM WebSphere platform version 6.1 (ND 6.1.0.17) (XD 6.1.0.3) was used for our experiments.

The traffic generator tool ran on a client machine with a single Xeon 2.8 GHz Intel processor, 512 KB cache and 2 GB RAM. Three different types of transaction classes were generated during the experiments. Each class was denoted by a different class ID in the HTTP request and was generated using different values for the traffic generator parameters. The classes were simply named as Class a, Class b and Class c. The servlet application ran on a server node with a single Xeon 3.06 GHz Intel processor, 512 KB cache and 2 GB RAM. The servlet processed different classes of transactions differently, through unique values of servlet parameters that resulted in unique values of service times and delays for each class.

6 Problems with Multiple Classes of Workload

It is demonstrated here that the use of EKF (in the lines of the work in [15–17]) for tracking model parameters of an AS system with multiple classes of workload has convergence problems. For this purpose, two different types of experiments were conducted:

1. *Low Variation in Workload (LVW) experiment*: As part of gateway management in an AS system (Fig. 1), one of the goals of a typical admission control mechanism is to ensure a smooth workload profile (see [23] and references there-in). The mechanism would attempt to remove spikes in the incoming user request rate leading to a smooth workload with low variations in the admitted request rate. This was the motivation for conducting the LVW experiment in which the admission control lead to a workload with low coefficients of variation for the three classes.
2. *Step-change in System Parameters (SSP) experiment*: Reconfiguration of the software architecture, components and functions in an AS system in order to accommodate sudden changes in the execution environment can lead to step-changes in the service time and queueing delay parameters. This was the motivation for conducting the SSP experiment in which the servlet parameters were altered to simulate adaptive reconfiguration.

6.1 Low Variation in Workload (LVW) Experiment

Consider the scenario when the coefficient of variation for inter-arrival time of in-coming workload is much less than one. Such was the case for the LVW experiment whose workload profile is shown in Fig. 4. The three different time series depict the transactional workload for classes a, b and c. Their coefficients of variation are 0.176, 0.143 and 0.104 for classes a, b and c, respectively. Figures 5 and 6 show the response time and CPU utilization measurements. All three measurements were taken as per recommendations for the sampling time T provided in [15–17] papers. The three sets of data were fed in to the Java implementation of the fil-ter proposed in Sect. 4 to estimate service time and network delay parameters for the three classes. Figures 7 and 8 show the computed estimates. The flat horizon-tal lines in both plots are the expected, actual values of service time and delay, for the compute-sleep micro-benchmarking servlet. These values are estimated as per the discussion in Sect. 5.2. This experiment does not require any measurement seg-mentation since the whole experiment is stationary in nature. The filter was tuned based on the recommended values for Q and R matrices provided in [15–17] pa-

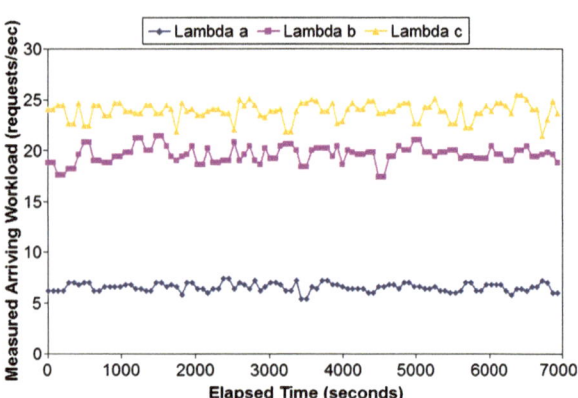

Fig. 4 Workloads (LVW experiment)

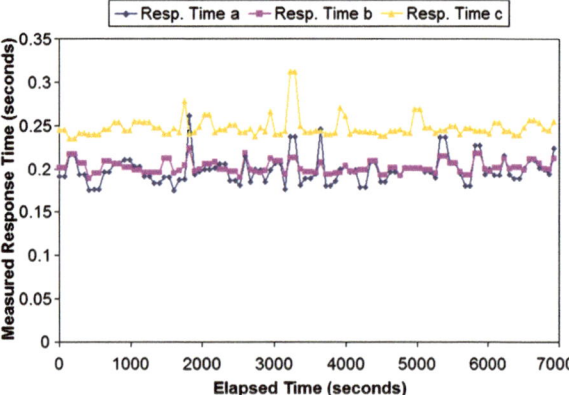

Fig. 5 Response times (LVW experiment)

Fig. 6 CPU utilization (LVW experiment)

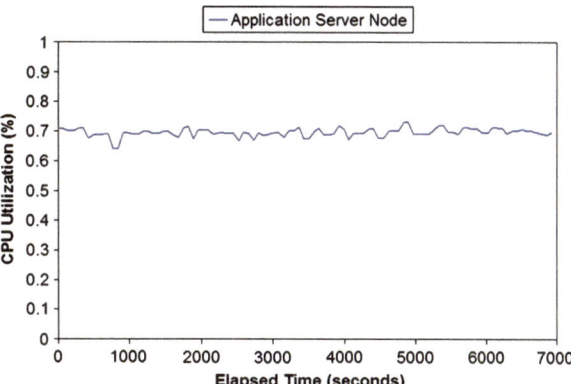

Fig. 7 Service time estimates (LVW)

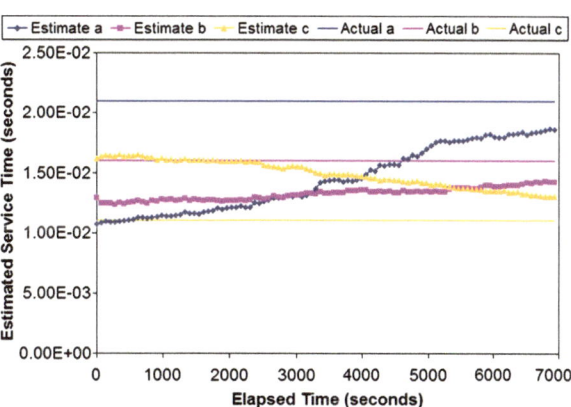

Fig. 8 Network delay estimates (LVW)

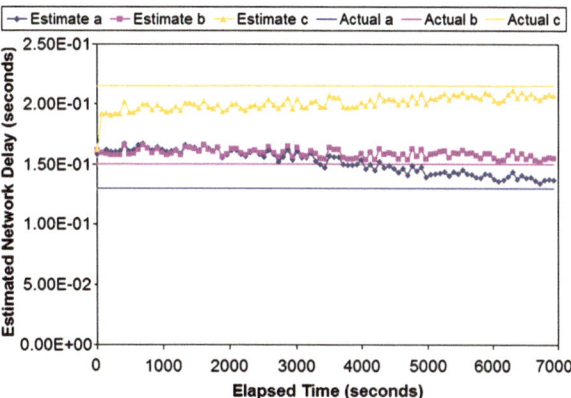

pers. In spite of following the tuning recommendations, both service time and delay estimates in Figs. 7 and 8 tend to converge to the actual values very slowly. Even after 6000 seconds of elapsed time the estimates for all classes have not reached the actual values. As a quantitative measure of the performance of the filter, Figs. 9

Fig. 9 Service time
estimation error (LVW)

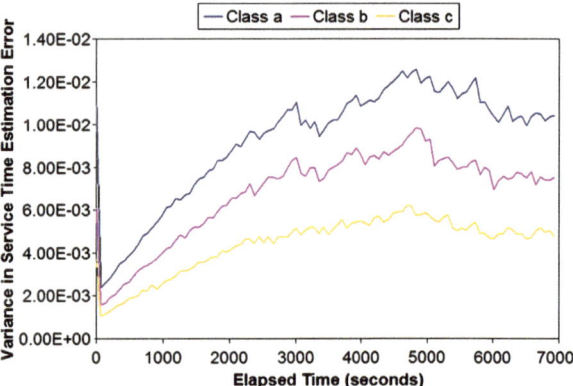

Fig. 10 Network delay est.
error (LVW)

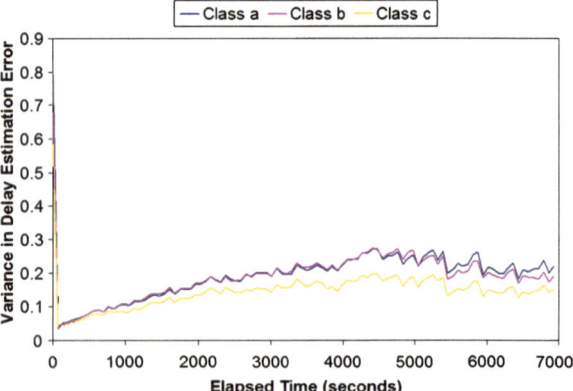

and 10 show the variances in estimation error which are essentially the diagonal el-
ements of $P_{k|k}$ matrix as time step k evolves. Clearly the variances do not converge
and instead gradually increase and only slightly decrease thereafter. Qualitatively,
non-convergence of the variances to a low steady-state value indicates the 'badness'
of the estimates [14].

6.2 Step-Change in System Parameters (SSP) Experiment

Consider here the scenario when there is a step-change in the actual parameters
caused by adaptive reconfiguration of the software. Such an adaptive reconfiguration allows the software to adapt to changes in the incoming workload, execution
environment, etc. We carried out the SSP experiment in which this step-change was
simulated by manually exchanging the servlet parameters twice between two of the
classes a and c. Instead of a mere exchange, the parameters for the two classes could

Fig. 11 Improved serv. time est. (LVW)

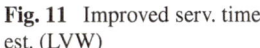
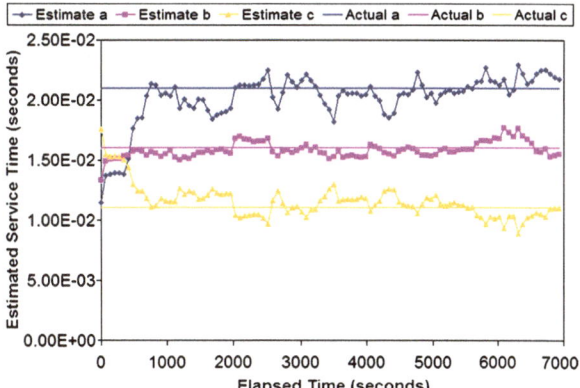

Fig. 12 Improved delay estimates (LVW)

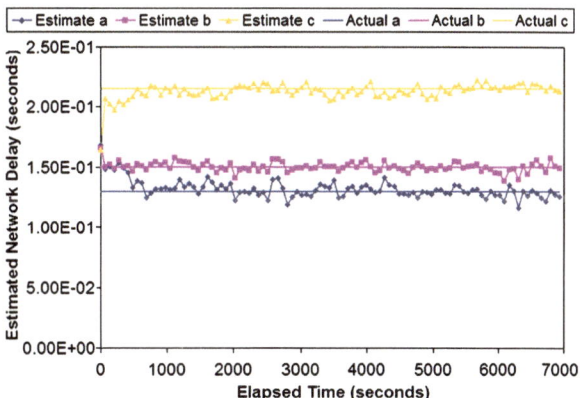

have also been changed to other different values. However, exchange of parameters was done for the sake of simplicity and easy presentation.

Figures 15, 16 and 17 show the workload, response time and CPU utilization measurements for this experiment. Notice the periodic and high varying nature of the workload. Figures 18 and 19 show the service time and delay estimates using the EKF proposed in Sect. 4 along with their expected actual values depicted by the flat lines. These values were again estimated as per the discussion in Sect. 5.2. Notice the manually introduced step-change in the actual values, twice. This experiment required segmentation of measurements in to three different sets as per the manually introduced step-changes. The filter was again tuned based on the recommended values for Q and R matrices and measurement sampling interval chosen as per [15–17]. In Figs. 18 and 19 it is seen that in the beginning of the experiment the service time and delay estimates converge to their expected values much faster than in the LVW experiment discussed previously. Thus, having a high varying workload improves the tracking of parameters by the filter. The service time and delay estimates also follow the switch in actual values at around 3000 and 4800 seconds of elapsed time. However, after the switch the estimates take a while to get close to the new values. Though the Kalman filter detects and tracks the switch in parameters,

Fig. 13 Improved service time estimation error (LVW)

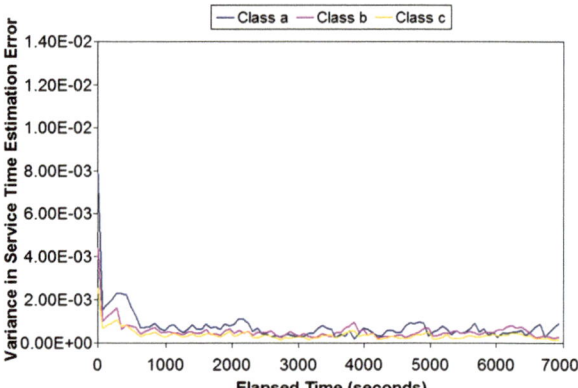

Fig. 14 Improved delay estimation error (LVW)

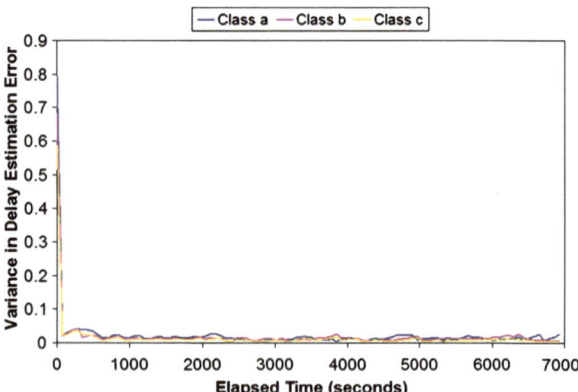

Fig. 15 Workloads (SSP experiment)

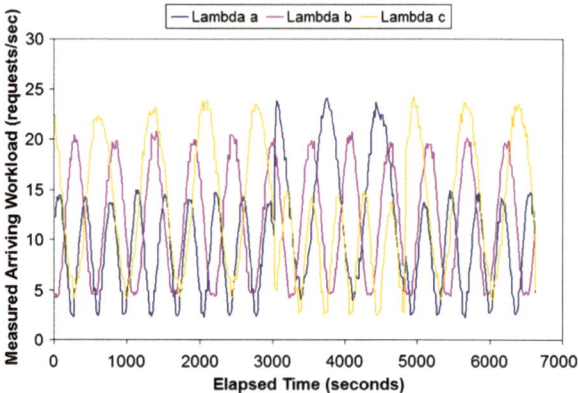

the convergence of estimates to new values is quite slow. Figures 20 and 21 show the variances in estimation error that converge to low values, but exhibit a saw-tooth type increase and decrease pattern. The variances do not converge to a steady-state value and could be further improved.

Fig. 16 Response times (SSP experiment)

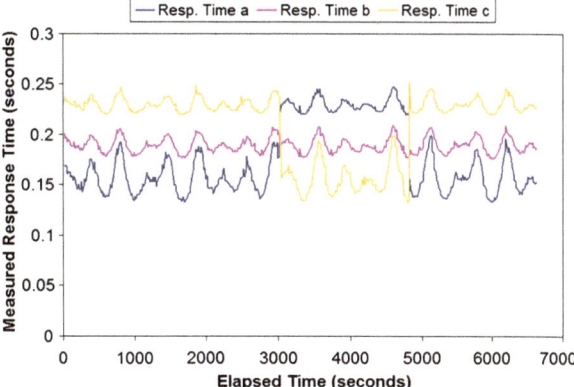

Fig. 17 CPU utilization (SSP experiment)

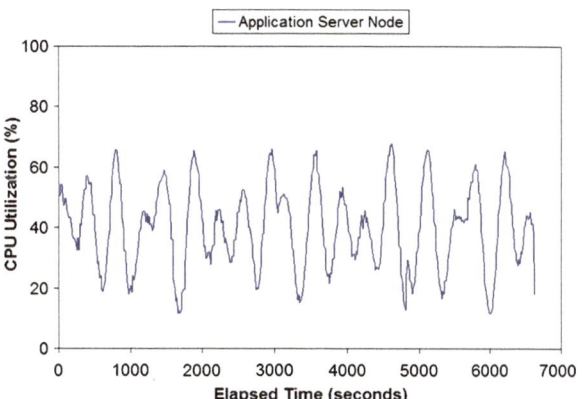

Fig. 18 Service time estimates (SSP)

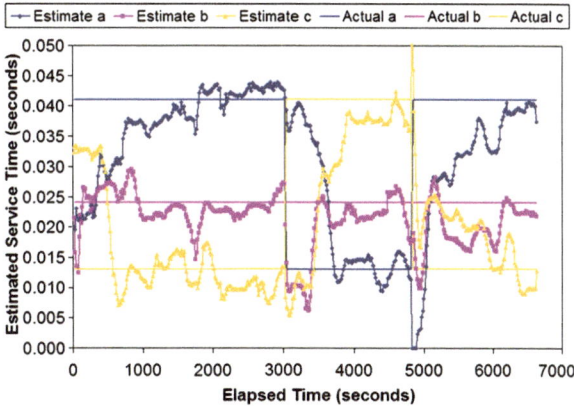

Fig. 19 Network delay
estimates (SSP)

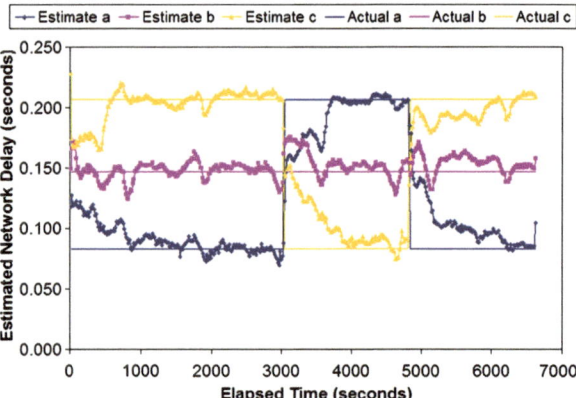

Fig. 20 Service time
estimation error (SSP)

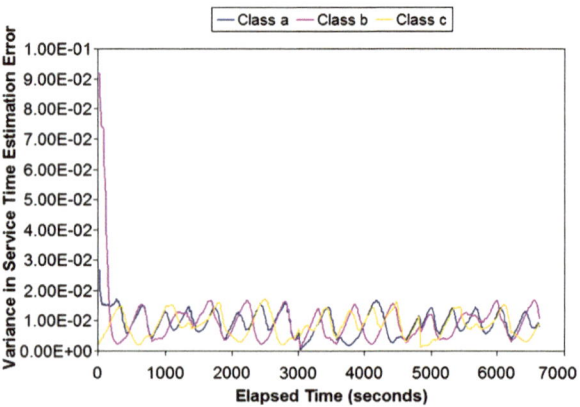

Fig. 21 Network delay
estimation error (SSP)

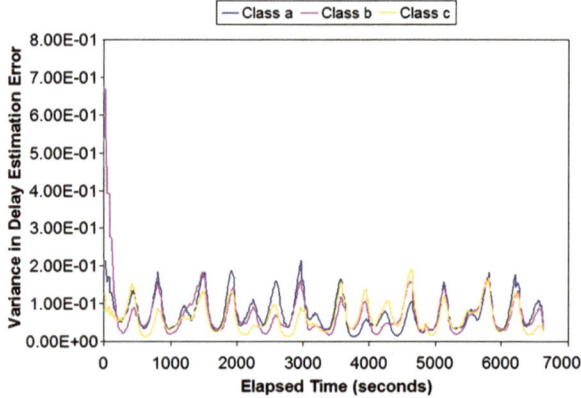

6.3 Problem Analysis

Let us carefully analyze the convergence problems discussed in the foregoing discussion. For the single class case, Zheng et al. [15–17] demonstrated through exper-

Fig. 22 Improved serv. time est. (SSP)

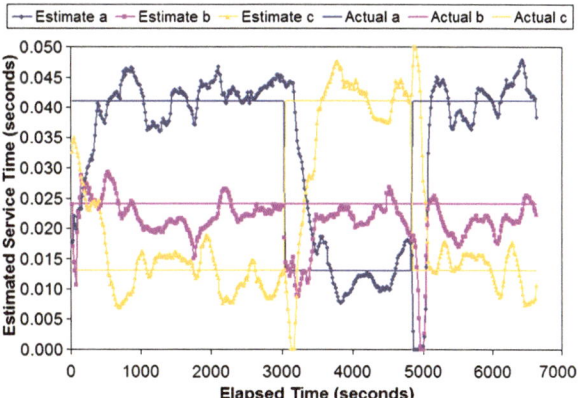

Fig. 23 Improved delay estimates (SSP)

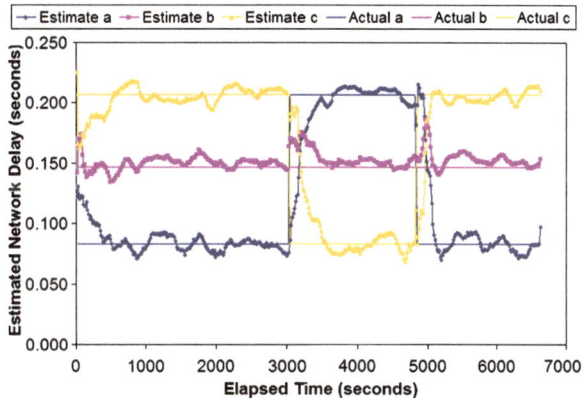

imental results that their Kalman filter is well able to track the step-change in parameters without any convergence problems. For a single class they used response time and CPU utilization measurements to estimate service time and user think time (instead of network delay). Thus they used two different measurements to estimate two different unknowns. This would work fine since they were trying to estimate as many unknowns as the known measurable quantities.

In general, if we have c classes then we would have $2c$ unknowns to be estimated, i.e., service time and delay (or think time) parameters for each class. Whereas, the number of measurements available would be only $c + 1$, i.e., response time for each class and CPU utilization for the single server node. User request rate measurements can not be used in the left hand side of the measurement model (Equation (4.2)) to increase the total number of knowns to $2c + 1$ instead of $c + 1$. Each measurable or known quantity corresponds to a constraint on the state in the measurement model. For a single class ($c = 1$), there would be sufficient measurable knowns to estimate the unknown variables. However, for multiple classes ($c \geq 2$) this would lead to an *under-determined* system since the number of measurable knowns would be less than the number of unknowns. This would result in lack of unique solution for the

Fig. 24 Improved service
time estimation error (SSP)

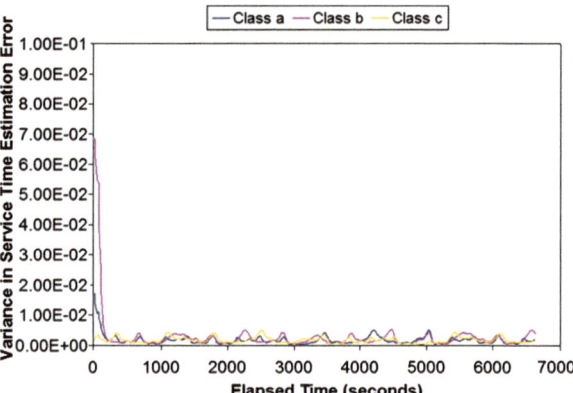

Fig. 25 Improved delay
estimation error (SSP)

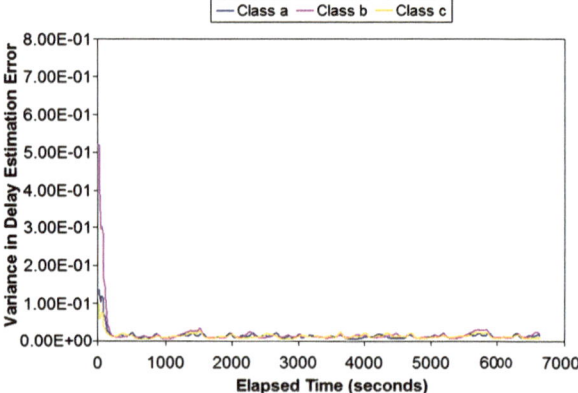

filter estimates at each time step. The filter would fail to compute a unique estimate for the service time and delay parameters and instead propose feasible but undesirable solution estimates. This explains the undesirable estimates obtained in both the experiments, leading to slow convergence towards the actual expected values.

Figures 26, 27 and 28 show the workload, response time and CPU utilization measurements from another SSP experiment with $c = 4$ classes. Figures 29 and 30 again show the service time and delay estimates as per Sect. 4 along with their expected actual values depicted by the flat lines. Let us compare the convergence of these estimates to their expected values between this and the previous SSP experiment for $c = 3$ classes. It can be observed that in the beginning of the 4 class experiment, service time estimates diverge far away from their expected values as compared to the 3 class experiment. This observation further validates our discussion in the previous paragraph. Higher number of classes would lead to a greater difference between the number of unknowns to be estimated and the number of available measurements. This would lead to an increased under-deterministic system and hence slower convergence to actual expected values.

Fig. 26 Workloads (SSP experiment)

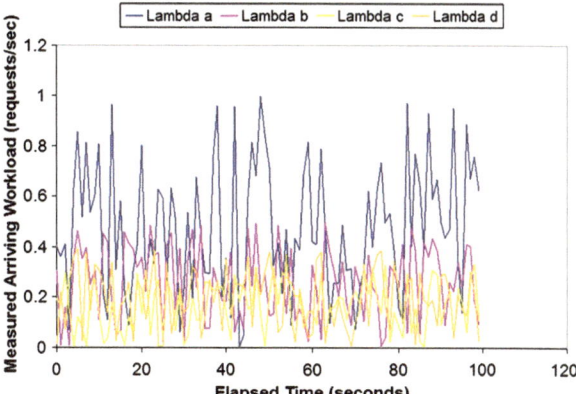

Fig. 27 Response times (SSP experiment)

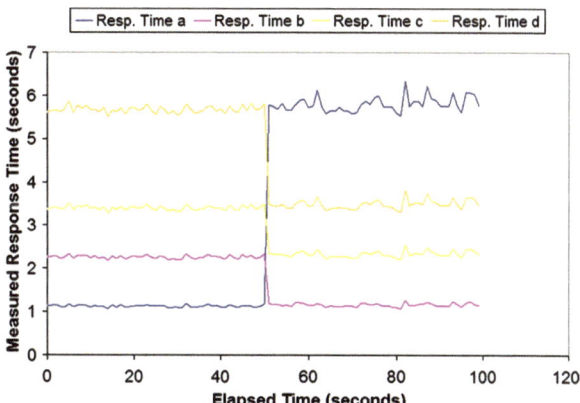

Fig. 28 CPU utilization (SSP experiment)

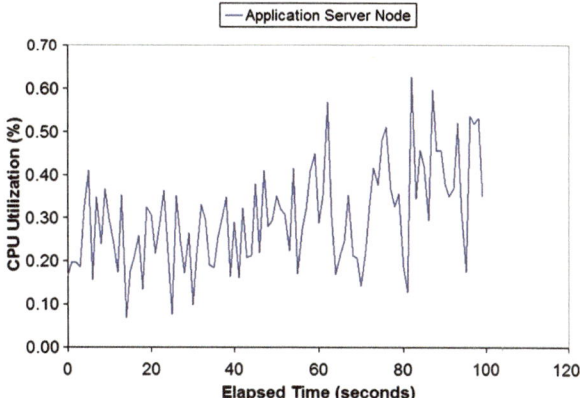

Comparing the LVW experiment with the SSP experiment, we observed in Sect. 6.2 that high varying workload in the latter improved the tracking of parameters. High varying workload has the possibility to generate higher number of *linearly*

Fig. 29 Service time
estimates (SSP)

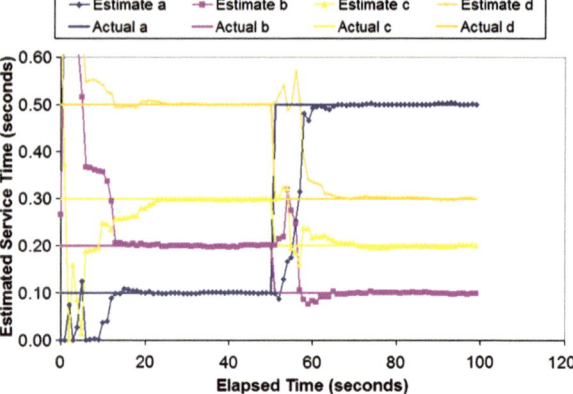

Fig. 30 Network delay
estimates (SSP)

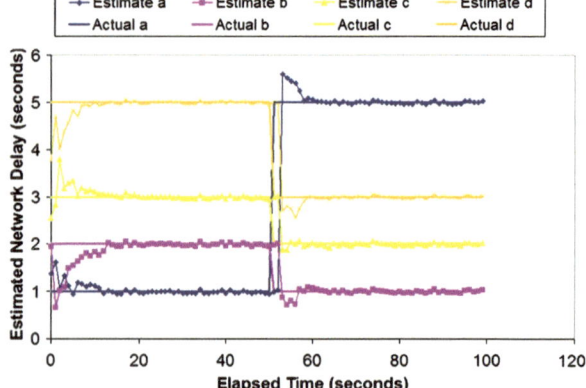

independent set of measurements at each time step k, as compared to low varying
workload (see [24] and references there-in). This would work towards reducing the
under-determined nature of the estimation problem and eventually lead to a reduced
set of feasible solutions. This explains the improvement in parameter tracking in the
SSP experiment.

7 Modified Filter Design & Improved Results

The under-determined nature of the estimation problem discussed in previous section can be addressed by increasing the number of observations in the measurement
model. This can be done by using measurements from recent past to construct *constraints* on the current state x_k and augmenting them as perfect measurements (see
Sect. 7.5.2 in [14]) to the measurement model. Assuming that the state vector remains stationary over the past $l_1 + l_2 + \cdots + l_N$ sampling intervals, the state at time
k must perfectly satisfy (i.e., without noise) the measurement equation based on

measurements from the last $l_1 + l_2 + \cdots + l_N$ sampling intervals. Here, N is the number of constraints and each l_i, $i = 1, \ldots, N$ is the number of sampling intervals whose measurements are averaged to build each of the N constraints. The measurement model for time step k can thus be augmented with a set of constraints $Dx_k = d$ in the following manner,

$$\begin{bmatrix} z_k \\ d \end{bmatrix} = \begin{bmatrix} H_k \\ D \end{bmatrix} x_k + \begin{bmatrix} v_k \\ 0 \end{bmatrix} \tag{7.1}$$

where,

$$d = [d_1 \ d_2 \ \cdots \ d_N]^T \quad \text{and} \quad D = [D_1 \ D_2 \ \cdots \ D_N]^T.$$

Here,

$$d_i = \bar{z}_{l_i} = \frac{1}{l_i} \sum_{j=p}^{q} z_{k-j} \quad \forall i = 1, \ldots, N$$

where,

$$p = 1 + \sum_{r=1}^{i-1} l_r \quad \text{and} \quad q = \sum_{r=1}^{i} l_r.$$

Similarly,

$$D_i = \bar{H}_{l_i} = \frac{1}{l_i} \sum_{j=p}^{q} H_{k-j} \quad \forall i = 1, \ldots, N$$

where, p and q are defined above. Instead of augmenting the constraints as perfect measurements with zero measurement noise, it is also possible to generalize further and consider them as noisy measurements with a non-zero noise term in (7.1). Also note that this augmented measurement model of (7.1) is different from the standard theory on constrained Kalman filtering in Sect. 7.5.2 of [14]. The difference being that here we use actual measurements from recent past to construct the constraints instead of relying on any a-priori knowledge about constraints on the state space. The EKF design proposed in Sect. 4 was modified to incorporate the augmented measurement model of (7.1). LVW and SSP experiments were repeated with this modified EKF design. The obtained results are presented after we provide some insights for choosing the values of N and each l_i.

7.1 Insights for Choosing N and Each l_i

The main purpose of incorporating additional constraints is to have at least as many linearly independent knowns or observations as the number of unknowns. The number of unknowns in our problem will always be $2c$. With one more additional set of constraints, i.e., $N = 1$, the number of observations will become $2(c + 1)$. This is

Table 1 Values chosen for
the constrained EKF

Experiment	N	l_1	l_2
LVW	2	4	3
SSP	1	3	n/a

sufficient to have a determined system if at least $2c$ of these $2(c + 1)$ observations are linearly independent. From our experience with various experiments we have observed that this is usually the case, i.e., $N = 1$ additional constraint is usually sufficient. In some experiments it was observed that $N = 1$ was not enough and two additional set of constraints were required for improved results.

Choice of each l_i is very specific to a given experiment. It depends on the rate of change of the software system parameters (due to their time-varying nature) and the sampling interval T. In fact, some systems may require updating the value of l_i at each time step k. Deriving an explicit expression for the optimal choice of l_i is a separate research problem in itself and is outside the scope of this paper.

For the experimental results that follow, values of N and l_i were chosen intuitively through empirical observation of results. They are given in Table 1.

7.2 Improved LVW Experiment Results

Figures 11 and 12 show service time and delay estimates for the LVW experiment using the modified EKF. $N = 2$ additional constraints were used for results in these figures. Observe the relatively fast convergence of estimates to the actual values as compared to Figs. 7 and 8. The additional constraints in the augmented measurement model increase the number of linearly independent knowns. This tends to reduce the under-determined nature of the estimation problem and the filter converges to the desirable, unique solution much faster. The fluctuations of estimates around the actual values in Figs. 11 and 12, reflect changes in the server node due to any background processes, context switching and fluctuating CPU cycles consumed for memory management.

With the modified EKF, estimates reach close to their actual expected values within around 700 seconds. Compare this number with Figs. 7 and 8 where the estimates do not converge to their actual values even after 6000 seconds. The order of improvement here is more than 8X in terms of the time to converge. This is substantial improvement with the modified EKF design. Figures 13 and 14 show the improvement quantitatively, in terms of the variances in estimation error that converge to very low and steady-state values.

7.3 Improved SSP Experiment Results

Figures 22 and 23 show service time and delay estimates for the SSP experiment using the modified EKF. $N = 1$ additional constraint was sufficient this time since the high varying workload already contributed towards generating higher number of linearly independent set of measurements at each time step k [24]. Service time estimates here converge to the new actual values only about 200 seconds after the 2nd switch in parameters which occurs at around 4800 seconds of elapsed time. Compare this with Fig. 18 where it takes more than around 1200 seconds. Similarly, delay estimates converge to the new actual values in only about 300 seconds in Fig. 23 as compared to more than approximately 1400 seconds in Fig. 19. Thus, for SSP experiment the order of improvement is about 4X to 6X in terms of the time to converge. Figures 24 and 25 show the quantitative improvement in terms of the variances in estimation error that converge to very low and steady-state values.

For the 4 class SSP experiment, Figs. 31 and 32 exhibit faster and improved convergence of service time and delay estimates to their expected values using the modified EKF algorithm. Comparing with Figs. 29 and 30, the improvement is about 3X in terms of the time to converge.

The results presented here confirm that our modified EKF design is very effective in solving the convergence problems encountered with the original EKF design. Our

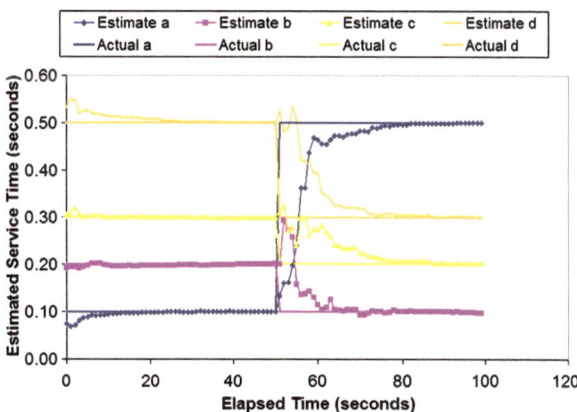

Fig. 31 Improved serv. time est. (SSP)

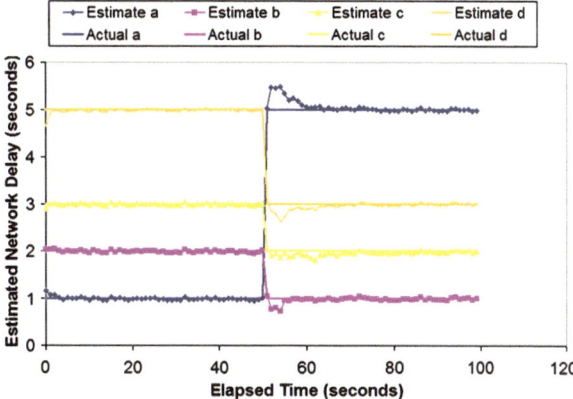

Fig. 32 Improved delay estimates (SSP)

modified design is crucial for a successful implementation of EKF for real-time performance modeling of AS systems that process multiple classes of workload.

8 Conclusion

Real-time performance modeling for AS systems is an emerging area of research. Prior work has demonstrated the effective use of Extended Kalman filters for tracking (estimating) model parameters in a system with single class of workload. However, in this work we have presented experiments that demonstrate the ineffectiveness of prior approaches for multiple classes of workload. We have further proposed a simple yet powerful modification to the existing filter design. Our modification eliminates the problems encountered with the original filter design, with a very high degree of improvement. To the best of our knowledge, ours is the first attempt to propose such a modification. Results presented in this paper can have a significant impact in improving performance of Kalman filters for the purpose of real-time performance modeling of AS systems.

References

[1] Solomon, B., Ionescu, D., Litoiu, M., Mihaescu, M.: A real-time adaptive control of autonomic computing environments. In: CASCON '07: Proceedings of the 2007 conference of the center for advanced studies on Collaborative research, pp. 124–136 (2007)

[2] Ionescu, D., Solomon, B., Litoiu, M., Mihaescu, M.: A robust autonomic computing architecture for server virtualization. In: INES 2008: International Conference on Intelligent Engineering Systems, pp. 173–180 (2008)

[3] Ionescu, D., Solomon, B., Litoiu, M., Mihaescu, M.: All papers. In: SEASS '07: Proceedings of First IEEE International Workshop on Software Engineering for Adaptive Software Systems. http://conferences.computer.org/compsac/2007/workshops/SEASS.html (July 2007)

[4] Hamann, T., Hübsch, G., Springer, T.: A model-driven approach for developing adaptive software systems, pp. 196–209 (2008)

[5] Chen, W.K., Hiltunen, M.A., Schlichting, R.D.: Constructing adaptive software in distributed systems. In: Proceedings of the 21st International Conference on Distributed Computing Systems, IEEE Computer Society, pp. 635–643 (2001)

[6] Zhang, L., Liu, Z., Riabov, A., Schulman, M., Xia, C., Zhang, F.: A comprehensive toolset for workload characterization, performance modeling, and online control. In: Computer Performance Evaluations, Modelling Techniques and Tools. LNCS, vol. 2794, pp. 63–77. Springer, Berlin (2003)

[7] Zhang, L., Liu, Z., Riabov, A., Schulman, M., Xia, C., Zhang, F.: Application Resource Measurement—ARM. http://www.opengroup.org/tech/management/arm/

[8] Zhang, L., Xia, C., Squillante, M., III, W.M.: Workload Service Requirements Analysis: A Queueing Network Optimization Approach. In: 10th IEEE International Symposium on Modeling, Analysis, and Simulation of Computer and Telecommunications Systems (MASCOTS) (2002)

[9] Liu, Z., Xia, C.H., Momcilovic, P., Zhang, L.: AMBIENCE: Automatic Model Building using InferEnce. In: Congress MSR03, Metz, France (Oct. 2003)

[10] Bemporad, A.: Model-based predictive control design: New trends and tools. In: Proc. 45th IEEE Conf. on Decision and Control, pp. 6678–6683 (2006)

[11] Pacifici, G., Spreitzer, M., Tantawi, A., Youssef, A.: Performance management for cluster based web services. IEEE J. Sel. Areas Commun. **23**(12), 2333–2343 (2005)
[12] Urgaonkar, B., Pacifici, G., Shenoy, P., Spreitzer, M., Tantawi, A.: Analytic modeling of multitier internet applications. ACM Trans. Web **1**(1), 1–35 (2007)
[13] Pacifici, G., Segmuller, W., Spreitzer, M., Tantawi, A.: CPU demand for web serving: Measurement analysis and dynamic estimation. Perform. Eval. **65**(6–7), 531–553 (2008)
[14] Simon, D.: Optimal State Estimation: Kalman, h Infinity and Nonlinear Approaches. Wiley, New York (2000)
[15] Zheng, T., Yang, J., Woodside, M., Litoiu, M., Iszlai, G.: Tracking time-varying parameters in software systems with extended Kalman filters. In: CASCON '05: Proceedings of the 2005 Conference of the Centre for Advanced Studies on Collaborative Research, pp. 334–345. IBM Press, Raleigh (2005)
[16] Zheng, T., Woodside, M., Litoiu, M.: Performance model estimation and tracking using optimal filters. IEEE Trans. Softw. Eng. **34**(3), 391–406 (2008)
[17] Woodside, M., Zheng, T., Litoiu, M.: The use of optimal filters to track parameters of performance models. In: QEST '05: Proceedings of the Second International Conference on the Quantitative Evaluation of Systems, Torino, Italy, p. 74 (September 2005)
[18] Woodside, M., Zheng, T., Litoiu, M.: Service system resource management based on a tracked layered performance model. In: ICAC '06: Proceedings of the third International Conference on Autonomic Computing, pp. 175–184. IEEE Press, New York (2006)
[19] Kumar, D., Zhang, L., Tantawi, A.: Enhanced Inferencing: Estimation of a Workload Dependent Performance Model. In: ICST Valuetools, Pisa, Italy (2009)
[20] Chang, J., Kumar, D., Pitts, A., Zhang, L.: Modeling Rational Asset Manager (RAM) Performance using AMBIENCE. IBM Technical Report, Lexington, USA (2008)
[21] Gross, D., Harris, C.M.: Fundamentals of Queueing Theory, 3rd edn. Wiley-Interscience, New York (1998)
[22] IBM: IBM websphere extended deployment. http://www.ibm.com/software/webservers/appserv/extend/
[23] Zhang, Z., Kurose, J., Salehi, J., Towsley, D.: Smoothing statistical multiplexing and call admission control for stored video. IEEE J. Sel. Areas Commun. **15**, 1148–1166 (1997)
[24] Stewart, C., Kelly, T., Zhang, A.: Exploiting nonstationarity for performance prediction. SIGOPS Oper. Syst. Rev. **41**(3), 31–44 (2007)

D. Kumar (✉)
IBM Research, 19 Skyline Drive, Hawthorne, NY 10532, USA
e-mail: kumardi@us.ibm.com

A. Tantawi
IBM Research, 19 Skyline Drive, Hawthorne, NY 10532, USA
e-mail: tantawi@us.ibm.com

L. Zhang
IBM Research, 19 Skyline Drive, Hawthorne, NY 10532, USA
e-mail: zhangli@us.ibm.com

A Control-Theoretic Approach for the Combined Management of Quality-of-Service and Energy in Service Centers

Charles Poussot-Vassal, Mara Tanelli, and Marco Lovera

Abstract The complexity of Information Technology (IT) systems is steadily increasing and system complexity has been recognised as the main obstacle to further advancements of IT. This fact has recently raised energy management issues. Control techniques have been proposed and successfully applied to design Autonomic Computing systems, trading-off system performance with energy saving goals. As users behaviour is highly time varying and workload conditions can change substantially within the same business day, the Linear Parametrically Varying (LPV) framework is particularly promising for modeling such systems. In this chapter, a control-theoretic method to investigate the trade-off between Quality of Service (QoS) requirements and energy saving objectives in the case of admission control in Web service systems is proposed, considering as control variables the server CPU frequency and the admission probability. To quantitatively evaluate the trade-off, a dynamic model of the admission control dynamics is estimated via LPV identification techniques. Based on this model, an optimisation problem within the Model Predictive Control (MPC) framework is setup, by means of which it is possible to investigate the optimal trade-off policy to manage QoS and energy saving objectives at design time and taking into explicit account the system dynamics.

Keywords Performance evaluation · Admission control · Dynamic voltage and frequency scaling · Linear parameter varying models · Model predictive control

Mathematics Subject Classification (2000) Primary 99Z99 · Secondary 00A00

1 Introduction

The steady increase in the complexity of Information Technology (IT) systems led IBM to release, in mid-October 2001, the "Autonomic Computing Manifesto" [1] observing that current applications have reached the size of several millions of lines

D. Ardagna, L. Zhang (eds.), *Run-time Models for Self-managing*   73
Systems and Applications, 73–96,
Autonomic Systems, DOI 10.1007/978-3-0346-0433-8_4, © Springer Basel AG 2010

of code while physical infrastructures include thousands of heterogeneous servers and require skilled IT professionals to install, configure, tune, and maintain. Due to this fact, system complexity has been recognised as the main obstacle to further advancement of IT.

Another emerging problem in this context is related to energy management. The growth in the number of servers has caused an enormous spike in electricity usage. IT analysts predict that, by 2012, up to 40% of an enterprise technology budget will be consumed by energy costs. From an environmental point of view, overall, IT accounts for 2% of global CO_2 emissions, i.e., IT pollutes to the same extent as the global air traffic [2].

Furthermore, system operation has to cope with the variability of users' behaviour and application workloads. Nowadays, IT systems have to provide to their users prescribed Quality of Service (QoS) levels usually defined in terms of application performance, such as requests response time or system throughput. QoS requirements are difficult to satisfy, since workload may vary by several orders of magnitude within the same business day [3, 4]. To handle workload variations and meet QoS requirements, resources have to be dynamically allocated among running applications and the IT architecture has to be re-configured at run-time.

Control-theoretic techniques have been proposed and successfully applied to the design of Autonomic Computing systems [5, 6]. The main actuation mechanisms which have been implemented are: (i) *Dynamic Voltage and Frequency Scaling* of server CPU, (ii) *admission control*, and (iii) *resource allocation in virtualised environments*. This chapter will focus on the first two of them.

Dynamic Voltage and Frequency Scaling (DVFS) is a mechanism which can be exploited to reduce the energy consumption of a server [7–9]. Modern CPUs allow varying both the CPU supply voltage and operating frequency. The adoption of DVFS as a control variable is very promising, as power consumption is proportional to the cube of the operating frequency, while server performance varies linearly with the operating frequency. Hence, under light load conditions energy consumption can be effectively reduced by lowering CPU frequency without worsening the provided QoS level.

Admission control is an overload protection mechanism which rejects requests under peak workload conditions in order to provide performance guarantees to the running applications [10–12]. Admission control is effective if the admitted requests are served according to their QoS constraints. However, QoS constraints need to be traded-off with energy saving objectives. To this end, it is of great importance to establish the optimal policy at *design time*, *i.e.*, when the strategies to manage the Web service infrastructure are evaluated and designed. This chapter presents a control oriented methodology to handle such issue. Furthermore, the runtime behaviour of the resulting policies will be evaluated.

In the utility-based context developed within the autonomic computing framework, approaches have been introduced to analyse and optimise the degree of users' satisfaction, expressed in terms of user-level performance metrics, which typically use performance models based on queueing theory, [13–15] (see the first chapter). These approaches can handle multiple decision variables (e.g., joint admission control and resource allocation [16]) but rely on the assumption that the system is at *steady state*. Hence, the optimal trade-off management policies that such approaches convey do not take into account the dynamic nature of the underlying physical system, which can have a decisive importance in selecting the management policies at machine level. As a matter of fact, in the formulation of autonomic computing as a control problem, the most critical issue is the variability of the dynamics of the Web server as a function of workload.

To capture such a variability and take it into account in the trade-off analysis, we propose to model the Web service dynamics via Linear Parametrically Varying (LPV) models, which have proved effective—in the control community—to deal with such parameter dependent systems, see e.g., [17, 18].

Recent work has shown that the LPV framework is very general, since it allows describing the performance of an IT system by exploiting all of the available technological mechanisms to manage QoS [19, 20]. Thus, in this work we first perform identification and validation experiments aimed at estimating an LPV dynamic model of the admission control dynamics. Such a model constitutes the basis for formulating the optimisation problem, the solution of which provides the optimal policy to manage the QoS/Energy trade-off. Specifically, the model of the server dynamics is derived using as inputs the admission probability and the CPU frequency, which are the two control variables employed to evaluate the optimal trade-off between QoS and energy saving. Based on the identified model, the trade-off evaluation problem is solved within the Model Predictive Control (MPC) framework, which is a widely used control approach allowing to formulate the control problem as a constrained optimisation one, see e.g., [21, 22]. Thus, the performance evaluation problem associated with the Web service system under study will be formulated in terms of a suitable cost function expressing the QoS/Energy saving trade-off and of a number of constraints further specifying the control objectives.

Notably, the proposed approach is quite general, in that it can accommodate different QoS measures together with other energy-related constraints within the same framework, and, most importantly, it can be applied to all available technological mechanisms to manage QoS with no conceptual differences. Another advantage is that the *ideal* formulation of the MPC control problem used for performance evaluation can be easily adapted to obtain a controller which can be actually run on the real system, so as to provide the possibility of analysing and quantifying the discrepancy between the optimal trade-off policy and the performance which can be achieved on the real system at policy *design time*.

The structure of this chapter is as follows. Section 2 provides the necessary background and defines the notation for the problem under study. Section 3 illustrates the LPV state space models employed for identification and shows the approach used to identify reliable models of the admission control dynamics, together with the experimental setting employed for identification and validation experiments. In Sect. 4 the proposed MPC-based approach to the analysis of the QoS/Energy trade-off is illustrated, and simulation results are shown to assess its suitability for the considered application.

2 Problem Statement and Notation

In the following, a Web service system endowed with DVFS and admission control functionalities will be considered. For the sake of simplicity, Web service applications are configured to serve requests according to the FIFO policy and run on a single CPU. In the queueing theory context, [23], the following quantities are commonly employed to describe the incoming workload over a time interval $[k\Delta t, (k+1)\Delta t]$, where Δt is the sampling interval:

- λ_k denotes the average requests arrival rate for the Web service application in the k-th time interval;
- s_k is the average requests service time, i.e., the overall CPU time needed to process a request for the considered application in the k-th time interval when the CPU runs at the maximum frequency and the CPU is fully dedicated to the execution of the application;
- T_k is the average server response time, i.e., the overall time a request stays in the system in the k-th time interval;
- f_k is defined as the *scaled frequency*, i.e., the ratio between the frequency adopted by the server CPU in the time interval k with respect to an intermediate CPU frequency value of the considered DVFS technology assumed to be the nominal one;
- $\mathcal{P}_k$ is the probability that a request will be admitted to the system in the k-th time interval.

The service time represents the overall server CPU time needed to serve a customer. Note that, generally speaking, the service time can be regarded as inversely proportional to the server CPU frequency. When physical servers are endowed with DVFS capabilities, in fact, the effect of, say, lowering the CPU frequency when a light workload is present in the system is an increase of the CPU time needed to serve a request (see [8]). This assumption is supported by current technology trends, since in modern systems (e.g., AMD Opteron 2347HE Barcelona core) CPUs and RAM clock can be scaled independently. Thus, in what follows it will be assumed that the effective service time can be defined as $s_{f,k} = s_k/f_k$. This assumption has been validated experimentally on a Web server endowed with the DVFS capability; the results of the validation experiment are depicted in Fig. 1. As can be seen, the above relationship is accurate (with an approximation of about 2%) and therefore can be considered acceptable for the present purposes.

As already mentioned, classical queueing theory provides a description of the system which relies on steady-state assumptions. Such a description is therefore reliable only over long time horizons.

For control purposes, however, a dynamical model of the server capable of capturing transients must be derived. We recall, in fact, that one of the aims of the present work is to obtain a control-oriented dynamical description of the server behaviour to be employed for dynamic performance evaluation via MPC control.

Remark 2.1 As incoming requests—independently of the application they may try to access—wait in a queue before accessing the physical server, it is clear that the

Fig. 1 Experimental
verification of $s_{f,k} = s_k / f_k$ on
a Web server with DVFS
functionalities

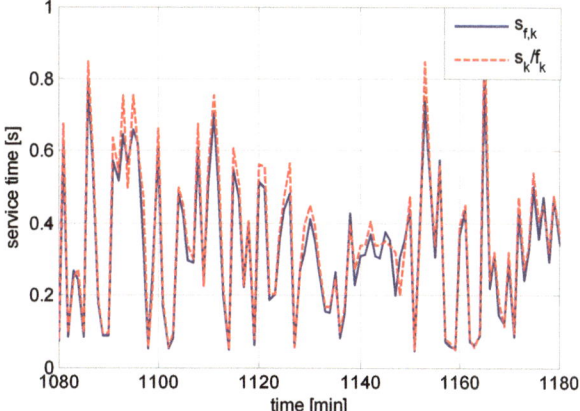

system dynamics will have a feedthrough term, i.e., a direct path from input to output. In fact, the response time T_k (i.e., the system output) is given by

$$T_k = \xi_k + s_{f,k}, \qquad (2.1)$$

where the queueing time ξ_k accounts for the time that the request spends in the queue. As such, the real dynamics of the system are to be found in the variable $\xi_k = T_k - s_{f,k}$. In what follows, LPV models will be identified for the dynamics of ξ_k only, and the final response time will then be retrieved via (2.1).

3 LPV State Space Models: Identification and Validation

In the considered application, an LPV modeling formulation has been adopted to handle the system nonlinearities due to workload variations. As shown in e.g., [19], this choice is essential since a simple Linear Time Invariant (LTI) model would not be precise enough to capture all the relevant dynamic behaviour of the considered system. In this section, the LPV model structure is described, and the identification approach used to model the dynamics of the admission control system are briefly presented (for more details on the identification approach, refer to [19, 20]). Further, the experimental setup employed for the identification and validation experiments is detailed, together with the obtained results.

3.1 LPV Model Identification Approach

LPV systems are linear and time-varying dynamical systems, characterised by state space matrices which are fixed functions of some vector of measurable, time varying parameters. LPV model identification algorithms are available in the literature both for input/output and state space representations of parametrically-varying dynamics. In particular, in the recent works [7, 24] an input–output modelling approach was adopted. If, however, the aim of the identification procedure is to eventually work out LPV models in state space form for control design purposes, one should keep in mind that the usual equivalence notions applicable to LTI systems cannot be directly used in converting LPV models from input-output to state space form, as the *time-variability* of LPV systems ought to be taken into account (see, e.g., the discussion in [25]). Bearing this in mind, in this work we focus on state space LPV models in the form

$$x_{k+1} = A(p_k)x_k + B(p_k)u_k$$
$$y_k = C(p_k)x_k + D(p_k)u_k, \tag{3.1}$$

where $p \in \mathbb{R}^s$ is the parameter vector, $x \in \mathbb{R}^n$ is the system state, $u \in \mathbb{R}^m$ is the control input, and $y \in \mathbb{R}^l$ is the measured output. It is often necessary to introduce additional assumptions regarding the way in which p_k enters the system matrices: in this work we focus on affine and input-affine models, defined as follows.

1. Affine parameter dependence (LPV-A):

$$A(p_k) = A_0 + A_1 p_{1,k} + \cdots + A_s p_{s,k} \tag{3.2}$$

   and similarly for B, C and D, and where by $p_{i,k}, i = 1, \ldots, s$ we denote the i-th component of vector p_k. This form can be immediately generalised to polynomial parameter dependence.
2. Input-affine parameter dependence (LPV-IA): this is a particular case of the LPV-A parameter dependence in which only the B and D matrices are considered as parametrically-varying, while A and C are assumed to be constant, i.e., $A = A_0$, $C = C_0$.

As far as LPV model identification is concerned, it is usually convenient to consider first the simplest form, i.e., the LPV-IA one, as its parameters can be retrieved using Subspace Model Identification (SMI) algorithms for LTI systems by suitably extending the input vector. In this work the MOESP class of SMI algorithms (see [26]) has been considered. LPV-IA models also provide a useful initial guess for iterative methods which can be used for the identification of fully parameterised models in LPV-A form, along the lines of [27, 28]. The classical way to perform linear system identification is by minimising the error between the real output and the predicted output of the model. A similar approach can be used for LPV state-space systems of the form (3.1). Letting the system matrices of (3.1) be completely described by a set of parameters θ, identification on the basis of N input/output samples can be carried out by minimising the cost function

$$V_N(\theta) := \sum_{k=1}^{N} \|y_k - \hat{y}_k(\theta)\|_2^2 = E_N^T(\theta)E_N(\theta),$$

with respect to θ, where

$$E_N^T(\theta) = \left[\left(y_1 - \hat{y}_1(\theta) \right)^T \quad \cdots \quad \left(y_N - \hat{y}_N(\theta) \right)^T \right]$$

y_k denotes the measured output and $\hat{y}_k(\theta)$ denotes the output of the LPV model to be identified.

3.2 Testbed Setting and Experimental Results

To perform the experiments needed for collecting identification and validation data, a workload generator and a micro-benchmarking Web service application have been used. The workload generator is based on a custom extension of the Apache *JMeter* 2.3.1 workload injector, [29], which allows to generate workload according to an open model [23] with a Poisson arrival process, which, see e.g., [30], can be used to model the user requests for individual Web pages (hence at session level) on a Web server. The micro-benchmarking Web service application is implemented as a Java servlet and is hosted within the Apache *Tomcat* 6.0 application server, [31]. The servlet has been designed to consume a given CPU time which allows to emulate the DVFS of the physical server (a Pentium D machine with no DVFS support). The benchmarking code has been embedded within the *synchronised* Java construct in order to schedule requests execution according to a FIFO policy. The application has been instrumented to measure the service time of each request. Note, that the service time determination can be done in practise based on techniques which can assess the number of CPU cycles consumed by requests both at application level (e.g., the Application Resource Measurement API, [32]) or at operating system level (e.g., kernel-based measurements, [12]). However, it must be said that kernel tracing might be difficult to be used in production environments, and that, at the application level, the known methods to estimate service times might have accuracy limitations when a multi-class system is considered, see e.g., [33].

To obtain an LPV model of the admission control dynamics, the identification experiments have been carried out employing a synthetic workload inspired by a real-world usage. The incoming workload has been chosen so as to reproduce a 24 hour trace obtained from a large Internet Web site including up to 100 physical servers. The workload injector has been configured to follow a Poisson process with request rate changing every minute according to the trace. Note that, even though the average request rate is only changed each minute, the arrival times of the single requests t_{req} do not uniformly span the time interval, but are generated as samples of an exponential distribution with parameter λ_k, i.e., $t_{req} \sim \mathcal{E}(\lambda_k)$.

As for the application service time s_k, it has been designed to follow a log-normal distribution (as observed for several real applications, [34]) such that, in each 1 minute time interval, the standard deviation $\sigma[s_k]$ is four times larger than the average service time $E[s_k]$, i.e., $\sigma[s_k] = 4\,E[s_k]$. To emulate the presence of a DVFS in the physical server, the generated average service time has then been

Fig. 2 Time histories of the
I/O data and scheduling
parameters in identification
experiments for admission
control. *Top plot*: scheduling
parameters λ_k (*solid line*) and
$s_{f,k}$ (*dotted line*); *middle plot*:
system input, admission
probability $\mathcal{P}_k$; *bottom plot*:
measured output, response
time T_k

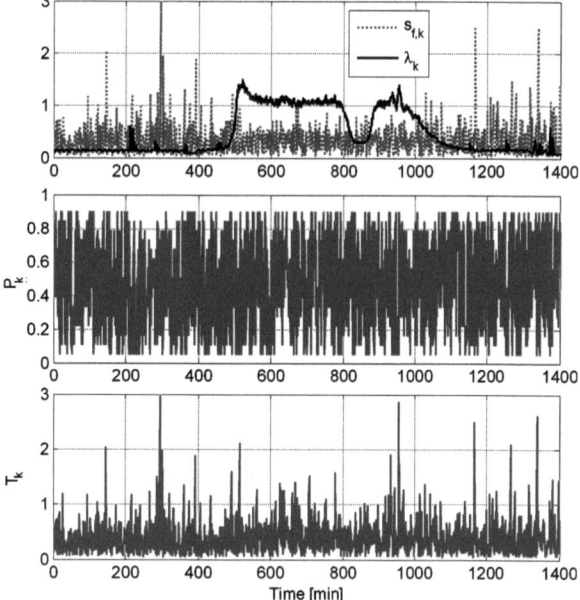

Fig. 3 Time history of the
server utilisation $\lambda_k \, s_k \, \mathcal{P}_k$
used in the identification
experiments for admission
control

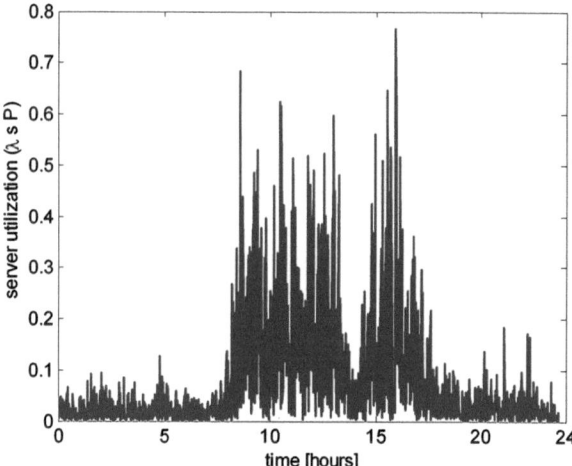

scaled by f_k to obtain $s_{f,k}$, where f_k emulates the DVFS of a physical server with
10 CPU frequency levels.

The admission probability $\mathcal{P}_k$ has been varied stepwise every 1 minute, with
values between 0.1 and 1. Figure 2 shows the time histories of the input, output
and scheduling parameters employed in the identification experiments, while Fig. 3
shows a plot of the overall server utilisation used in the identification experiments,
which, for admission control, is defined as $\lambda_k \, s_k \, \mathcal{P}_k$. As can be seen, the system was
subject to a varying workload, characterised by two peaks during the day occur-

ring approximately between 9 a.m. and 1 p.m. and between 2.30 and 5 p.m. (see Figure 3).

For validation purposes, different realisations of the same workload profile have been employed, while varying the parameters of the service time log-normal distribution. Specifically, two validation tests have been performed with the standard deviation of the log-normal $\sigma[s_k] = q\,E[s_k]$ and $q = \{2, 6\}$. This has been done to analyse whether the identified models are sensitive to the variability of the CPU time distribution.

To quantitatively evaluate the models, both on identification and validation data, two metrics are considered: the percentage Variance Accounted For (VAF), defined as

$$VAF = 100\left(1 - \frac{\mathrm{Var}[y_k - y_{sim,k}]}{\mathrm{Var}[y_k]}\right),\tag{3.3}$$

where y_k is the measured signal and $y_{sim,k}$ is the output obtained from the identified model, and the percentage average error e_{avg}, computed as

$$e_{avg} = 100\left|\frac{E[y_k - y_{sim,k}]}{E[y_k]}\right|.\tag{3.4}$$

This choice allows to assess the system performance both in a 1 and in a 2-norm sense.

Based on the identification data, an LPV-IA model for the admission control dynamics was estimated. To employ the model as a basis for a control problem tailored to analyse the trade-off between QoS and energy saving, we consider as inputs the admission probability and the effective service time, i.e., $u_k = [\mathcal{P}_k, s_k/f_k]$ and use the arrival rate λ_k and its square as scheduling parameters, that is $p_k = [\lambda_k\ \lambda_k^2]$. The system output is the server response time T_k. The model order was set to 4 via cross-validation analysis and the best sampling time for this application proved to be $\Delta t = 1\,\mathrm{min}$.

Based on the discussion in Sect. 2, an LPV-IA model for the dynamics of ξ_k was estimated, and the overall response times computed according to (2.1). A plot of the response time obtained with the identified model on validation data is compared to the measured one in Fig. 4 for the case of $q = 2$.

A summary of the identified model performance on validation data for both $q = 2$ and $q = 6$ is provided in Table 1, which confirms the validity of the proposed LPV model.

4 Dynamic Analysis of the QoS/Energy Trade-off

The main challenge related with QoS requirements can be stated as that of guaranteeing a given service time associated with a request, denoted with T_{ref}, which is defined and negotiated between the customers and the service provider, and a certain minimal amount of accepted requests (here modeled as an admission probability $\mathcal{P}_k$), while either:

Fig. 4 Detail of the
measured (*solid line*) and
simulated (*dashed line*)
response time obtained with
an LPV-IA model for the
admission control dynamics
on validation data

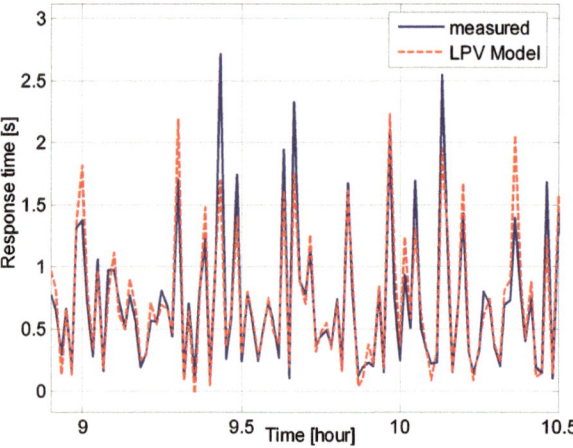

Table 1 Performance of the
identified models for
admission control with
$\Delta t = 1$ min on validation data

Valid. Performance $\Delta t = 1$ min	$q = 2$	$q = 6$
VAF on 24 h	65.46%	64.54%
VAF light load	88.94%	86.95%
VAF heavy load	57.89%	54.23%
e_{avg} on 24 h	7.27%	8.47%
e_{avg} light load	4.34%	6.78%
e_{avg} heavy load	9.40%	13.32%

1. Maximizing the number of served users: Quality of Service (QoS) objective.
2. Minimizing the power consumption: Energy saving objective.

These objectives reflect the natural QoS/Energy saving trade-off. Indeed, the first objective reflects the ability of a service provider to serve a large number of requests, while the second one reflects the ability of a service provider to achieve energy saving, and thus cost reduction.

In this section, the optimal performance level of the server is computed using an optimisation algorithm inspired by the Linear Parameter-Varying Model Predictive Control (LPV-MPC) approach.

To this purpose, the relevant background on MPC is first provided in Sect. 4.1, while the application of MPC to optimal performance computation is presented in Sect. 4.2.

4.1 Model Predictive Control for Performance Evaluation

Model Predictive Control (MPC) is a widely used approach to the solution of large scale, multivariable, possibly constrained control problems which has been developed in the Control community over the last three decades. The main idea of MPC can be summarised as follows: i) the control problem is formulated as an optimisation one, based on a mathematical model for the system to be controlled (and possibly of known external disturbances), a cost function expressing the desired performance of the system over a future time horizon and all the relevant constraints on the input, state and output variables; ii) the control action over the future horizon is computed by repeatedly solving the optimisation problem on line; iii) the implementation of the computed control action is based on the so-called *receding horizon* principle, i.e., at each time step only the first sample of the computed control sequence is actually applied and the control problem is re-solved at the subsequent time step, [21, 22].

MPC is a very attractive idea, as it allows a very natural formulation of control problems in terms of constrained optimisation. On the other hand, however, this approach leads to a number of issues when it comes to guaranteeing closed-loop stability, dealing with uncertainty in the mathematical model of the system to be controlled and ensuring that the optimisation problem is computationally tractable in view of the need to solve it online. Such issues are a subject of active research and have been successfully clarified in a number of frameworks, see e.g., [35–37]. Most of the attention in the literature focused on *standard* MPC problems in which the system under study is LTI and the cost function expressing the desired closed-loop performance is a quadratic one. In this respect, the literature on LPV-MPC is relatively recent, see e.g., [38–40].

When it comes to performance evaluation, MPC is a very valuable tool for a number of reasons. First of all, provided that the system for which a performance analysis is sought after falls within the assumptions under which MPC can be applied with some guarantees, an MPC controller can be set up and implemented fairly easily, as it requires little tuning with respect to other approaches. Furthermore, if, e.g., one is interested in assessing *optimal* performance in the face of external disturbances, the controller can be implemented by assuming that the future evolution of the disturbances is exactly known over the future horizon. Such setting provides the ability of analysing the optimal performance achievable on the considered system, but can be also easily adapted to provide a controller which can be actually implemented in the non ideal case. As an example, in the considered application, to translate the *ideal* LPV-MPC controller used for performance evaluation into a regulator which can be used on the real Web server it is sufficient to design a state estimator from input/output data—the MPC controller needs to have access to the state variables of the dynamical model which are often not measurable—and to let the controller work with no preview of the future evolution of the disturbances (which in the considered case are the service time and the requests arrival rate) or, possibly, with the evolution estimated by workload predictors, [41]. Of course, the resulting MPC controller performance will be fully and easily comparable with that provided by the ideal case used for performance evaluation, so that the degree of *sub-optimality* of the final implementation can be also investigated at policy design time.

In the following section the performance evaluation problem associated with the Web service system under study will be formulated in terms of a suitable cost function expressing the QoS/Energy saving trade-off and of a number of constraints further specifying the control objectives. As a mathematical model for the system under study, the identified LPV model described in Sect. 3 will be used.

4.2 Analysis for Optimal Performance

Let us consider the admission probability $\mathcal{P}_k$ and the scaled CPU frequency f_k as the control variables. The objective is to compute the theoretical optimal performance of a controlled server. To do so, we work under the following assumptions.

1. The request rate λ_k and the requests service time s_k are considered as known variables over a time horizon of N samples.
2. The state variables x_k of the system are assumed to be accessible.
3. The LPV model of the Web server dynamics is assumed to be perfectly fitting the real Web server system.
4. The desired response time T_{ref} is considered as a known variable over the time horizon N.

Based on these assumptions, the idea is to optimise an appropriate performance index representing either the QoS or the Energy saving objective while guaranteeing that the constraints on the system dynamics, control variables and system performance are fulfilled. Note that, as discussed in the previous section, assumptions 1), 2) and 3) are only valid in an ideal setting, whereas assumption 4) is always fulfilled in practise.

To apply the proposed LPV-MPC approach, one has to define the following.

1. A cost function to be minimised, representing the trade-off between the QoS and Energy saving objectives, see Sect. 4.3.
2. A set of dynamic equality constraints, denoted as $\Sigma(x_k, \lambda_k, s_k, \mathcal{P}_k, f_k)$, based on the LPV system model described in Sect. 3, see Sect. 4.4.
3. A set of inequality constraints, denoted as Λ, aimed at guaranteeing that the control signals evolve within physical bounds (input constraints) and that the tracking of the desired response time T_{ref} is achieved (performance constraints), see Sect. 4.5.

Once such quantities have been defined, the solution to the problem is obtained by solving a nonlinear constrained optimisation problem at each sampling step. The general scheme of the proposed approach is illustrated in Fig. 5.

4.3 Cost Function Definitions

To model the QoS/Energy saving trade-off, the following cost function can be introduced

Fig. 5 Optimal performance
computation scheme

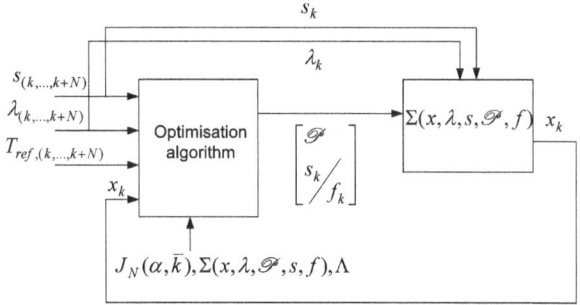

$$J_N(\alpha, \bar{k}) = \alpha J_{QoS}(\bar{k}) + (1 - \alpha) J_{ES}(\bar{k})$$

$$= \alpha \sum_{k=\bar{k}}^{\bar{k}+N-1} \left| \frac{\overline{\mathcal{P}} - \mathcal{P}_k}{\overline{\mathcal{P}} - \underline{\mathcal{P}}} \right| + (1 - \alpha) \sum_{k=\bar{k}}^{\bar{k}+N-1} \left| \frac{1/\underline{f} - 1/f_k}{1/\underline{f} - 1/\overline{f}} \right|, \qquad (4.1)$$

where $k \in \mathbb{N}$ is the current time instant, $\bar{k}$ and $N \in \mathbb{N}$ are the initial time instant and
the prediction horizon length over which the optimisation is carried out, respectively,
$\mathcal{P}_k \in [\underline{\mathcal{P}}, \overline{\mathcal{P}}]$ (resp. $f_k \in [\underline{f}, \overline{f}]$) represents the admission probability (resp. the CPU
scaled frequency) in the current time interval, and $\alpha \in [0, 1]$ is a design parameter
which allows to privilege either QoS or Energy saving objectives. Recall that $\mathcal{P}_k$ and
$s_{f,k} = s_k/f_k$, $k \in [\bar{k}, \bar{k} + N]$ are the control inputs to be computed by the LPV-MPC
controller.

The cost function $J_N(\alpha, \bar{k})$ describes a convex combination of the performance
objectives. More specifically, note that:

- $J_N(0, \bar{k}) = \sum_{k=\bar{k}}^{\bar{k}+N-1} \left| \frac{1/\underline{f}-1/f_k}{1/\underline{f}-1/\overline{f}} \right|$ represents the case where the objective is to min-
  imise the CPU frequency (Energy saving objective).
- $J_N(1, \bar{k}) = \sum_{k=\bar{k}}^{\bar{k}+N-1} \left| \frac{\overline{\mathcal{P}}-\mathcal{P}_k}{\overline{\mathcal{P}}-\underline{\mathcal{P}}} \right|$ represents the case where the objective is to max-
  imise the admission probability, hence to satisfy the largest possible number of
  requests (QoS objective).

Note that the objective function is given in discrete time, where the sampling
time $\Delta t \in \mathbb{R}^+$ is chosen according to the model description (here $\Delta t = 1$ min, see
Sect. 3).

4.4 Dynamic Equality Constraints

The dynamic equality constraints of the considered problem are simply given by
the LPV-IA model derived in Sect. 3. This results in a set of nonlinear dynamic

constraints, denoted by $\Sigma(x_k, \lambda_k, s_k, \mathcal{P}_k, f_k)$, namely

$$
\begin{cases}
x_{k+1} = Ax_k + \left(B_{10} + B_{11}\lambda_k + B_{12}\lambda_k^2\right)\mathcal{P}_k + \left(B_{20} + B_{21}\lambda_k + B_{22}\lambda_k^2\right)\frac{s_k}{f_k} \\
\xi_k = Cx_k + \left(D_{10} + D_{11}\lambda_k + D_{12}\lambda_k^2\right)\mathcal{P}_k + \left(D_{20} + D_{21}\lambda_k + D_{22}\lambda_k^2\right)\frac{s_k}{f_k} \quad (4.2) \\
T_k = \xi_k + \frac{s_k}{f_k},
\end{cases}
$$

where $A \in \mathbb{R}^{n \times n}$, $\{B_0, B_1, B_2\} \in \mathbb{R}^{n \times n_u}$, $C \in \mathbb{R}^{n_y \times n}$ and $\{D_0, D_1, D_2\} \in \mathbb{R}^{n_y \times n_u}$ are known matrices (here $n = 2$, $n_u = 1$ and $n_y = 1$). Further, x_k represents the state of the system, and the response time T_k is the overall system output (see (2.1)). Finally, λ_k and s_k will be considered as known variables (up to time $\bar{k} + N - 1$), even though, in practise, they are generally unknown (or only partially known thanks to some workload estimators).

4.5 Input and Performance Inequality Constraints

Now, let us define Λ as the set describing input and performance inequality constraints as follows

$$
\Lambda : \begin{cases}
0 \le \xi_k \\
\underline{\mathcal{P}} \le \mathcal{P}_k \le \overline{\mathcal{P}} \\
\underline{f} \le f_k \le \overline{f} \\
-\Delta \le T_k - T_{ref} \le \Delta
\end{cases} \quad (4.3)
$$

where T_{ref} is the desired value of the response time and Δ defines the admissible tracking error $T_k - T_{ref}$. Both T_{ref} and Δ are design parameters. Note that, for simplicity, the desired value of the response time T_{ref} has been defined as constant. In the same way, the proposed approach can handle a time-varying set-point trajectory, i.e., $T_{ref,k}$, which may be useful to handle QoS requirements which are functions, for example, of the time of day.

4.6 LPV-MPC Optimisation Problem

The considered constrained finite-time optimal control problem to be solved at each sampling time $\bar{k}$ is defined as

$$
J_N^*(\alpha, \bar{k}) = \min \ J_N(\alpha, \bar{k})
$$

$$
\text{subject to} \begin{cases}
\begin{bmatrix} x_{k+1} \\ \xi_k \\ T_k \end{bmatrix} = (4.2), \quad k \in [\bar{k}, \bar{k} + N - 1] \\
\Lambda = (4.3).
\end{cases}
$$

This problem is iteratively solved using the YALMIP parser and a standard non-linear constrained solver via interior point methods [42, 43]. The Reader should keep in mind that the proposed optimal performance computation is *ideal*, as perfect modeling, full state and workload parameters knowledge are assumed. Still, this approach provides an upper bound on the achievable server performance and can help both dynamic performance evaluation and controller design. As mentioned before, in fact, the ideal controller can be easily adapted to be employed on the real system via state estimation and assuming no knowledge of the workload parameters (or complementing the system with workload predictors).

When implemented in an online fashion, the proposed control system has of course to run in real-time, thus solving the optimisation problem discussed above at each sampling instant, i.e., every minute. Note that, as far as the LPV model update is concerned, it simply requires a matrix-vector product. The same is true for the state estimator, which results to be a linear and time-invariant dynamical system (see [44]). The most demanding phase, as far as computational complexity is concerned, is the constrained optimisation of the cost function: however, given that the controller would run on board of the Web server, the CPU and the memory available offer performance which are well beyond the usual embedded computing infrastructure on which most control systems commonly run. As such, we expect that the sampling time of one minute can be used also in real-time. Should the computational complexity be too large to solve the problem within this time interval, one could simply identify an LPV model for the system based on a larger sampling interval and formulate and solve the optimisation problem over this new time scale.

In the following, the LPV-MPC controller is used to evaluate the optimal performance of the considered application, based on the dynamical model identified in Sect. 3, both via time domain simulations and by analysing the performance index (4.1), which is representative of the QoS/Energy saving trade-off.

5 Simulation Results

In this section, the results of simulations carried out to analyse the influence of the parameter α in the cost function (4.1), i.e., the trade-off between QoS and Energy saving, are presented. To perform the analysis we assume that the system is subject to the requests rate λ_k (shown in Fig. 6-top) associated with the service time, s_k (Fig. 6-bottom).

Additionally, in order to quantitatively evaluate both QoS and Energy saving objectives, the following performance measures will be employed

$$
\begin{aligned}
P_{QoS} &= \sum_{k=1}^{N_f} \frac{\|\mathcal{P}_k - \underline{\mathcal{P}}\|_2}{\|\overline{\mathcal{P}} - \underline{\mathcal{P}}\|_2} \\
P_{ES} &= \sum_{k=1}^{N_f} \frac{\|1/\underline{f} - 1/f_k\|_2}{\|1/\underline{f} - 1/\overline{f}\|_2}
\end{aligned}
\tag{5.1}
$$

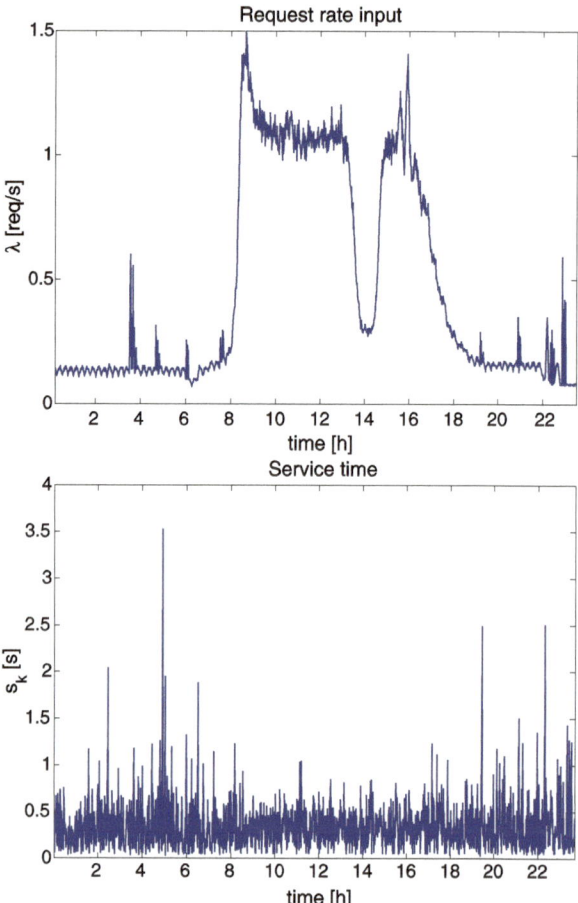

Fig. 6 Illustration of the request rate λ_k (*top*) and of the service time s_k (*bottom*) considered in the simulation study

where N_f is the final simulation sample and $\|v\|_2$ indicates the 2-norm of vector v. As a consequence:

- $P_{QoS} = 1$ (resp. 0) indicates that the maximum (resp. the minimum) number of requests has been served with the desired response time T_{ref}.
- $P_{ES} = 1$ (resp. 0) indicates that the power consumption of the server has been minimised (resp. maximised), i.e., the server CPU frequency has been lowered (resp. increased).

To perform the simulations, the following server configuration is considered:

- The upper and lower bounds on f_k (recall that it represents the ratio between the current CPU frequency and the nominal value of the CPU frequency according to the considered DVFS technology) are chosen as $[\underline{f}_k, \overline{f}_k] = [0.01, 4]$. This choice illustrates the fact that, when the server is running with f_k lower than one it saves energy with respect to the nominal configuration, while, when f_k is larger than one it consumes more energy. Note that these bounds can be viewed as a *system parameter*, as they depends on the DVFS settings of the server in use.

- The admission probability limits are chosen as $[\underline{\mathcal{P}}, \overline{\mathcal{P}}] = [0.1, 1]$. This configuration implies that the server system is at least constrained to accept 10% of the incoming requests. Note that this constitutes an additional *design parameter* for the overall policy, since it depends on the provider/customer QoS negotiation.
- The reference response time has been set to $T_{ref} = 1$s and the maximum tracking error to $\Delta = \frac{25}{100} T_{ref}$.
- The prediction horizon length has been set to $N = 10$. This variable modifies the optimisation problem by enlarging the time interval over which the controller has knowledge of the future evolution of the workload parameters, i.e., of the service time and requests arrival rate. Thus, in general, as N grows larger the optimisation results become (theoretically) better. In practise, experiments have shown that $N = 10$ is appropriate for our purposes (see also [45]).

5.1 QoS/Energy Trade-off Analysis

We now move to the analysis of the QoS/Energy trade-off. At first, the performance measures (5.1) are evaluated for different values of α. Figure 7 shows the values of P_{QoS} and P_{ES} in (5.1) for different values of α.

By inspecting Fig. 7, the trade-off between QoS and energy saving is apparent. When α is low (see also (4.1)) energy saving is a priority. Conversely, increasing

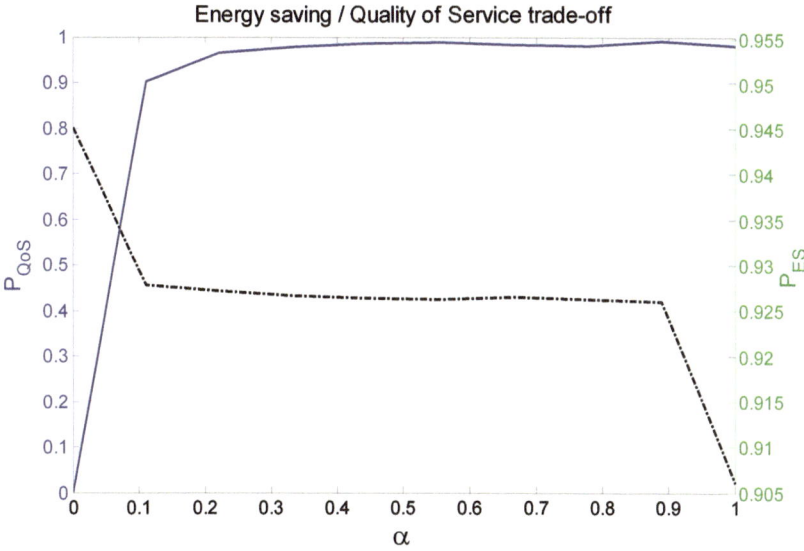

Fig. 7 Plot of the performance measures P_{QoS} (*solid line, left axis*) and P_{ES} (*dashed line, right axis*) as functions of α for $N = 10$

α leads to higher energy consumption but allows a larger number of requests to be admitted in the system, thus maximising QoS. According to these results, the following remarks are due.

- When $\alpha = 0$, P_{ES} is maximised, while the P_{QoS} is almost null, which means that the admission probability is almost always at its lower bound of $\underline{P} = 0.1$.
- When $\alpha = 1$, the P_{ES} is minimised, while P_{QoS} is maximised, which means that the admission probability is almost always at its upper bound $\overline{P} = 1$ and the effective service time is low.
- The maximal and minimal values of the P_{ES} curve are not reached. This is due to two main reasons:
  - first, according to the constraints described in the previous section, it is not possible for the system to guarantee an admission probability of $P_k = \underline{P} = 0.1$ while minimising the CPU frequency.
  - secondly, the requested response time should remain around $T_{ref} = 1$ s. To illustrate this point refer to top plots of Figs. 8 and 9. It is possible to fulfil this requirement by e.g., reducing the minimal admission probability or by increasing the desired response time value T_{ref}. This highlights the flexibility of the proposed approach, which allows to analyse the system performance for different designer choices, thereby providing a valuable means to evaluate different system settings.
- A reasonable trade-off between QoS and Energy saving is achieved, in our setting (with the considered request rate and service time profiles), for low values of α (e.g., $\alpha \cong 0.1$).

5.2 Time Domain Analysis

Finally, to illustrate performance of the proposed LPV-MPC controller in some representative test cases, the following examples are considered.

- Simulation 1: $N = 10$ and $\alpha = 0$; Energy saving objective.
- Simulation 2: $N = 10$ and $\alpha = 0.15$; Energy saving/QoS trade-off objective.

The optimal control-based server performance is compared with an open loop configuration (e.g., with no control) where the CPU frequency and the admission probability are fixed as follows.

- The CPU frequency is fixed to 1, which means that the CPU runs at a nominal speed.
- The admission probability is set to $P_k = \overline{P} = 1$, which is equivalent to accepting 100% of the incoming requests.
- The service time s_k and the request rate λ_k follow the evolution in time shown on Fig. 6.

The obtained results are shown in Figs. 8 and 9. Specifically, the top plots of Figs. 8 and 9 both confirm that the constraint on the response time T_k is always

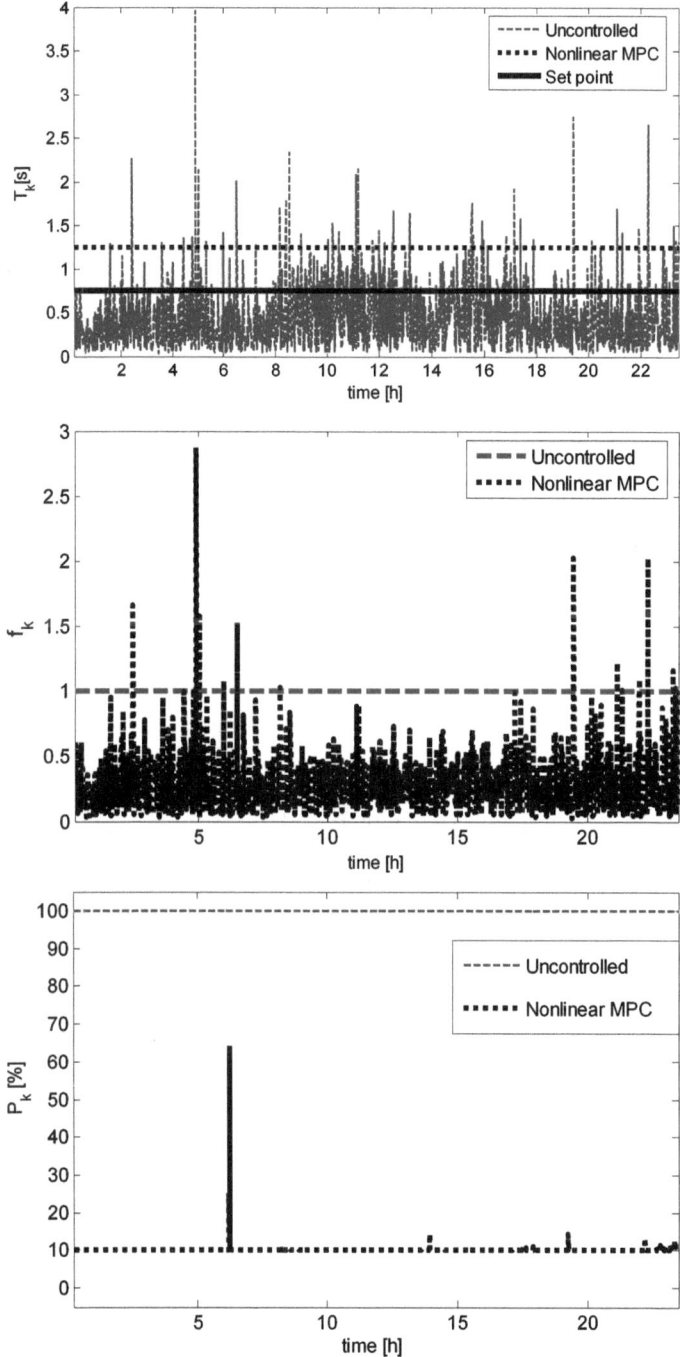

Fig. 8 Simulation 1: ($\alpha = 0$). *Top plot*: response time T_k. *Middle plot*: CPU scaled frequency f_k. *Bottom plot*: admission probability $\mathcal{P}_k$. Uncontrolled server (*dashed line*), LPV-MPC (*dotted line*)

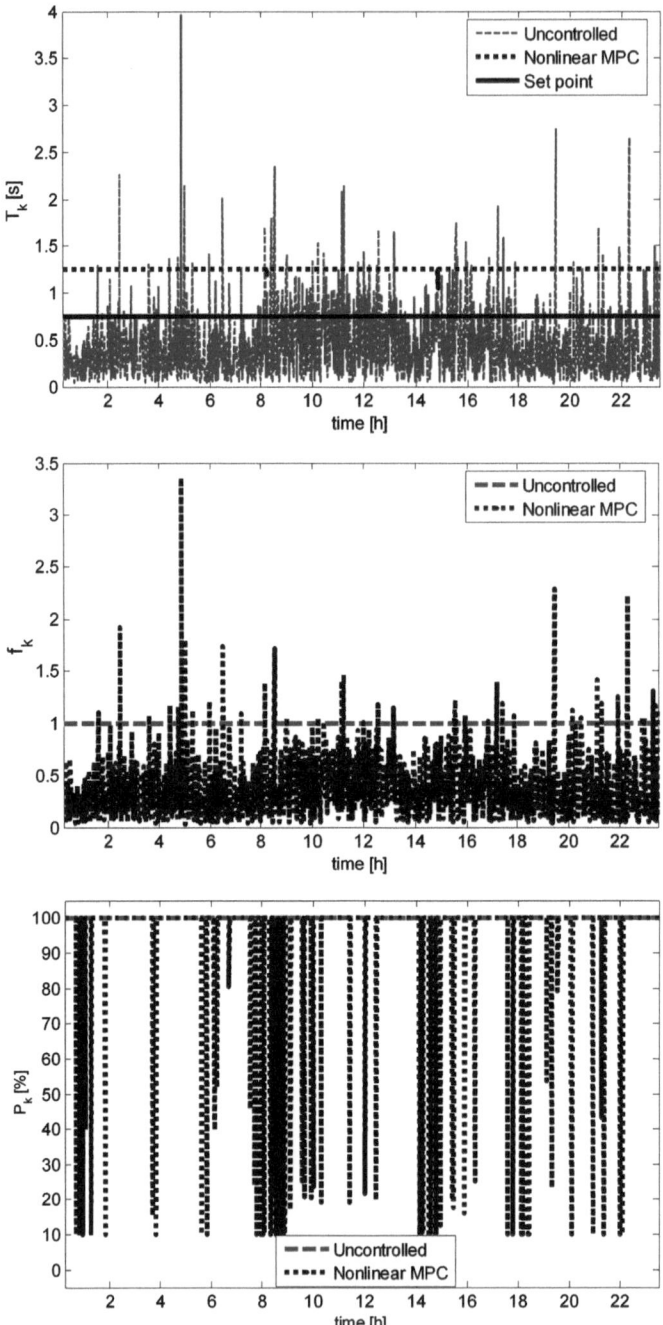

Fig. 9 Simulation 2: ($\alpha = 0.15$). *Top plot*: response time T_k. *Middle plot*: CPU scaled frequency f_k. *Bottom plot*: admission probability $\mathcal{P}_k$. Uncontrolled server (*dashed line*), LPV-MPC (*dotted line*)

fulfilled when the system is controlled. Moreover, these results also show that the uncontrolled server provides very poor performance when the number of requests increases, leading to poor QoS. This confirms the need of using a controller to enhance the system performance.

Further, the middle and bottom plot of Figs. 8 and 9 prove that input and performance constraints are satisfied. Additionally, they show how the admission probability and effective service time are adjusted to guarantee a good level of both QoS and energy saving. More specifically:

- Figure 8 (Simulation 1, Energy saving objective) shows that, over the whole experiment, the admission probability $\mathcal{P}_k$ (bottom plot) is kept constant at its lower bound, while f_k (middle plot) is modulated to maximise energy saving, i.e., to minimise the CPU frequency (consistently with the settings of the performed simulation test). As a matter of fact, over the time interval in which λ_k is low (see the top plot), the effective service time is increased, meaning that the CPU frequency is lowered, thus yielding energy saving. Also notice that the frequency adaptation is mostly dependent on the service time requested. As a matter of fact, remember that total treatment time is define by $T_k = \xi_k + s_{f,k}$, hence largely dependent on the magnitude of s_k itself.
- Figure 9 (Simulation 2, QoS/Energy saving trade-off objective) shows that, when the number of requests is large, i.e., between 9 and 16 h, the admission probability $\mathcal{P}_k$ (bottom plot) is reduced to allow obtaining a CPU frequency f_k reasonable, i.e. below one (middle plot), in order to save energy. Conversely, over the time interval in which λ_k is low the CPU frequency is lowered, thus resulting in reduced energy consumption and the admission probability $\mathcal{P}_k$ is at its upper bound to ensure good QoS. Indeed, since in this simulation the aim was to ensure a trade-off between QoS and energy saving, this behaviour is consistent with the objectives.

6 Concluding Remarks

In this chapter, a control-theoretic framework for the dynamic analysis of the QoS/Energy trade-off in Web service systems has been presented. Specifically, the contribution is twofold: first, an effective identification approach for modeling admission control dynamics has been presented. Secondly, an approach to evaluate the achievable server performance has been proposed using a numerical optimisation approach involving the estimated LPV dynamical model and an iterative optimisation procedure. This problem formulation leads to an *optimal closed-loop* performance analysis illustrating both the QoS/Energy saving trade-off and the interest in controlling both the service time and the admission rate to improve performance while guaranteeing a given desired service response time. Further, the analysis of such an optimal control solution can be very useful to design an actual LPV-MPC controller, as it allows to analyse its performance against such a benchmark so as to quantitatively evaluate its degree of sub-optimality at design time.

Future work will address the design of real-time LPV-MPC controllers by complementing the control system with state estimation and workload prediction capabilities.

References

[1] Kephart, J.O., Chess, D.M.: The vision of autonomic computing. IEEE Comput. **36**(1), 41–50 (2003)

[2] Metha, V.: A holistic solution to the IT energy crisis (2007). [Online]. Available: http://greenercomputing.com/

[3] Chase, J.S., Anderson, D.C.: Managing energy and server resources in hosting centers. In: ACM Symposium on Operating Systems Principles (2001)

[4] Raghavendra, R., Ranganathan, P., Talwar, V., Wang, Z., Zhu, X.: No power struggles: A unified multi-level power management architecture for the data center. In: Proceedings of the 13th International Conference on Architectural Support for Programming Languages and Operating Systems (ASPLOS), pp. 48–59 (2008)

[5] Abdelzaher, J.S.T., Lu, C., Zhang, R., Lu, Y.: Feedback performance control in software services. IEEE Control Syst. Mag. **23**(3), 21–32 (2003)

[6] Kusic, D., Kephart, J.O., Kandasamy, N., Jiang, G.: Power and performance management of virtualized computing environments via lookahead control. In: ICAC 2008 Proc. (2008)

[7] Qin, W., Wang, Q.: Modeling and control design for performance management of web servers via an LPV approach. IEEE Trans. Control Syst. Technol. **15**(2), 259–275 (2007)

[8] Kusic, D., Kandasamy, N.: Risk-aware limited lookahead control for dynamic resource provisioning in enterprise computing systems. In: ICSOC 2004 Proc. (2004)

[9] Kephart, J., Chan, H., Das, R., Levine, D., Tesauro, G., Rawson, F., Lefurgy, C.: Coordinating multiple autonomic managers to achieve specified power-performance tradeoffs. In: ICAC Proceedings (2007)

[10] Carlstrom, J., Rom, R.: Application-aware admission control and scheduling in web servers. In: Infocom Proc. (2002)

[11] Welsh M., Culler D.: Adaptive overload control for busy internet servers. In: USITS Proceedings (2003)

[12] Urgaonkar, B., Shenoy, P.: Sharc: managing CPU and network bandwidth in shared clusters. IEEE Trans. Parallel Distrib. Syst. **15**(1), 2–17 (2004)

[13] Pacifici, G., Spreitzer, M., Tantawi, A.N., Youssef, A.: Performance management for cluster-based web services. IEEE J. Sel. Areas Commun. **23**(12), 2333–2343 (2005)

[14] Urgaonkar, B., Pacifici, G., Shenoy, P.J., Spreitzer, M., Tantawi, A.N.: Analytic modeling of multitier Internet applications. ACM Trans. Web **1**(1) (2007)

[15] Zhang, L., Ardagna, D.: SLA based profit optimisation in autonomic computing systems. In: ICSOC 2004 Proceedings, New York, pp. 173–182 (2004)

[16] Abrahao, B., Almeida, V., Almeida, J., Zhang, A., Beyer, D., Safai, F.: Self-adaptive SLA-driven capacity management for internet services. In: Proc. NOMS06 (2006)

[17] Apkarian, P., Gahinet, P., Becker, G.: Self-scheduled H_∞ control of linear parameter-varying systems. Automatica **31**(9), 1251–1261 (1995)

[18] Shamma, J.S., Athans, M.: Analysis of gain-scheduled control for nonlinear plants. IEEE Trans. Autom. Control **35**(8), 898–907 (1990)

[19] Tanelli, M., Ardagna, D., Lovera, M., Zhang, L.: Model identification for energy-aware management of web service systems. In: ICSOC08 Proc. (2008)

[20] Tanelli, M., Ardagna, D., Lovera, M.: LPV model identification in virtualized service center environments. In: 15th IFAC Symposium on System Identification, Saint Malo, France (2009)

[21] Camacho, E., Bordons, C.: Model Predictive Control. Springer, New York (1999)

[22] Maciejowski, J.: Predictive Control with Constraints. Prentice-Hall, New York (2001)
[23] Kleinrock, L.: Queueing Systems. Wiley, New York (1975)
[24] Qin, W., Wang, Q.: An LPV approximation for admission control of an Internet web server: Identification and control. Control Eng. Pract. **15**(12), 1457–1467 (2007)
[25] Toth, R., Felici, F., Heuberger, P., den Hof, P.V.: Discrete time LPV I/O and state space representations, differences of behaviour and pitfalls of interpolation. In: Proceedings of the 2007 European Control Conference, Kos, Greece (2007)
[26] Verhaegen, M.: Identification of the deterministic part of MIMO state space models given in innovations form from input output data. Automatica **30**(1), 61–74 (1994)
[27] Lee, L., Poolla, K.: Identification of linear parameter-varying systems using nonlinear programming. ASME J. Dyn. Syst. Meas. Control **121**(1), 71–78 (1999)
[28] Verdult, V.: Nonlinear system identification: A state-space approach. PhD thesis, University of Twente, Faculty of Applied Physics, Enschede, The Netherlands (2002)
[29] Apache: Apache Jmeter. [Online]. Available: http://jakarta.apache.org/jmeter/index.html
[30] Arlitt, M., Williamson, C.: Internet web servers: workload characterization and performance implications. IEEE/ACM Trans. Netw. **5**(5), 815–826 (1997)
[31] Apache: Apache Tomcat. [Online]. Available: http://tomcat.apache.org/
[32] The Open Group: Application Resource Measurement—Arm. [Online]. Available: http://www.opengroup.org/tech/management/arm/
[33] Rolia, J., Vetland, V.: Correlating resource demand information with ARM data for application services. In: Proceedings of the 1st International Workshop on Software and Performance, pp. 219–230 (1998)
[34] Almeida, J., Almeida, V., Ardagna, D., Cunha, I., Francalanci, C., Trubian, M.: Joint admission control and resource allocation in virtualized servers. J. Parallel Distrib. Comput. **70**(4), 344–362 (2010)
[35] Magni, L., Scattolini, R.: Robustness and robust design of MPC for nonlinear discrete-time systems. Lect. Notes Control Inf. Sci. **358**, 239–254 (2007)
[36] De Nicolao, G., Magni, L., Scattolini, R.: Stabilizing receding-horizon control of nonlinear time-varying systems. IEEE Trans. Autom. Control **43**, 1030–1036 (1998)
[37] Mayne, D.Q., Rawlings, J.B., Rao, C.V., Scokaert, P.O.M.: Constrained model predictive control: Stability and optimality. Automatica **36**, 789–814 (2000)
[38] Besselmann, T., Lofberg, J., Morari, M.: Explicit model predictive control for linear parameter-varying systems. In: 47th IEEE Conference on Decision and Control, pp. 3848–3853 (2008)
[39] Lu, Y.H., Arkun, Y.: Quasi-Min-Max MPC algorithms for LPV systems. Automatica **36**, 527–540 (2000)
[40] Chisci, L., Falugi, P., Zappa, G.: Gain-scheduling MPC of nonlinear systems. Int. J. Robust Nonlinear Control **13**(3–4), 295–308 (2003)
[41] Andreolini, M., Casolari, S.: Load prediction models in web-based systems. In: Proceedings of the 1st International Conference on Performance Evaluation Methodologies and Tools, Pisa, Italy (2006)
[42] Lofberg, J.: YALMIP: a toolbox for modeling and optimization in MATLAB. In: Proceedings of the CACSD Conference, Taipei, Taiwan (2004). [Online]. Available: http://control.ee.ethz.ch/~joloef/yalmip.php
[43] Coleman, T., Zhang, Y.: Optimization Toolbox (for Use with MATLAB), v2.11 ed., June 2001
[44] Poussot-Vassal, C., Tanelli, M., Lovera, M.: Linear parametrically varying MPC for combined quality of service and energy management in web service systems. In: Proceedings of the American Control Conference, ACC 2010, Baltimore, MD, USA, pp. 3106–3111 (2010)
[45] Poussot-Vassal, C., Tanelli, M., Lovera, M.: Dynamic analysis of the trade-off between QoS and energy savings in admission control for web service systems. In: Proceedings of the 1st Workshop on Run-time Model for Self managing Systems and Applications, Pisa, Italy (2009)

C. Poussot-Vassal
ONERA / DCSD, BP 74025, Toulouse Cedex, France
e-mail: charles.poussot-vassal@onera.fr

M. Tanelli (✉)
Dipartimento di Elettronica e Informazione, Politecnico di Milano, Piazza Leonardo da
Vinci, 32, 20133 Milano, Italy
e-mail: tanelli@elet.polimi.it

M. Lovera
Dipartimento di Elettronica e Informazione, Politecnico di Milano, Piazza Leonardo da
Vinci, 32, 20133 Milano, Italy
e-mail: lovera@elet.polimi.it

The Emergence of Load Balancing in Distributed Systems: the SelfLet Approach

Nicolò M. Calcavecchia, Danilo Ardagna, and Elisabetta Di Nitto

Abstract Complex pervasive systems are typically composed of a large number of heterogeneous nodes, pervasively distributed across the environment. These systems pose several new challenges such as the need for nodes to autonomously and dynamically manage themselves in order to achieve some common goal, despite to the continuous evolution of the surrounding environment. An important research area for these systems regards the identification of proper load balancing mechanisms that, depending on the current utilization of resources at a node and on its knowledge of the neighbourhood, aim at optimizing at runtime the global system state with simple local actions without a centralized intelligence.

The `SelfLet` environment is a framework that provides an architectural model and a runtime infrastructure to support the development of distributed and autonomic systems. In this paper we extend the `SelfLet` approach by defining two optimization policies that, based on a prediction of the future load of a `SelfLet` node and of its neighbours, compute the most profitable autonomic load balancing action to be actuated. We show that adopting this approach, a system-wide load balancing behaviour emerges from the local actions.

Keywords Autonomic systems · Distributed workload management

Abbreviations

$\mathcal{N}$	Set of logical nodes of the network
n	`SelfLet` index
$\mathcal{N}_n$	Set of neighbours for `SelfLet` n
$\mathcal{S}_n$	Services offered at `SelfLet` n
$\mathcal{O}_n^s$	Set of neighbours of n offering service s
a_n^s	Revenue received for the execution of service s at `SelfLet` n
$c_n^{s,b}$	Incurred cost for the execution of service s implemented by behavior b at `SelfLet` n
$\tilde{\lambda}_{n_i,n_j}^s$	Request rate from `SelfLet` n_i to `SelfLet` n_j for service s

D. Ardagna, L. Zhang (eds.), *Run-time Models for Self-managing Systems and Applications*, 97–124,
Autonomic Systems, DOI 10.1007/978-3-0346-0433-8_5, © Springer Basel AG 2010

$\Lambda_{n_i}^s$ Cumulative request rate for service s at `SelfLet` n_i
$\lambda_{i,n}^b$ Request rate for state i of behaviour b in `SelfLet` n
$\mathcal{I}^b$ Set of states composing the behaviour b
i Index for behaviour states
p_{ij} Probability to go from state i to state j
$\boldsymbol{P}^b$ Routing matrix for behaviour b
$\overline{R}_n^s$ Response time threshold for service s at `SelfLet` n
$U_{i,n}^b$ Utilization generated by behaviour b in state i at `SelfLet` n
U_n^b Total utilization generated by behaviour b at `SelfLet` n
U_n Total utilization at `SelfLet` n
$\hat{U}_n$ Total predicted utilization at `SelfLet` n

1 Introduction

Modern software systems are increasingly complex and distributed. Moreover, they tend to be more and more dynamic to cope with the high dynamicity of the environment in which they operate. These characteristics make the runtime management of these systems cumbersome, error prone, and highly time consuming. One of the objectives of autonomic computing is to address these issues by equipping systems with self-* abilities (self-configuration, self-healing, self-optimization and self-protection) [31]. Within this context, a number of autonomic frameworks have been proposed which enable the design and execution of self-* abilities [4, 7]. They usually offer either predefined self-management policies or programmatic mechanisms for creating new policies at design time. Some other works also propose the adoption of prediction models [51] as a way to anticipate the evolution of the system and to make timely decisions on the execution of self-* activities. Our work differentiates from existing ones because it focuses on distributed decentralized environments in which predictions are produced at each site starting from local knowledge and self-* actions are performed as well.

We propose a framework called `SelfLet` [12, 23]. Its main assumption is that a system is composed of many cooperating components, the `SelfLets`. They can provide and consume services offered by other `SelfLets` and are able to make decisions based on a local knowledge of the surrounding environment. The ability to make local decisions is crucial for highly decentralized environments where a centralized control mechanism may easily become a critical bottleneck. A `SelfLet` can be easily programmed for what concerns both its *normal behaviour* and its *autonomic policies*.

In this chapter we study the problem of load balancing among `SelfLets` and propose and evaluate a decentralized solution. The idea is that, by monitoring local resources, each `SelfLet` decides the actuation of certain optimization actions such as redirecting requests, teaching service implementations to other `SelfLets`, or learning service implementations from others. The solution we propose takes into account revenues and costs generated as the result of service execution in a `SelfLet` according to multiple Quality of Service (QoS) levels. After evaluating a set of candidate optimization actions, each `SelfLet` can act following a greedy or a non-greedy strategy depending on the state of its neighbours.

In the literature several other approaches to support load balancing have been presented. Most of them, however, adopt a centralized paradigm in which the optimizing actions are decided by a single node that knows about the state of the entire system. Moreover the load balancing action usually supported by these approaches is the redirection of requests to other nodes. By adopting a decentralized approach we offer a solution that is more compatible with the overall philosophy of the underlying distributed software system. Moreover, by enabling the possibility for `SelfLets` to teach/learn service implementations, we add a new degree of freedom to the load balancing solution.

The remainder of the chapter is organized as follows. Sections 2 and 3 introduce the `SelfLets` framework and the related performance model. The distributed autonomic load balancing algorithms are presented in Sect. 4. Section 5 is dedicated to the experimental results. Section 6 reviews other approaches proposed in the literature. Conclusions are finally drawn in Sect. 7.

2 The SelfLet Approach

The autonomic framework that we use as a starting point for our work is presented in more details in [12, 23]. It is based on an autonomic infrastructure and architectural model called `SelfLets`.

According to the `SelfLets` model, a software system is composed of various autonomous elements, each of which is a `SelfLet`. Every `SelfLet` is defined in terms of the elements described below.

Offered Services   Services represent high level tasks a `SelfLet` is able to accomplish. The implementation of a service in the `SelfLet` is called *behaviour*. Designers program the behaviours using UML state diagrams (with some restrictions that have been introduced to formalize their semantics). A service can have more than one implementation. One of these is the *default behaviour*.

We distinguish two kinds of behaviours, complex and elementary; *complex behaviours* have a generic number of internal states while *elementary behaviours* are restricted to have a single internal state. More specifically, elementary behaviours execute the actual computation which is contained in OSGi bundles [1] called *abilities*.

Figure 1 shows an example of a complex behaviour taken from a `SelfLet` controlling consumption of energy in a home environment [13]. In the initial state the current level of energy consumption is monitored and, depending on this value the behaviour can move to the lack state where it asks for the possibility of using more energy by invoking the need of an appropriate ability, or it may enter in an over consumption state where it remains until the situation gets stabilized. The conditions over the arcs define what the next state is by comparing the sensed energy value to an internal threshold.

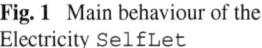

Fig. 1 Main behaviour of the
Electricity `SelfLet`

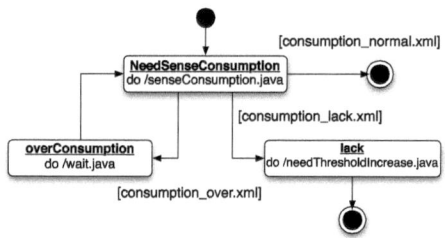

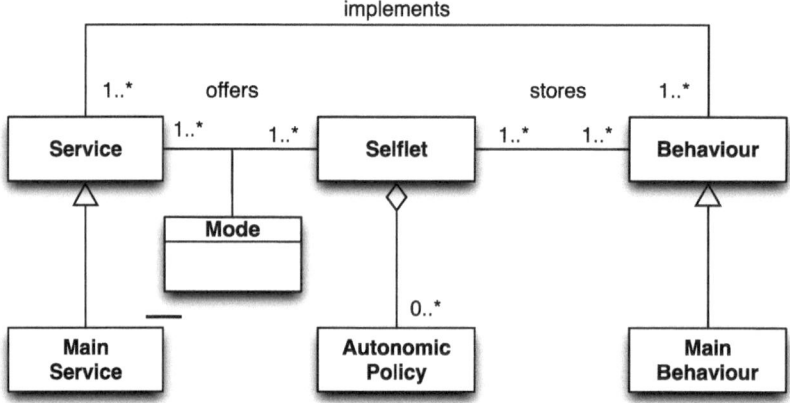

Fig. 2 `SelfLets` framework

In our approach, services can be offered in different ways. A `SelfLet` can
directly fulfill a service request and return the result to the caller: in this case the
service is offered in a "Can Do" way. Alternatively, the `SelfLet` can be available
to *teach* the service, so that the requester is able to execute the service by itself from
then on. We call this the "Can Teach" way. A `SelfLet` can offer a service even
if it does not know it directly, by using the "Know Who Can Do" and "Know Who
Can Teach" ways: in this case, the `SelfLet` will give the requester information
about the `SelfLets` able to either offer the service or provide directions for the
execution of the service. Any combination of these "offer modes" is allowed.

`SelfLets` can spontaneously advertise their offered services to inform the other
`SelfLets` about them. Indeed, when issuing a service request, a `SelfLet` can
specify the offer mode it would prefer. The main relationships characterizing services, behaviours and policies of `SelfLets` are summarized in Fig. 2.

Each `SelfLet` maintains a list of known providers for each service it requires
(and cannot offer itself). Then, when a need for such a service arises, the `SelfLet`
selects one of these providers according to a given policy, and directly asks it for the
service. The `SelfLets` in a network cooperate to keep such lists always up-to-date
with information about the availability of providers.

A *main service* represents the objective of the `SelfLet`. The main service is
proactively executed after the `SelfLet` has been initialized.

Autonomic Policies   *Autonomic policies* define reactions to abnormal situations that can occur during the life-time of the `SelfLet`. The reactions include the possibility of changing the main service, disabling/enabling the execution of the other services, disabling/enabling the interaction with some neighbours, etc.

The `SelfLet` offers to policy writers a list of actions that enable the transformation of several aspects of the `SelfLet` itself. These methods are the way the decisions made by the policies are put in action to adapt to a changed situation. The actions offered in the current implementation include, besides the methods related to service execution:

- changing the way a service is offered or asked. In particular, a service could be offered or asked in a *teach, do, know who can do* or *know who can teach* mode, or in several modes at the same time;
- install action of a new service within the `SelfLet`;
- install action new abilities, i.e. basic atomic service implementations;
- switch from a service implementation to another;
- modification of a given behaviour, directly deleting and replacing its component states and transitions.

`SelfLet` Internal Architecture   The heart of the `SelfLet` architecture (see Fig. 3) is the *Autonomic Manager*, which is responsible for the evolution of a `SelfLet` depending on the set of *Autonomic Policies* it has installed; this set can

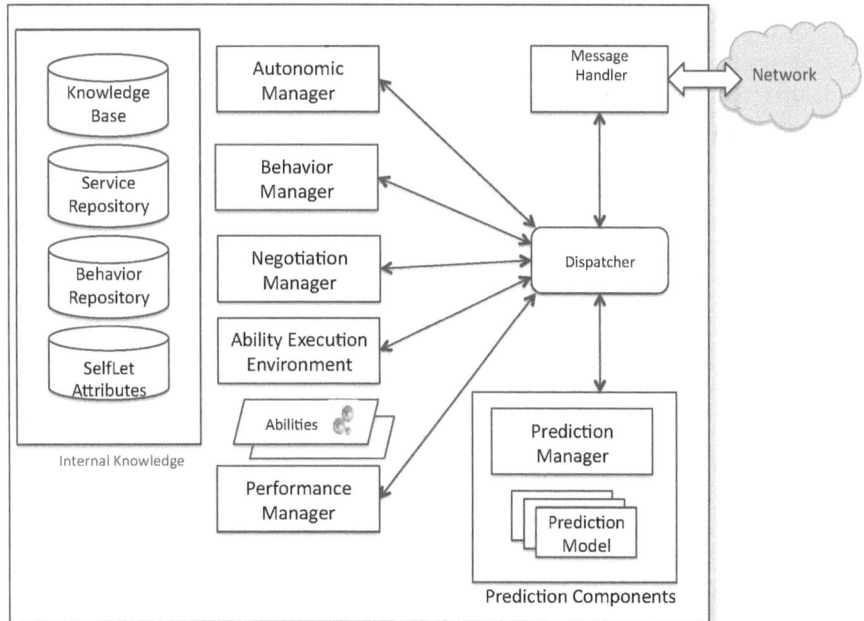

Fig. 3 The internal architecture of a `SelfLet`

evolve over time. The *Autonomic Manager* is implemented exploiting *Drools* [27], a Java *Production Rule System*. The well-known features of the Production Rule Systems, along with the advanced nature of the Drools language, allow the `SelfLet` programmers to write sophisticated autonomic policies, using a simple, declarative style.

The *Behaviour Manager* controls the execution of the `SelfLet`'s behaviour. Whenever a request for a service arises, the Autonomic Manager triggers the execution of a rule that verifies whether the service is locally available or not and, if not, asks the *Negotiation Manager* to retrieve the Service and negotiate with the corresponding `SelfLet` a proper offer mode.

The *Internal Knowledge* is composed of four parts: *Knowledge Base*, which can be used to store and retrieve any kind of information needed by any of the `Self-Let` components; *Service Repository*, which lists services the `SelfLet` can offer (to itself or to other `SelfLets`); *Behaviours Repository*, which contains all the behaviours specifications the `SelfLet` is able to run; *Attribute Repository*, which stores descriptions about the `SelfLet`.

The *Ability Execution Environment* is in charge of executing *Abilities*, that can be activated as part of behaviours. The *Performance Manager* provides the functionalities to monitor the execution of internal services and offers a unified interface to access this information. The communication internal to the `SelfLet` and among `SelfLets` follows a publish/subscribe approach. All `SelfLet` architectural components are connected to a *Dispatcher* which is in charge of receiving subscriptions for events and event publications. It asynchronously delivers all published events to those components that have subscribed to them. The dispatcher is, in turn, connected to the *Message Handler*, which manages the communication with the external environment and with other `SelfLet` through the REDS [20] middleware. The usage of a publish/subscribe communication paradigm does not require `SelfLets` to know each other's identity: a relevant advantage in large-scale, self-managing, distributed systems.

In [17] we have extended the `SelfLet` architecture by incorporating prediction models that allow the `SelfLets` autonomic policies to be activated not only when something happens, but also when there is a reasonably high probability that something will happen in the near future. Each `SelfLet` produces and actuates predictions independently from the others. Predictions are based on the events that are produced within a `SelfLet` and on those that arrive from the external environment. These events are received as input by prediction models that, in turn, generate new events that represent the forecast. Such forecast is then received by the Autonomic Manager and can activate a proper autonomic policy. The framework allows for two degrees of freedom: the first is constituted by the choice of the prediction model to adopt (e.g., based on moving average, splines). The second is represented by the definition of the autonomic policy that implements the reaction to a prediction.

The `SelfLets` approach has been implemented both on a full fledged Java platform and on wireless sensors running the TinyOS operating system and adopting the NesC programming language. This second implementation, known as `Tiny-`

SelfLet, implements a smaller set of functionalities due to the physical constraints of the devices and is currently being consolidated [41].

3 Performance Model of a SelfLet System

In this section, we formalize those aspects of the SelfLet framework that are related to the load balancing aspects that we consider in this paper.

3.1 Network Topology

As discussed in [22], an overlay network is maintained in a SelfLet distributed system; it defines the set of SelfLets reachable from any given SelfLet. The overlay can be represented by an undirected graph $S = (\mathcal{N}, \mathcal{E})$ where $\mathcal{N}$ denotes the set of nodes while $\mathcal{E} = (\mathcal{N} \times \mathcal{N})$ defines the neighbourhood relation. For each SelfLet $n \in \mathcal{N}$ we associate a set of neighbours denoted by $\mathcal{N}_n \subseteq \mathcal{N}$, $\mathcal{N}_n = \{m | (n, m) \in \mathcal{E}\}$. Each SelfLet in $\mathcal{N}_n$ can be directly contacted by n (and vice versa) for example, requesting the execution of a service. Figure 4 shows an example of a network including six SelfLets. The relationships defined by $\mathcal{E}$ are employed for load balancing purposes (actuated by means of redirects and teaching of services).

3.2 SelfLet Workload

In the following, as in [6, 49], among the many SelfLet resources, we consider CPU as representative for the load balancing problem. Furthermore, for the sake of simplicity, we assume that physical machines running SelfLets are homogeneous and each machine hosts a single SelfLet. Requests for different services are executed either in a First-Come First-Serve (FCFS) or a Processor Sharing (PS) manner

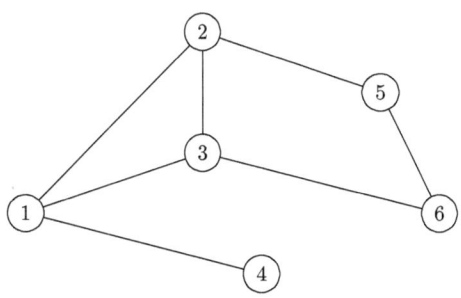

Fig. 4 A graph representing a network of distributed SelfLets. The neighbours sets are the following: $\mathcal{N}_1 = \{2, 3, 4\}, \mathcal{N}_2 = \{1, 3, 5\}, \mathcal{N}_3 = \{1, 2, 6\}, \mathcal{N}_4 = \{1\}, \mathcal{N}_5 = \{2, 6\}, \mathcal{N}_6 = \{3, 5\}$

[16]. Under FCFS, we assume that the service time for each request has an exponential distribution whereas, under PS, the service time follows a general distribution, including heavy-tail distributions of Web systems [38].

Each `SelfLet` is characterized by a certain QoS level in terms of response time and by a certain pricing scheme. We take the perspective of a software provider where revenues are gained for the execution of service requests, while some costs are also due to the infrastructure providers which host the `SelfLets` execution in physical machines.

The set of services available at a `SelfLet` n is denoted by $\mathcal{S}_n$ and represents the functionalities the `SelfLet` is able to achieve and offer to other `SelfLets`. Each service can be requested and executed by the `SelfLet` itself or by some remote `SelfLets`. In the latter case, the service is executed remotely and then the result of the computation is sent back to the requester after the execution, according to a client/server paradigm.

We denote the set of `SelfLets` reachable from n and offering a certain service s with the symbol $\mathcal{O}_n^s$. Services can be requested only between neighbours, i.e. $\mathcal{O}_n^s \subseteq \mathcal{N}_n$.

We assume that a price a_n^s is associated with each service s at `SelfLet` n and that a full revenue is gained if the requests are served within a response time threshold $\overline{R}_n^s$. Otherwise, revenues are lost. The request execution cost depends on the specific behaviour b adopted and will be denoted by $c_n^{s,b}$.

The system we are modelling allows `SelfLets` to send requests to peers with the aim of executing some services. In order to capture this characteristic we must introduce some notation.

We denote with $\widetilde{\lambda}_{n_i n_j}^s$ the request rate from a `SelfLet` n_i to `SelfLet` n_j for service s, with $n_j \in \mathcal{O}_{n_i}^s$, $s \in S_{n_j}$; since the `SelfLet` itself can generate service requests for some local services we also consider the case in which $\widetilde{\lambda}_{n_i n_i}^s > 0$ at `SelfLet` n_i.

We define the set $Out_{n_i} = \{n_j | \widetilde{\lambda}_{n_i n_j} > 0\}$ and the set $In_{n_i} = \{n_j | \widetilde{\lambda}_{n_j n_i} > 0\}$ containing the `SelfLet`'s indexes generating or receiving workload toward n_i respectively.

Moreover, we denote with $\Lambda_{n_i}^s$ the *aggregated* request rates for service s at `SelfLet` n_i which is calculated according to:

$$\Lambda_{n_i}^s = \sum_{n_j \in In_{n_i}} \widetilde{\lambda}_{n_j n_i}^s \tag{3.1}$$

Figure 5 shows a network example where request rates are highlighted.

$$\Lambda_2^s = \widetilde{\lambda}_{12}^s + \widetilde{\lambda}_{22}^s + \widetilde{\lambda}_{32}^s$$

Fig. 5 Example of request rates among three `SelfLets` for service s

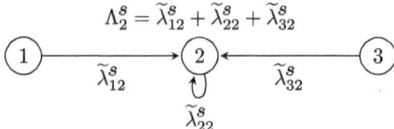

3.3 Behaviour Performance Model

As discussed in Sect. 2, behaviours describe the implementation of services in terms of state diagrams; the current implementation (i.e., default behaviour) of a service s is denoted by the symbol $\overline{b}(s)$.

We recall that a behaviour is defined by a state diagram in which each state represents a service invocation. Each service can be implemented either by a simple ability or by a complex behaviour including several states.

A directed edge from a state i_1 to a state i_2 indicates that the service contained in i_1 must be achieved before service contained in i_2 starts. More formally, we will use the symbol $\mathcal{I}^b = \{i_1, i_2, \ldots\}$ to denote the set of services composing the behaviour b. It must be noticed that given a behaviour b, the corresponding implemented service is uniquely determined.

Certain states of the behaviour can have more than one outgoing arc; this situation is typical when the choice of the next state depends on a condition on internal variables. For each arc going from state i_1 to state i_2 we associate a number $p_{i_1 i_2}$ representing the probability to execute the transition (see Fig. 6). The values can be given by the designer or estimated at runtime by the `SelfLet` monitoring subsystem. Probabilities obey to the normalization constraint:

$$\sum_{i_2 \in \mathcal{I}^b} p_{i_1 i_2} = 1, \quad \forall i_1 \in \mathcal{I}^b \tag{3.2}$$

A behaviour b (implementing service s) composed of N states can be represented by a $N \times N$ matrix whose elements (i_1, i_2) are the probabilities $p_{i_1 i_2}$. We call it the routing matrix and it will be denoted by $\boldsymbol{P}^b$.

If a service is implemented by a complex behaviour including several states, its request rate influences the request rates of the implementing services. Request rates are regulated by the following flow conservation equation [16]:

$$\lambda_n^b = \boldsymbol{P}^b \lambda_n^b + \Lambda_n^s \mathbf{e}_1 \quad \forall b, n \tag{3.3}$$

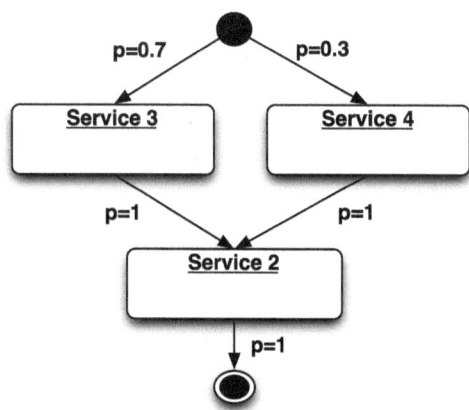

Fig. 6 A simple behaviour with probability associated to arcs

where the column vector $\boldsymbol{\lambda}_n^b = (\lambda_{1,n}^b, \ldots, \lambda_{|\mathcal{I}^b|,n}^b)$ represents the request rates of each state within behaviour b and the column vector $\mathbf{e_1} = (1, 0, \ldots, 0)$ represents the fact that the initial state receives all requests. For each service, the aggregate request rate Λ_n^s is computed by (3.1), where $\boldsymbol{P}^b$ is the routing matrix of the behaviour b implementing service s.

During the behaviour execution, the computation goes through a subset of states in $\mathcal{I}^b$; behaviour diagrams can be recursively expanded up to the point in which each state represents a local elementary behaviour (i.e., its implementation is available as a local ability) or a remote service. For both cases we define the service demand as follows:

$$D^s = \begin{cases} DL^s & \text{if service } s \text{ is implemented by a local elementary behavior.} \\ DR^s & \text{if service } s \text{ is executed remotely.} \end{cases} \quad (3.4)$$

The demanding time DL^s is defined as the overall CPU time needed to serve a request for service s and is specified at design time and updated at runtime by the monitoring system e.g., by adopting Kalman filters as discussed in the fourth chapter. The demanding time for services executed remotely includes the time employed for parameters marshalling and unmarshalling and for sending and receiving requests.

3.4 Behaviour Utilization

In order to compute the utilization due to a behaviour execution, the behaviour internal structure and in particular its composing states have to be considered. Utilization of each state i in the behaviour description $\overline{b}$ at the SelfLet n is given by:

$$U_{i,n}^{\overline{b}(s)} = \begin{cases} D^s \lambda_{i,n}^{\overline{b}(s)} & \text{if the state } i \text{ represents a service implemented by a local ability or by a remote service.} \\ \sum_{i \in \mathcal{I}^b} U_{i,n}^{\overline{b}(s)} & \text{if the state } i \text{ represents a local complex service.} \end{cases} \quad (3.5)$$

Once the utilization of each service is established, the utilization associated with each behaviour execution is given by:

$$U_n^{\overline{b}(s)} = \sum_{i \in \mathcal{I}^b} U_{i,n}^{\overline{b}(s)} \quad (3.6)$$

Finally, the SelfLet utilization can be computed as the sum over all services available at SelfLet:

$$U_n = \sum_{s \in \mathcal{S}_n} U_n^{\overline{b}(s)} \quad (3.7)$$

Table 1 State of a `SelfLet` at node n

Symbol	Description
S_n	Services available at the `SelfLet`
$\mathcal{O}_n^s$, $\forall s \in S_n$	`SelfLet` neighbours offering service s
U_n	Total utilization
a_n^s, $\forall s \in S_n$	Cost for offered services

3.5 State of a SelfLet

The decentralized nature of a `SelfLet` system impose a peer-to-peer communication paradigm within the overlay network. In particular, each `SelfLet` periodically exchanges its current state with neighbours. Information are shared in a loosely coupled way; these information represent a way for `SelfLets` to monitor the surrounding environment.

The relevant state of a generic `SelfLet` n is defined by the data reported in Table 1.

Values composing the state are retrieved from various internal subsystems of the `SelfLet`. In particular, available services are stored within the service repository together with their costs while the neighbours set is discovered at run-time by the middleware capabilities. Finally, the total utilization is evaluated by the performance monitor component.

4 Autonomic Policies for Load Balancing

`SelfLets` live in highly dynamical contexts in which workloads can change for many reasons. For example some `SelfLets` might appear or fail at runtime or services request rates can vary due to some external factors.

Under ideal conditions, in a network of homogeneous physical machines, the utilization should be the same at each `SelfLet` component thus avoiding bottlenecks and underutilized `SelfLets`. The autonomic policies we adopt aim at achieving this theoretical goal, of course, taking into account all constraints imposed by the environment in which the `SelfLets` system is actually running. In particular, our policies allow `SelfLets` to promptly adapt to changes by forecasting future demand for services and actuating the most appropriate actions among redirecting service requests, teaching services to other `SelfLets` or changing service implementation.

In `SelfLets`, policies work according to the ECA paradigm: when an Event is received and a Condition is satisfied then an Action is taken. Policies can also be executed periodically to adapt the system configuration according to workload/events predictions. In particular, we decided to actuate the policy when the current level of CPU utilization violates a certain critical threshold; moreover, the policy is also periodically activated and a prediction of the utilization is used.

In the following we describe in detail our policy for equalizing the utilization of `SelfLet` systems. We first formalize the concept of prediction and utilization thresholds (see Sects. 4.1 and 4.2). Then we provide details on the cost of each load balancing action (see Sect. 4.3) and on how the policy selects the most appropriate action to be taken (see Sect. 4.4).

4.1 Prediction Model

The forecast is typically produced as a function of the past w observations (values resulted from a prediction are denoted with the hat symbol,^); we use the symbol $f_{\Lambda_n^s}$ to refer to the function computing the prediction for request rate.

$$\hat{\Lambda}_n^s = f_{\Lambda_n^s}(\Lambda_n^s(t), \Lambda_n^s(t-1), \dots, \Lambda_n^s(t-w)) \tag{4.1}$$

As discussed in the second chapter, forecasts can be produced by different prediction techniques; in particular, the availability of different prediction schemes gives also the possibility to switch among them at runtime according to their precision (e.g., for example minimizing the mean square error as in [40]).

Similarly to the work described in [15], once workload prediction is available at each `SelfLet`, it is possible to produce utilization prediction by simply applying the equations introduced in Sect. 3.4.

In particular, we compute the predicted utilization contribution of service s to `SelfLet` n with the following formula:

$$\hat{U}_n^s = f_{U_n^s}(\hat{\Lambda}_n^s) \tag{4.2}$$

while the total predicted utilization at `SelfLet` n is given by:

$$\hat{U}_n = \sum_{s \in \mathcal{S}_n} \hat{U}_n^s \tag{4.3}$$

4.2 Utilization Thresholds

The objective of our autonomic policy is to redistribute the resource utilization over all `SelfLets` while keeping a high revenue. In order to achieve this objective the CPU utilization is monitored at runtime and two utilization thresholds are defined: $\overline{U}_{\min}$ and $\overline{U}_{\max}$. The value of utilization thresholds also reflects the ability of the `SelfLet` to complete requests in a timely way; indeed, a high CPU utilization typically implies a high response time. We fix the value of these thresholds $\overline{R}_n^s$ for each service such that the probability of violating the threshold on response time is bounded by a probability α. Let be $\overline{R}_n = \min_{s \in \mathcal{S}_n} \overline{R}_n^s$. We use the following standard result from the queuing theory (e.g. see [37]) which bounds the probability for response time R to be greater than a value R_n as a function of utilization $\hat{U}_n$:

$$P[R > \overline{R}_n] \le e^{-\sum_{s \in \mathcal{S}_n} \Lambda_n^s(\frac{1}{\hat{U}_n}-1)\overline{R}_n} = \alpha \tag{4.4}$$

The previous equation can be rewritten as $\hat{U}_n \leq \dfrac{1}{1-\frac{\ln\alpha}{\overline{R}_n \sum_{s\in\mathcal{S}_n}\Lambda_n^s}}$. We set the $\overline{U}_{\max}$ threshold equal to the right-hand part of the previous inequality, while $\overline{U}_{\min}$ is set heuristically equal to $0.8\overline{U}_{\max}$ (see [47]).

Depending on the current *predicted* utilization value (see (4.3)), a SelfLet can be in one of the following states:

- Normal: $\overline{U}_{\min} < \hat{U}_n < \overline{U}_{\max}$
- Over-utilization: $\hat{U}_n \geq \overline{U}_{\max}$
- Under-utilization: $\hat{U}_n \leq \overline{U}_{\min}$

The threshold R_n impacts on generated net revenues at the SelfLet; indeed, whenever the response time violates this threshold the service provider does not generate any revenue. More specifically, net revenues are proportional to the service execution rates. In particular the net revenues at SelfLet n for the execution of the set of services s implemented through the behaviour b can be evaluated as:

$$netRev_n = \sum_{s\in\mathcal{S}_n}(a_n^s(P[R < \overline{R}_n]) - c_n^{s,b})\Lambda_n^s T \quad \forall n \in \mathcal{N} \tag{4.5}$$

where $P[R < \overline{R}_n]$ denotes the probability that service s request response time is lower than the threshold $\overline{R}_n$ while T indicates the system control time.

4.3 Actions and Their Costs

In this section we identify the actions that can be taken by a SelfLet and quantify the costs and revenues these actions generate as well as the corresponding impact on the SelfLet. Such impact is expressed in terms of CPU utilization and profits generated.

4.3.1 Change Service Implementation

This action substitutes the implementation of a service with a new one (i.e., changes the default behaviour). This action is available for service s at SelfLet n only if there are alternative implementations.

Given two behaviours b_1, b_2 implementing service s, switching from b_1 to b_2 (identified by the notation $b_1 \rightarrow b_2$) can cause some modification of the SelfLet utilization. We are interested in comparing the utilization of current behaviour with the new behaviour; to do so we calculate the utilization delta between the actual situation and the new action (see formula (4.6)).

$$\Delta U_n^{b_1 \rightarrow b_2} = U_n^{b_2} - U_n^{b_1} \tag{4.6}$$

The profit delta is given by the difference of costs as reported in formula (4.7):

$$\Delta netRev_n = (a_n^s P[R < \overline{R}_n] + c_n^{s,b2} - c_n^{s,b1})\hat{\Lambda}_n^s \tag{4.7}$$

4.3.2 Service Redirect

When a `SelfLet` is over-utilized ($U_n > \overline{U}_{\max}$) a good strategy to actuate is the redirection of service requests to other `SelfLets`. For example, if `SelfLet` n_1 issues requests for service s to `SelfLet` n_2, n_2 can actuate a redirect to any other neighbour `SelfLet` provided that it offers service s. This solution is commonly adopted in large web server systems [44].

Redirects are intended to be performed in probability; the redirecting `SelfLet` will choose among its candidate providers according to a given weight. The initial values for the weights are the same, but as soon the network evolves they dynamically adapt to the workload condition.

In order to implement the redirect action, a couple of choices must be made; in particular, in our case we distinguish the following three degrees of freedom:

- Which service requests have to be redirected
- Which set of `SelfLets` can receive redirected service requests
- Which portion of service requests is redirected (i.e., the probability to redirect a request toward a `SelfLet`).

Here we assume that redirect is actuated by the `SelfLet` receiving requests; moreover, we limit the forwarding to only one `SelfLet` instead of a set of `SelfLets`. Algorithm 1 generates a set of redirect candidate actions; these actions will be added to the general set of candidate actions together with teach and change implementation candidate actions.

Input : $\mathcal{S}_n, \mathcal{N}_n$
Output: candidateActions

1 redirectActions $\longleftarrow \emptyset$;
2 **for** $s \in Services$ **do**
3     $\Delta U = U_n - \overline{U}_{\max}$;
4     $\Delta \Lambda_n^s = \frac{\Delta U}{D^s}$;
5     $p = \min(\frac{\Delta \Lambda_n^s}{\Lambda_n^s}, 1)$;
6   **for** $m \in \mathcal{N}_n$ **do**
7   action $\longleftarrow$ generateRedirectAction(s, m, p);
8   redirectActions $\longleftarrow$ redirectActions $\cup$ {action};
     end
9
  end
10 **return** redirectActions;

Algorithm 1: Generation of redirect actions at `SelfLet` n. The probability of redirecting a service is computed by taking into account the value of the current utilization with respect of the utilization threshold $\overline{U}_{\max}$

The utilization delta obtained by a redirect action can be computed as follows:

$$\triangle U_n = (1 - p)U_n^{\overline{b}} \qquad (4.8)$$

where $\overline{b}$ is default implementation for redirected service s. Similarly, the profit delta is given by:

$$\triangle netRev_n = (1 - p)(a_n^s(P[R < \overline{R}_n]) - c_n^{s,\overline{b}})T \qquad (4.9)$$

where we put the term $P[R < \overline{R}_n]$ to consider only requests satisfying the threshold on response time.

4.3.3 Service Teach

Services can be taught among SelfLets. The teaching can be *active* or *passive*: an active teaching happens when a SelfLet asks another SelfLet to provide the service code (i.e., request in teach mode). Conversely, a passive teaching happens when a SelfLet forces the teaching toward a second SelfLet (i.e., it is not asked). Since services can be implemented by different behaviours, we assume that the service teach just replicates the current implementation of the service, i.e., its default behaviour. Algorithm 2 generates the set of candidate teach actions.

The main goal of teach is to create another provider for the taught service. There is an associated computational burden due to the dimension of the behaviour; in particular, complex behaviours are just a description of a composition of other services, thus their dimension is limited. However, elementary behaviours, contain the actual logic and data implementing the service and their dimension can be considerable.

It is important to say that not every service can be taught (e.g., a service sensing a temperature through a sensor physically installed in the machine), indeed the service provider has the possibility to specify in which way the service is offered (i.e., *CanDo, CanTeach, None* etc.).

Input : $\mathcal{S}_n, \mathcal{N}_n$
Output: candidateActions

1 candidateActions $\longleftarrow$ ∅;
2 **for** $s \in$ *Services* **do**
3   **for** $m \in \mathcal{N}_n$ **do**
4   action $\longleftarrow$ generateTeachAction(s, m);
5   candidateActions $\longleftarrow$ candidateActions $\cup$ {action};
      end
  end
6 **return** candidateActions;

Algorithm 2: Generation of teach actions at SelfLet n

Actuating a teach action can have a direct impact on the request rate of the taught service. For example, if $\mathtt{SelfLet}$ n teaches service s to $\mathtt{SelfLet}$ m, it will not receive anymore the portion of requests coming from m; the new request rate is thus given by $\Lambda_n'^s = \Lambda_n^s - \tilde{\lambda}_{m,n}^s$. The CPU utilization of the teach action is evaluated as described in Sect. 3.3 where in formula (3.3) the new value of $\Lambda_n'^s$ is used to obtain the new utilization $U_n(\Lambda_n'^s)$.

$$\Delta U_n = U_n - U_n(\Lambda_n'^s) \tag{4.10}$$

The same reasoning applies to revenues, since requests issued by m are lost and hence the net revenues are given by:

$$\Delta netRev_n = \sum_{s' \in \mathcal{S}_n \wedge s' \neq s} ((a_n^{s'} P[R < \overline{R}_n] - c_n^{s',b})\Lambda_n^{s'} + (a_n^s P[R < \overline{R}_n] - c_n^{s,b})\Lambda_n'^s)T$$

$$\tag{4.11}$$

It is important to point out that our estimates for deltas in this case are optimistic; indeed, they assume that external nodes do not change their current decisions about service requests. For example, if a service is taught to another $\mathtt{SelfLet}$, say from n_1 to n_2, not only requests issued by n_2 are missed but also requests from neighbours shared between n_1 and n_2 can change. In fact, other $\mathtt{SelfLets}$ can decide to switch their service provider from n_1 to n_2 thus modifying revenues and utilization at n_1.

4.4 General Policy

The autonomic policy monitors the situation of the $\mathtt{SelfLet}$ and of its neighbours and, if this appears to be going toward a critical situation, activates proper actions. The policy is activated periodically (i.e., every 60 seconds). At each activation the utilization value of the $\mathtt{SelfLet}$ is checked against the thresholds (see Sect. 4.2). In order to devise a stable network without continuous fluctuations, the $\mathtt{SelfLet}$ monitors also the state of neighbouring $\mathtt{SelfLets}$. In fact, by knowing the state of other $\mathtt{SelfLets}$ we can take actions aiming at optimizing utilization at system-level instead of $\mathtt{SelfLet}$-level.

According to the predicted utilization value (normal, over-utilization, under-utilization), the $\mathtt{SelfLet}$ actuates one of the following strategies:

Greedy The objective is to maximize revenues within the $\mathtt{SelfLet}$ without taking into account the effects on other $\mathtt{SelfLets}$. This strategy is adopted when the utilization of a $\mathtt{SelfLet}$ n and of its neighborhood are between the two thresholds (i.e., are under normal operating conditions), that is:

$$(\overline{U}_{\min} < \hat{U}_m < \overline{U}_{\max}) \quad \forall m \in \mathcal{N}_n \cup \{n\} \tag{4.12}$$

Non-Greedy The objective is, again, to maximize revenues on a $\mathtt{SelfLet}$. In this case, however, the actions to be executed are selected depending also on their impact on other $\mathtt{SelfLets}$. In particular, actions causing a threshold violation in other `SelfLets` are discarded. The non-greedy strategy is selected by a `Self-Let` n iff:

$$\exists\, m \in \mathcal{N}_n \cup \{n\} \quad \text{s.t.} \quad \neg(\overline{U}_{\min} < \hat{U}_m < \overline{U}_{\max}) \tag{4.13}$$

In this condition, the system predicts that the utilization of the `SelfLet` or one of its neighborhood is going to violate the thresholds.

Based on one of the two strategies above, a set of candidate optimization actions is generated. These candidates depend on: (i) the predicted profit, (ii) the predicted CPU utilization obtained if the action would be actuated, and (iii) the actuation cost due to the infrastructure provider. Then, the policy selects the action to be actuated following a probability-based approach: given the set of candidates, the probability to actuate an action is proportional to the profit generated by it. Selecting in probability allows the system to be more stable. For example if all `SelfLets` decide to redirect their requests to the most under-utilized `SelfLet`, very likely, this will introduce a bottleneck in the system [3]. On the contrary, if `SelfLets` choose their redirect receiver according to a probability distribution the probability to overload one specific `SelfLet` is lower.

The set of candidate actions is divided into four sets (not necessarily not-empty or disjoints) depending on their economical convenience and the threshold violation on local and remote `SelfLets` (see formula (4.14)). More precisely, once established the profitability (positive or negative) an action is classified depending on the overloading of local `SelfLet` and of remote `SelfLets`.

$Profitable = \{a \in candidates \mid \Delta netRevenues(a) > 0\}$

$NonProfitable = \{a \in candidates \mid \Delta netRevenues(a) \leq 0\}$

$OverloadNeighbours = \left\{ a \in candidates \,\middle|\, \begin{array}{l} a \text{ triggers threshold violation in some} \\ \text{neighbour } m; \, \hat{U}_m > \overline{U}_{\max} \end{array} \right\}$

$OverloadLocal = \left\{ a \in candidates \,\middle|\, \begin{array}{l} a \text{ triggers at } \texttt{SelfLet } n \text{ local threshold} \\ \text{violation } \hat{U}_n > \overline{U}_{\max} \end{array} \right\}$

$$\tag{4.14}$$

The first two sets partition actions only with respect to their profitability; indeed, if obtained net revenues overcome the action cost, then actuating the action is advantageous in economical terms. The last two sets classify actions by taking into account its resource utilization; in particular, it is checked whether actuating the action causes the CPU threshold to be violated in neighbours and in local `SelfLet` respectively. Notice that $Profitable \cap NonProfitable = \emptyset$ while possibly $OverloadNeighbour \cap OverloadLocal \neq \emptyset$.

```
 1  strategy ← getCurrentStrategy();
 2  if strategy == "noAction" then
 3      return ;
    end
 4  candidateActions ← actionsChangingImplementation ∪ actionsTeachingServices
    ∪ actionsRedirectingRequests ∪ actionsLearningServices;
 5  Profitable ← getProfitableActions(candidateActions);
 6  NonProfitable ← getNonProfitableActions(candidateActions);
 7  OverloadNeighbours ← getOverloadNeighbours(candidateActions);
 8  OverloadLocal ← getOverloadLocal(candidateActions);
 9  if strategy = "greedy" then
10      a ← pickBestGreedyAction(Profitable,
        OverloadNeighbours, NonProfitable, OverloadLocal);
11  else
12      a ← pickBestNon-GreedyAction(Profitable,
        OverloadNeighbours, NonProfitable, OverloadLocal);
    end
13  actuateAction(a);
```
Algorithm 3: The load balancing policy at SelfLet n

Algorithm 3 shows the load balancing policy. Initially (line 1), the strategy to adopt is established; the function *getCurrentStrategy()* checks whether the current predicted utilization violates the thresholds locally and remotely and after that returns the strategy. If the strategy is *noAction* then the current situation is optimal and there is no need to take further actions (line 3). For each type of optimization action (e.g. change implementation, redirect and teach) a set of candidate actions is produced; all candidates are inserted in the *candidateActions* set (line 4).

The set of candidate actions is then used to classify actions depending on their profitability and their utilization (lines from 5 to 8). At this point the algorithm selects an action according to the strategy initially selected by using one of the two functions *pickBestGreedyAction* and *pickBestNon-GreedyAction* which are described in Algorithms 4 and 5. Finally the action is actuated (line 13).

The two strategies represents two ways of optimizing the system; the main difference is represented by the potential impact on neighbours. Indeed, when acting according to a *greedy strategy*, neighbours can be overloaded because the main objective is to improve local SelfLet regardless of neighbours conditions. The *non-greedy strategy* instead can have impact only on local SelfLet leaving neighbours utilization unaltered.

Both algorithms are divided in two phases: in the first one the most convenient candidate action set is created by establishing an order on candidate sets; in the second phase a single action is selected with a probability proportional to its profit and CPU utilization. Actions causing a local threshold violation are not taken into account since a SelfLet should not spontaneously go into an overloaded state.

Input : *Profitable, OverloadNeighbour, NonProfitable, OverloadLocal*
Output: An action chosen according to a greedy strategy

1 $S_0 \leftarrow \{a \mid a \in \text{Profitable} \cap \neg\text{OverloadNeighbour} \cap \neg\text{OverloadLocal}\}$;
2 $S_1 \leftarrow \{a \mid a \in \text{Profitable} \cap \text{OverloadNeighbour} \cap \neg\text{OverloadLocal}\}$;
3 $S_2 \leftarrow \{a \mid a \in \text{NonProfitable} \cap \neg\text{OverloadNeighbour} \cap \neg\text{OverloadLocal}\}$;
4 $S_3 \leftarrow \text{NonProfitable}$;
5 candidateActionsSet $\leftarrow \emptyset$;
6 **if** $S_0 \neq \emptyset$ **then**
7   candidateActionsSet $\leftarrow S_0$;
8 **else if** $S_1 \neq \emptyset$ **then**
9   candidateActionsSet $\leftarrow S_1$;
10 **else if** $\hat{U}_m \geq \hat{U}_{\max}$ **then**
11   **if** $S_2 \neq \emptyset$ **then**
12   candidateActionsSet $\leftarrow S_2$;
13   **else if** $S_3 \neq \emptyset$ **then**
14   candidateActionsSet $\leftarrow S_3$;
       end
    end
15 **return** pickInProbability(candidateActionsSet);

Algorithm 4: The *pickBestGreedyAction* algorithm

Input : *Profitable, OverloadNeighbour, NonProfitable, OverloadLocal*

1 $S_0 = \{a \mid a \in \text{Profitable} \cap \neg\text{OverloadNeighbour} \cap \neg\text{OverloadLocal}\}$;
2 $S_1 = \{a \mid a \in \text{NonProfitable} \cap \neg\text{OverloadNeighbour} \cap \neg\text{OverloadLocal}\}$;
3 candidateActionsSet $\leftarrow \emptyset$;
4 **if** $S_0 \neq \emptyset$ **then**
5   candidateActionsSet $\leftarrow S_0$;
6 **else if** $S_1 \neq \emptyset$ **then**
7   candidateActionsSet $\leftarrow S_1$;
   end
8 **return** pickInProbability(candidateActionsSet);

Algorithm 5: The *pickBestNon-GreedyAction* algorithm

In the *pickBestGreedyAction*, the candidate set is chosen according to the following priority order:

1. Actions improving net revenues and not overloading any neighbours. These are the best candidate actions, since the local situation is improved without affecting neighbours.
2. Actions improving net revenues and overloading some neighbour. Since the local strategy is greedy, these actions are allowed.
3. Actions not improving net revenues and not overloading some neighbour. This set, as well as the next one, is considered only when the current utilization overcomes the utilization threshold. The rationale behind this choice is that the SelfLet is willing to renounce to some profits in favour of a better CPU utilization and response time.

4. The last set differs from the previous one since it takes all possible negative actions, even if they cause a threshold violation in neighbours.

The *pickBestNon-GreedyAction* works similarly to the greedy version with the exception that actions overloading neighbours are ruled out.

5 Experimental Results

In this section we present the results of some preliminary analyses we performed to validate the effectiveness of our framework. The main objective is to quantitatively evaluate the benefits in terms of system performance and revenues which can be achieved by implementing optimization policies.

In order to validate our approach, we built a case study involving two SelfLets offering and requesting services to each other. The physical system supporting experiments is based on VMWare ESXi 4.0, running on an Intel Nehalem dual socket quad-core system with 32 GB of RAM. SelfLets are deployed in two virtual machines running Ubuntu 8.04 Linux distribution. Each VM has a physical core dedicated with guaranteed performance and 1 GB of memory reserved.

The configuration of services at each node is shown in Figs. 7(a) and 7(b). States depicted in grey color represent abilities thus containing the actual computation. Each ability implements a micro-benchmarking application which consumes CPU time according to an exponential distribution. Requests are served according to FCFS scheduling.

The first SelfLet offers three services: S_1, S_2 and S_3. More specifically, S_1 incorporates the two sub-services S_2 and S_3. Service S_2 is implemented by three elementary behaviours differing by their service demand and cost, while service S_3 is provided with a single elementary behaviour. SelfLet 2 offers the service S_4 which can be implemented by two different behaviours.

Abilities cost and demanding times have been chosen with the rationale that implementations offering better performance (i.e., lower CPU time) have a higher cost with respect to abilities with lower performance.

Revenues for services are reported in Table 2 and are independent from the actual implementation of the service.

Both SelfLets have a main service structured as a loop in which an external service is called; in particular, SelfLet 1 sends requests for the execution of service S_4 to SelfLet 2, vice versa SelfLet 2 sends requests for the execution of service S_1. Notice that S_1 is a complex behaviour and in order to be completed its two sub-services need to be executed. For each SelfLet we generated a request workload with requests interarrival time extracted from an exponential distribution; the extracted value is used as think time in the wait state to put the SelfLet in temporary sleep. The requests load has been varied in three different time intervals lasting 10 minutes each, the overall experiment lasted 30 minutes (see Table 3).

For each service a maximum allowed response time is fixed (see Table 2). Whenever the service provider violates this threshold the SelfLet does not receive any

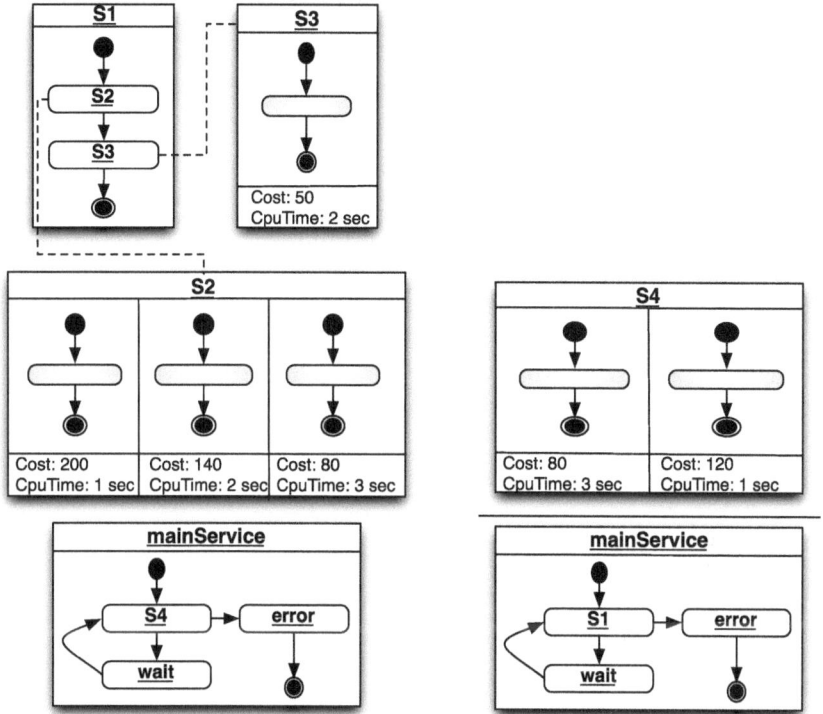

(a) Services configuration at SelfLet 1.   (b) Services configuration at SelfLet 2.

Fig. 7 The services installed at each SelfLet in the case study

Table 2 Case study service revenues and response times

Name	Revenues	Max response time (msec)
S_1	300	20,000
S_2	230	10,000
S_3	80	10,000
S_4	150	8,000

revenue for the service request, and the service execution cost is incurred (see Table 2). In our case study we limit the optimization to the change service implementation action; more specifically, the optimization policy switches among different implementations depending on the current workload. Note that, the evaluation of the policy requires only few milliseconds hence we guess that our approach can scale to consider more complicated setting including a larger number of SelfLets.

Experiments have been performed in two settings: with optimization policy and without the policy. The policy actuates actions changing the implementation of services according to the actual CPU load and the current generated revenues as described in Sect. 4. For the case without the optimization policy, we decided to adopt

Table 3 Service requests
rates (requests per second)
used in the case study

Service requested	Time interval (min)		
	0–10	10–20	20–30
$S1$ in SelfLet 1	0.2	0.05	0.1
$S4$ in SelfLet 2	0.4	0.16	0.3

as static configuration the most profitable implementation which is not further modified during the experiment. The most profitable behaviour is the one maximizing the ratio between revenues and the required CPU time: S_2 is then implemented by the second behaviour, while S_4 by the first one.

Figures 8(a) and 8(b) depict the CPU utilization of the two SelfLets in the two experimental settings. The plots show that during the initial time interval, which corresponds to heavy workload conditions, the setting with the policy enabled achieves sensibly better results with respect the other; this result is expected because the policy changes the service implementation with a behaviour requiring lower CPU time. In SelfLet 2 both configurations have a quite similar trend; this can be explained by the fact that the static assignment of behaviours is the same of the dynamic policy and the second SelfLet remains always under light load conditions.

A further confirmation of the effectiveness of the approach is given by response times of service requests reported in Figs. 8(c) and 8(d). Especially in the case of service $S1$ there is a substantial improvement in the response time where only 6.9% of requests violates the response time threshold, while the static assignment leads to a 51.4% threshold violations.

In Fig. 8(e) the instantaneous net revenues for the whole system are reported. The overall net revenues are given by the integral of the two curves and the solution with the optimization policy obtains 2.73 times more revenues than the static solution. The highest improvements are achieved during the period of heavy workload. In that case, the optimization policy modifies the implementation of services and requests are satisfied respecting the thresholds thus generating positive net revenues reducing the SelfLets utilization.

6 Related Work

Several research groups are being investigating the various areas of autonomic computing and are building frameworks to support the development of systems showing some self-* property. A recent survey of autonomic computing systems and an analysis of self-* properties have been provided in [11, 32]. Besides the seminal Manifesto [34], IBM contributed to the Autonomic Computing research field with a reference architectural model [33]; this model represents autonomic computing systems as a layered architecture together with an autonomic control loop. A different approach to the autonomic computing is the one known as *emergence*; it takes inspiration from the biological world which contains many examples of successful distributed systems. More precisely, the emergence refers to complex behaviors

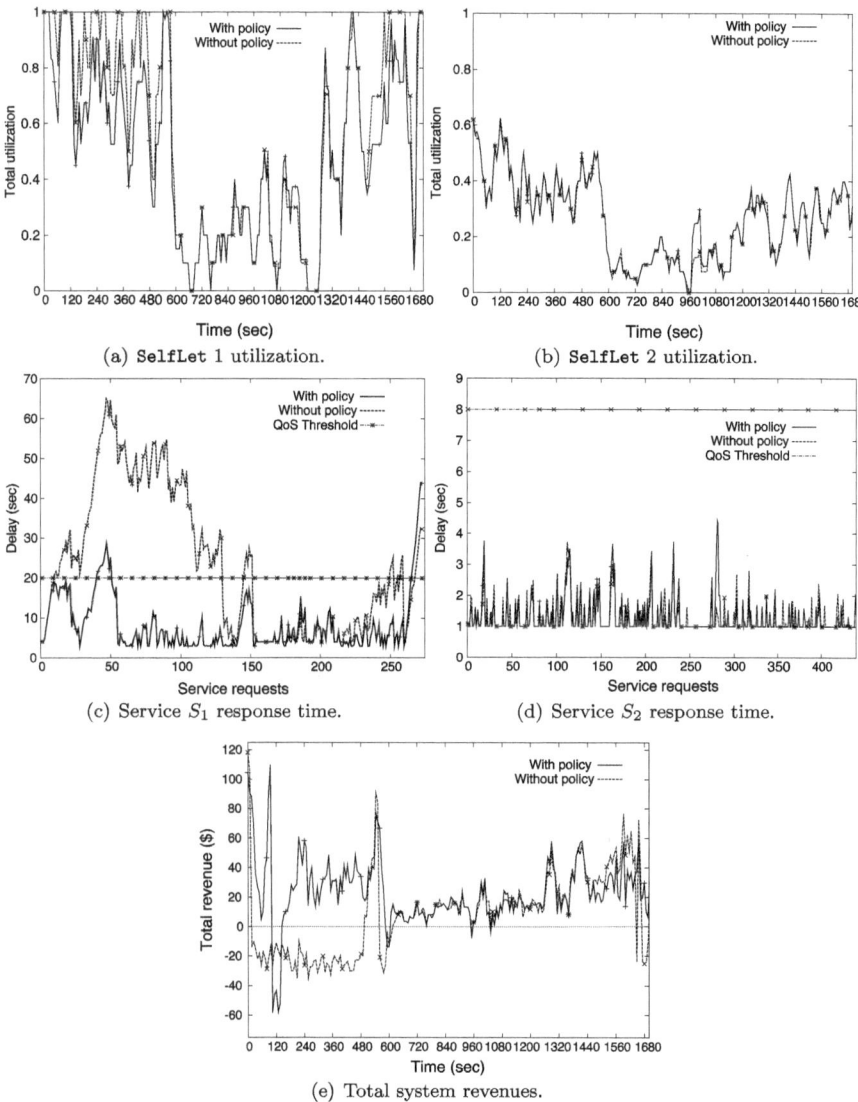

(a) SelfLet 1 utilization.

(b) SelfLet 2 utilization.

(c) Service S_1 response time.

(d) Service S_2 response time.

(e) Total system revenues.

Fig. 8 Performance metrics obtained in the experimental environment

emerging from the interaction of many elements performing very simple actions. Reference work for this approach are [5] and [55].

Examples of implementation of autonomic architectural frameworks have been provided in [39, 42] where a component based approach is taken. In service based systems, the work in [45] faced the problem of service live-migration introducing virtualized WSRF containers (see [53]), while authors in [35] provided some basic mechanisms for the runtime dynamic replacement of service implementations.

Referring to more theoretical approaches, an important part of the work performed on prediction models regards the management of Web systems [2, 19]. These works study the issues involved in creating a representative view of a web system by detecting significant and non-transient load changes. A similar work has been carried out in [43] in which periods of high utilization or poor performance are predicted using data mining and machine learning techniques. The study aims at optimizing the resources assignment and the computation of opportunistic job scheduling by using auto-regressive methods, multivariate regression methods and bayesian network classifiers. In [36] the authors present an approach to obtain response time predictions regarding a web application.

Concerning self-optimizing resource management, the solutions proposed in the literature can be classified in centralized and distributed. In a centralized approach, a dedicated entity is in charge of establishing a "desired global property" and has a global knowledge of the resources state in the whole system.

"Global properties" are usually evaluated by introducing utility functions which quantify the degree of user satisfaction by expressing their goals in terms of user-level performance attributes (e.g., request response time [50]). Typically, the system is modelled by means of a performance model embedded within an optimization framework [6, 50].

Centralized solutions are not suitable for geographically distributed systems, such as SelfLets, the Internet, cloud based systems or more in general massively distributed systems [3, 28, 30], since no one entity has global information about all of the system resources. Indeed, the communication overhead required to share the resource state information is not negligible and the delay to achieve state information from remote nodes could lead a centralized resource scheduler to very inaccurate decisions due to dynamic changes in system conditions, as well as resource consumption fluctuations or unexpected events [30].

Distributed resource management policies have been proposed to govern efficiently geographically distributed IT architectures that cannot implement centralized decisions and support strong interactions among the remote nodes [3]. Distributed resource management is very challenging, since one node's decisions may inadvertently degrade the performance of the overall system, even if they greedily optimize the node's performance. Sometimes, local decisions could lead the system even to unstable oscillations [29]. It is, thus, difficult to determine the best control mechanism at each node in isolation, so that the overall system performance is optimized. Dynamically choosing when, where and how allocate resources and coordinating the resource allocation accordingly is an open problem and is becoming more and more relevant with the advances of Cloud Computing [28].

One of the first contributions for resource management in geographically distributed systems has been proposed in [3], where novel autonomic distributed load balancing algorithms have been proposed. The algorithms aim to reduce the communication overhead among the system components and to gradually shift portions of requests among the distributed nodes. Authors have proposed a trend-based activation scheme that is based on local system information and exploit cooperation among other nodes. In the work [44] mechanisms to optimize performance within a geographical node and to redirect requests to the best remote node have been proposed. In distributed streaming networks, authors in [30] have proposed a joint admission control and resource allocation scheme, while [52] has proposed optimal scheduling techniques. Scheduling in streaming systems faces the problem that the incoming workload would far exceed system capacity much of the time.

In the distributed resource management area, researches are borrowing some ideas also from the biological world [46]. For instance, studies on the capability of various species to evolve in order to better adapt to the environment they are living in and analyses of the behaviour of colonies of insects and their capability to self-organize have been proposed [18, 21]. In this latter case, the main goal is to apply similar capabilities to software systems of interconnected components that singularly, like ants for their anthill [8], have limited information and reasoning power, but, all together, contribute to the high-level goals for the whole system. Using this approach, many complex problems can be solved by executing simple rules locally to each component of the system, regardless of the system size and without the need of a centralized control [14]. These algorithms have been used to improve system availability [26] by continuously reconfiguring groups and also to support load balancing in a distributed setting [14]. Bio-inspired techniques have been recently applied in several computer science fields, spanning the robot self-organization [48], the behaviour of autonomic network [9], the actions of swarms of autonomous vehicles performing dangerous tasks [54], and to organize sensors network deployment [26]. Biology-inspired techniques have been used in self-aggregation algorithms to establish and maintain groups of software components that cooperate to reach a common goal [24, 25] and to implement performance and energy-aware virtual machines live migration to minimize the number of overloaded and underloaded servers [10].

With respect to the above mentioned works, which usually focus on a single mechanism or resource management goal (e.g., load balancing, service migration), the main novelty of our work is to provide a unifying a framework able to support the development of distributed autonomic policies taking into account jointly several resource management actuation mechanisms.

7 Conclusion

In this paper we have presented our approach to deal with load balancing within the SelfLets framework. A system built in terms of SelfLets is usually highly decentralized and requires decisions to be taken on a local basis. For this reason, in our load balancing approach each SelfLet exploits the changing implementation, implementation teach, and request redirect actions in order to distribute the load evenly within its neighborhood. The SelfLet also exploits its prediction capabilities in order to actuate any action in advance. The experimental results, even though they evaluate the approach only partially, considering small networks of SelfLets performing only changing implementation actions, already show clear advantages with respect to the case in which the optimal `SelfLets` configuration is chosen but it is kept fixed for the entire duration of the system operation.

Our future work is focusing on the following directions: i) validate our proposal on a significant case study characterized by a high number of `SelfLets` in a real Cloud system, ii) implement all the three actions that we have identified in the current contribution, iii) adopt advanced prediction models that can be easily incorporated into the `SelfLets` framework.

Acknowledgement The work presented in this paper is sponsored by the European Commission, Programme IDEAS-ERC, Project 227977-SMScom.

References

[1] OSGi Alliance: OSGi Alliance Specifications. http://www.osgi.org/Specifications/release4v41

[2] Andreolini, M., Casolari, S., Colajanni, M.: Models and framework for supporting runtime decisions in web-based systems. ACM Trans. Web **2**(3), 1–43 (2008)

[3] Andreolini, M., Casolari, S., Colajanni, M.: Autonomic request management algorithms for geographically distributed internet-based systems. In: SASO 2008, pp. 171–180 (2008)

[4] Agarwal, M., Bhat, V., Liu, H., Matossian, V., Putty, V., Schmidt, C., Zhang, G., Zhen, L., Parashar, M., Khargharia, B., Hariri, S.: Automate: enabling autonomic applications on the grid. In: Autonomic Computing Workshop, 2003, pp. 48–57, June 2003

[5] Anthony, R.: Emergence: a paradigm for robust and scalable distributed applications. In: Proceedings of the 1st International Conference on Autonomic Computing (2004)

[6] Ardagna, D., Trubian, M., Zhang, L.: Sla based resource allocation policies in autonomic environments. J. Parallel Distrib. Comput. **67**(3), 259–270 (2007)

[7] Babaoğlu, Ö., Meling, H., Montresor, A.: Anthill: A framework for the development of agent-based peer-to-peer systems. In: International Conference on Distributed Computing Systems, p. 15 (2002)

[8] Babaoglu, O., Meling, H., Montresor, A.: Anthill: A framework for the development of agent-based peer-to-peer systems, pp. 15–22 (2002)

[9] Balasubramaniam, S., Botvich, D., Donnelly, W., Strassner, J.: A biologically inspired policy based management system for survivability in autonomic networks, pp. 160–168, Sept. 2007

[10] Barbagallo, D., Di Nitto, E., Dubois, D., Mirandola, R.: A bio-inspired algorithm for energy optimization in a self-organizing data center. In: Weyns, D., Malek, S., de Lemos, R., Andersson, J. (eds.) Self-Organizing Architectures. Lecture Notes in Computer Science, vol. 6090, pp. 127–151. Springer, Berlin/Heidelberg (2010). doi:10.1007/978-3-642-14412-7_7

[11] Berns, A., Ghosh, S.: Dissecting Self-* Properties. In: Proceedings of SASO, pp. 10–19 (2009)

[12] Bindelli, S., Nitto, E.D., Mirandola, R., Tedesco, R.: Building autonomic components: the SelfLets approach. In: Proc. ASE—Workshops, pp. 17–24 (2008)

[13] Bindelli, S., Di Nitto, E., Furia, C., Rossi, M.: Using compositionality to formally model and analyze systems built of a high number of components. In: 5th IEEE International Conference on Engineering of Complex Computer Systems. IEEE Computer Society, Los Alamitos (2010)

[14] Beckers, R., Holl, O.E., Deneubourg, J.L.: From local actions to global tasks: Stigmergy. In: Collective Robotics. Proceedings Artificial Life IV MA, pp. 181–189. MIT Press, Cambridge (1994)

[15] Bennani, M., Menascé, D.: Resource allocation for autonomic data centers using analytic performance models. In: IEEE Int'l Conf. on Autonom. Computing (2005)

[16] Bolch, G., Greiner, S., de Meer, H., Trivedi, K.: Queueing Networks and Markov Chains. Wiley, New York (1998)

[17] Calcavecchia, N., Di Nitto, E.: Incorporating prediction models in the SelfLet framework: a plugin approach. In: 1st International Workshop on Run-Time Models for Self-managing Systems and Applications

[18] Camazine, S., Deneubourg, J.L., Franks, N.R., Sneyd, J., Theraulaz, G., Bonabeau, E.: Self-organization in Biological Systems. Princeton University Press, Princeton (2001)

[19] Casolari, S., Andreolini, M., Colajanni, M.: Runtime prediction models for web-based system resources. In: IEEE International Symposium on Modeling, Analysis and Simulation of Computers and Telecommunication Systems, 2008. MASCOTS (2008)

[20] Cugola, G., Picco, G.P.: Reds: A reconfigurable dispatching system. In: Proc. of the 6th Int. Workshop on Software Engineering and Middleware SEM06, pp. 9–16. ACM, New York (2006)

[21] Detrain, C., Deneubourg, J., Pasteels, J.: Information Processing in Social Insects. Birkäuser, Basel (1999)

[22] Devescovi, D., Di Nitto, E., Dubois, D., Mirandola, R.: Self-organization algorithms for autonomic systems in the selflet approach. In: Autonomics '07: Proceedings of the 1st International Conference on Autonomic Computing and Communication Systems, pp. 1–10, ICST, Brussels, Belgium (2007). ICST (Institute for Computer Sciences, Social-Informatics and Telecommunications Engineering)

[23] Devescovi, D., Di Nitto, E., Mirandola, R.: An infrastructure for autonomic system development: the selflet approach. In: Proc. ASE, pp. 449–452 (2007)

[24] Di Nitto, E., Dubois, D., Mirandola, R.: Self-aggregation algorithms for autonomic systems, pp. 120–128, Dec. 2007

[25] Di Nitto, E., Dubois, D., Mirandola, R., Saffre, F., Tateson, R.: Self-aggregation techniques for load balancing in distributed systems, pp. 489–490, Oct. 2008

[26] Dolev, S., Tzachar, N.: Empire of colonies: Self-stabilizing and self-organizing distributed algorithm. Theor. Comput. Sci. **410**(6–7), 514–532 (2009)

[27] http://www.jboss.org/drools/

[28] Erdogmus, H.: Cloud computing: Does nirvana hide behind the nebula? IEEE Softw. **26**(2), 4–6 (2009)

[29] Felber, P., Kaldewey, T., Weiss, S.: Proactive hot spot avoidance for web server dependability. In: SRDS '04: Proceedings of the 23rd IEEE International Symposium on Reliable Distributed Systems, pp. 309–318. IEEE Computer Society, Washington (2004)

[30] Feng, H., Liu, Z., Xia, C.H., Zhang, L.: Load shedding and distributed resource control of stream processing networks. Perform. Eval. **64**(9–12), 1102–1120 (2007). Performance 2007, 26th International Symposium on Computer Performance, Modeling, Measurements, and Evaluation

[31] Ganek, A.G., Corbi, T.A.: The dawning of the autonomic computing era. IBM Syst. J. **42**(1), 5–18 (2003)

[32] Huebscher, M.C., McCann, J.A.: A survey of autonomic computing–degrees, models, and applications. ACM Comput. Surv. **40**(3), 7 (2008)

[33] IBM. An Architectural Blueprint for Autonomic Computing, 4th edn. (2006)

[34] IBM. Autonomic computing manifesto

[35] Irmert, F., Fischer, T., Meyer-Wegener, K.: Runtime adaptation in a service-oriented component model. In: Proceedings of SEAMS, pp. 49–56 (2008)

[36] Kirtane, S., Martin, J.: Application performance prediction in autonomic systems. In: Proceedings of the 44th Annual Southeast Regional Conference, pp. 566–572. ACM, New York (2006)

[37] Kleinrock, L.: Queuing Systems, vol. I. Wiley, New York (1975)

[38] Liu, Z., Squillante, M., Wolf, J.L.: On maximizing service-level-agreement profits. In: Proc. of ACM Electronic Commerce Conference, October 2001

[39] Linner, D., Pfeffer, H., Jacob, C., Kress, A., Krüssel, S., Steglich, S.: SmartWare: framework for autonomic application services. In: Proceedings of Autonomics, pp. 17–23 (2008)

[40] Menascé, D.A., Dubey, V.: Utility-based QoS Brokering in Service Oriented Architectures. In: IEEE International Conference on Web Services Proceedings, pp. 422–430 (2007)
[41] Panzeri, M.: Studio di un approccio per la realizzazione di agenti autonomici in reti di sensori wireless. Master's thesis, Politecnico Di Milano (2008)
[42] Peper, C., Schneider, D.: Component engineering for adaptive ad-hoc systems. In: Proceedings of SEAMS, pp. 49–56 (2009)
[43] Powers, R., Goldszmidt, M., Cohen, I.: Short term performance forecasting in enterprise systems. In: KDD '05: Proceedings of the Eleventh ACM SIGKDD International Conference on Knowledge Discovery in Data Mining, pp. 801–807. ACM, New York (2005)
[44] Ranjan, S., Knightly, E.: High-performance resource allocation and request redirection algorithms for web clusters. IEEE Trans. Parall. Distrib. Syst. **19**(9), 1186–1200 (2008)
[45] Reich, C., Banholzer, M., Buyya, R., Bubendorfer, K.: Engineering an autonomic container for WSRF-based web services. In: Proceedings of ADCOM, pp. 277–282 (2007)
[46] Shackleton, M., Marrow, P.: Editorial, special issue on nature-inspired computation. BT Technol. J. **18**(4), 9–11 (2000)
[47] Rolia, J., Cherkasova, L., McCarthy, C.: Configuring workload manager control parameters for resource pools. In: 10th IEEE NOMS, Vancouver, Canada, April 2006
[48] Shen, W.-M., Salemi, B., Will, P.: Hormone-inspired adaptive communication and distributed control for conro self-reconfigurable robots. IEEE Trans. Robot. Autom. **18**(5), 700–712 (2002)
[49] Tang, C., Steinder, M., Spreitzer, M., Pacifici, G.: A scalable application placement controller for enterprise data centers. In: WWW2007 (2007)
[50] Urgaonkar, B., Pacifici, G., Shenoy, P., Spreitzer, M., Tantawi, A.: Analytic modeling of multitier internet applications. ACM Trans. Web **1**(1), 2 (2007)
[51] Vilalta, R., Apte, C.V., Hellerstein, J.L., Ma, S., Weiss, S.M.: Predictive algorithm in the management of computer systems. IBM Syst. J. **41**(3), 461–474 (2002)
[52] Wolf, J., Bansal, N., Hildrum, K., Parekh, S., Rajan, D., Wagle, R., Wu, K.-L., Fleischer, L.: Soda: an optimizing scheduler for large-scale stream-based distributed computer systems. In: Middleware '08: Proceedings of the 9th ACM/IFIP/USENIX International Conference on Middleware, pp. 306–325. Springer, New York (2008)
[53] http://www.globus.org/wsrf/
[54] Xi, W., Tan, X., Baras, J.: A stochastic algorithm for self-organization of autonomous swarms, pp. 765–770, Dec. 2005
[55] De Wolf, T., Holvoet, T.: Emergence as a general architecture for distributed autonomic computing (2004)

N.M. Calcavecchia (✉)
Dipartimento di Elettronica e Informazione, Politecnico di Milano, Pizza Leonardo da Vinci 32, 20133, Milano, Italy
e-mail: calcavecchia@elet.polimi.it

D. Ardagna
Dipartimento di Elettronica e Informazione, Politecnico di Milano, Pizza Leonardo da Vinci 32, 20133, Milano, Italy
e-mail: ardagna@elet.polimi.it

E. Di Nitto
Dipartimento di Elettronica e Informazione, Politecnico di Milano, Pizza Leonardo da Vinci 32, 20133, Milano, Italy
e-mail: dinitto@elet.polimi.it

Run Time Models in Adaptive Service Infrastructure

Marco Autili, Paola Inverardi, and Massimo Tivoli

Abstract Software in the near ubiquitous future will need to cope with variability, as software systems get deployed on an increasingly large diversity of computing platforms and operates in different execution environments. Heterogeneity of the underlying communication and computing infrastructure, mobility inducing changes to the execution environments and therefore changes to the availability of resources and continuously evolving requirements require software systems to be adaptable according to the context changes. Software systems should also be reliable and meet the user's requirements and needs. Moreover, due to its pervasiveness, software systems must be dependable. Supporting the validation of these self-adaptive systems to ensure dependability requires a complete rethinking of the software life cycle. The traditional division among static analysis and dynamic analysis is blurred by the need to validate dynamic systems adaptation. Models play a key role in the validation of dependable systems, dynamic adaptation calls for the use of such models at run time. In this paper we describe the approach we have undertaken in recent projects to address the challenge of assessing dependability for adaptive software systems.

1 Introduction

The near future envisions a pervasive heterogeneous computing infrastructure that makes it possible to provide and access software services on a variety of devices, from end-users with different needs and expectations. To ensure that users meet

This work is a revised and extended version of [28]. It has been partially supported by the IST project PLASTIC No 026955, the FET project CONNECT No 231167, and the Italian Prin D-ASAP. We acknowledge all the members of the consortium for PLASTIC, CONNECT, and D-ASAP, and of the SEALab at University of L'Aquila for joint efforts on all the research efforts reported in this paper.

D. Ardagna, L. Zhang (eds.), *Run-time Models for Self-managing*
Systems and Applications, 125–152,
Autonomic Systems, DOI 10.1007/978-3-0346-0433-8_6, © Springer Basel AG 2010

their non-functional requirements by experiencing the best Quality of Service (QoS) according to their needs and specific contexts of use, services need to be context-aware, adaptable, and dependable. The development and the execution of such services is a big challenge and it is far to be solved.

Software services and systems in the near ubiquitous future (Softure) cannot rely on the classical desktop-centric assumption that the system execution environment is known a priori at design time and, hence, the execution environment of a Softure cannot be statically anticipated. Softure will need to cope with variability, as software systems get deployed on an increasingly large diversity of computing platforms and operates in different execution environments. Heterogeneity of the underlying communication and computing infrastructure, mobility inducing changes to the execution environments and therefore changes to the availability of resources and continuously evolving requirements require software systems to be adaptable according to the context changes.

Context awareness and adaptation have become two key aspects to be considered while developing and running future software. While providing/consuming services, Softure need to be aware of and adaptive to their context, i.e., the combination of user-centric data (e.g., requested QoS, information of interest for users according to their current circumstance) and resource/computer-centric data (e.g., resources and conditions of devices and network). At the same time, Softure should be dependable and meet the users performance requirements and needs. Moreover, due to its pervasiveness and in order to make adaptation effective and successful, adaptation must be considered in conjunction with dependability, i.e., no matter what adaptation is performed, the system must continue to guarantee a certain degree of QoS.

Supporting the development and execution of Softure systems raises numerous challenges that involve languages, methods and tools for the systems through design, analysis, and validation in order to ensure dependability of the self-adaptive systems that are targeted.

In this paper we describe three completely different instantiations of a development process model for Softure systems. We report our experience in assessing dependability for adaptive software systems within the context of three different projects. Although completely different, it is worthwhile considering the three scenarios since each of them focus on different dependability requirements. However, due to their different nature and aims, neither a common example cannot be used to discuss them nor it is meaningful for them to give an integrated view.

The first one, that we will describe in detail, concerns the IST PLASTIC [36] project that can be considered as a specific instance of Softure as context-aware software for next generation networking environments. Another scenario concerns the FET CONNECT [21] project that aims at enabling continuous composition of networked systems to respond to the evolution of functionalities provided to and required from the networked environment. Since the project is still in a preliminary stage, we cannot provide a detailed description of it. In the last scenario we describe how to manage the performance of the Siena publish/subscribe middleware [16, 19] by using the Performance Management Framework (PFM). PFM allows the management of the system performance at run time based on monitoring and model-based performance evaluation [17]. We will keep also the description of the PFM scenario short since it concerns a particular activity of a development process model for Softure, i.e., dynamic reconfiguration driven by the run-time exploitation of performance models.

Our thesis is that Softure requires to rethink the whole software development process since it never stabilizes, but it is permanently under maintenance. Software evolution, which is traditionally practiced as an off-line activity, must often be accommodated at run time for Softure. This requires to reconcile the static view with the dynamic view by breaking the traditional division among development phases by moving some activities from design time to deployment and run time hence asking for new and more efficient verification and validation techniques. Dependability is achieved with a comprehensive life cycle approach from requirements to operation, to maintenance by analyzing *models*, testing code, monitor, and repair execution. Many software models are involved, from requirements to specification, to code. In order to support dependability of adaptable applications new modeling notations are required. These should permit to express and deal with characteristics that are crucial for a Softure, i.e., QoS, resource-awareness, evolution, reconfiguration, variability, and uncertainty. At the same time they should allow for validation techniques affordable at run time. Their cost must be sustainable under the execution environment resource constraints, e.g. time and computational resources. In order to easily and consistently integrate the modeling layer with the analysis and implementation ones, model transformation and evolution techniques should be exploited.

The paper is structured as follows. In the following section we discuss the Softure characteristics in order to identify the two key challenges, i.e., *adaptability* and *dependability*, and to highlight the crucial role that models play, at run time, for adaptive software. This discussion will bring us to consider the Softure issues in a software process perspective. In Sect. 3, we propose a new software process for Softure, where models play a key role in dynamic adaptation and dependability validation. In Sect. 4, we show the application of the proposed process to three different scenarios we borrowed from three projects we participate(d) to. In Sect. 5 we conclude by summarizing the thesis originating from the discussion carried on throughout the paper.

2 Setting the Context

Softure is supposed to execute in an ubiquitous, heterogeneous infrastructure under mobility constraints. This means that the software must be able to carry on operations while changing different execution environments or *contexts*. Execution contexts offer a variability of resources that can affect the software operation. *Context awareness* refers to the ability of an application to *sense* the context in which it is executing and therefore it is the base to consider (self-)adaptive applications, i.e., software systems that have the ability to change their *behavior* in response to external changes.

It is worthwhile stressing that although a change of context is measured in quantitative terms, an application can only be adapted by changing its behavior, i.e., its functional/qualitative specification. For instance, (Physical) Mobility allows a user to move out of his proper context, traveling across different contexts and, to our purposes, the difference among contexts is determined in terms of available resources like connectivity, energy, software, etc. However other dimensions of contexts can exist relevant to the user, system and physical domains, which are the main context domains identified in the literature [8, 9, 20, 26, 38, 40]. In the software development practice when building a system the context is determined and it is also part of the (non-functional) requirements (operational, social, organizational constraints). If context changes, requirements change therefore the system needs to change. In standard software, the pace at which context changes is slow and they are usually taken into account as evolutionary requirements. For Softure, context changes occur due to physical mobility while the system is in operation. This means that if the system needs to change this should happen dynamically. This notion leads to consider different ways to modify a system at run time that can happen in different forms namely *(self-)adaptiveness/dynamicity* and at different levels of granularity, from software architecture to line of code.

Softure needs also to be dependable. *Dependability* is an orthogonal issue that depends on QoS attributes, like performance and all other *-bilities*. Dependability impacts all the software life cycle. In general dependability is an attribute for software systems that operate in specific application domains. For Softure we consider dependability in its original meaning as defined in [27], that is *the trustworthiness of a computing system which allows reliance to be justifiably placed on the service it delivers ... Dependability includes such attributes as reliability, availability, safety, security.* Softure encompasses any kind of software system that can operate in the future ubiquitous infrastructure. The dependability requirement is therefore extended also to applications that traditionally have not this requirement. Dependability in this case represents the user requirement that states that the application must operate in the unknown world (i.e., out of a confined execution environment) with the same level of reliance it has when operating at home. At home means in the controlled execution environment where there is complete knowledge of the system behavior and the context is fixed. In the unknown world, the knowledge of the system is undermined by the absence of knowledge on contexts, thus the dependability requirement arises also for conventional applications. Traditionally dependability is achieved with a comprehensive approach all along the software life cycle from requirements to operation to maintenance by analyzing models, testing code, monitor and repair execution.

Therefore the overall challenge is to provide dependable assurance for highly adaptable applications. Since dependability is achieved throughout the life cycle many software artifacts are involved, from requirements specification to code. In the rest of this paper, as such artifacts, we will consider *models*, i.e., an idealized view of the system suitable for reasoning, developing, validating a real system. Models can be functional and non-functional and can represent different level of abstractions of the real system, from requirements to code. Our research bias is on Software Architecture, therefore we will often consider software architectural systems' models. An architectural model allows the description of the static and dynamic components of the system and explains how they interact. Software architectures support early analysis, verification and validation of software systems. Software architectures are the earliest comprehensive system model along the software lifecycle built from requirements specification. They are increasingly part of standardized software development processes because they represent a system abstraction in which design choices relevant to the correctness of the final system are taken. This is particularly evident for dependability requirements like security and reliability and quantitative ones like performance.

3 The Process View: the Role of Models at Run Time

In this section we cast the above discussed challenges in a development process view. The process view focuses on the set of activities that characterize the development and the operation of a software system. These activities are traditionally divided into activities related to the actual production of the software system and activities that are performed when the system can be executed and goes into operation. Specification, Design, Validation, and Evolution activities vary depending on the organization and the type of system being developed. Each Activity requires its Language, Methods and Tools and works on suitable artefacts of the system. For validation purposes each artefact can be coupled with a *model*. Models are an idealized view of the system suitable for reasoning, developing, validating a real system. To achieve dependability a large variety of models are used from behavioral to stochastic. These models represent the systems at very different levels of abstraction from requirements specification to code. The ever growing complexity of software has exacerbated the dichotomy development/static/compile time versus execution/dynamic/interpreter time concentrating as many analysis and validation activities as possible at development time.

Softure puts new requirements on this standard development process. The evolutionary nature of Softure makes infeasible a standard approach to validation since it would require before the system is in execution to predict the system behavior with respect to virtually any possible change. Therefore, in the literature most approaches that try to deal with the validation of dynamic software system concentrate the changes to the structure by using graph and graph grammars formalisms or topological constraints [11, 14, 22, 23, 25, 30, 32, 39]. As far as changes to behavior are concerned, only few approaches exist that make use either of behavioral equivalence checks or of the type system [2–4] or through code certification [12, 33]. If dependability has to be preserved through adaptation, whatever the change mechanism is, at the time the change occurs a validation check must be performed. This means that all the models necessary to carry on the validation step must be available at run time and that the actual validation time becomes now part of the execution time. In this direction, it is worth to mention the work in [24] where the authors present a model-driven approach (D-KLAPER) that, building on the KLAPER (Kernel LAnguage for PErformance and Reliability analysis) intermediate language, allows for capturing the core features for the performance and reliability analysis of a dynamically

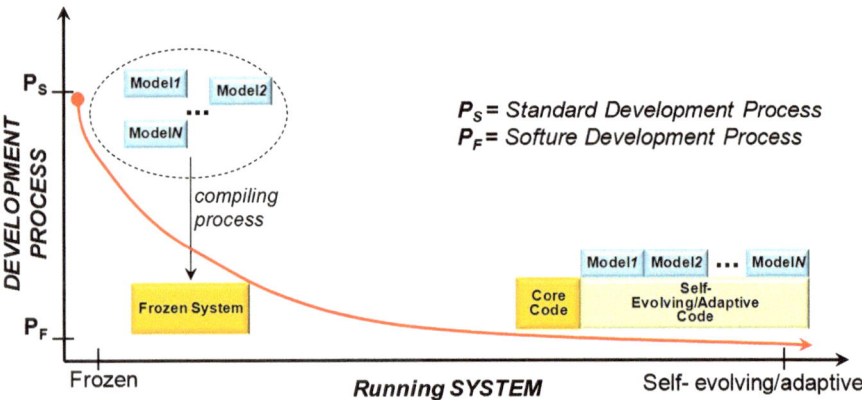

Fig. 1 The softure development process

reconfigurable component-based system. Indeed, this approach goes into a similar direction as the projects later on described (specifically, PLASTIC and PFM) and, in particular, KLAPER has been also used in PLASTIC for performance analysis.

The Softure development process therefore has to explicitly account for complex validation steps at run time when all the necessary information are available. Figure 1 represents the process development plane delimited on the left-hand side by the standard development process and on the right-hand side by the softure development one. The vertical dimension represents the static versus dynamic time with respect to all the activities (e.g., analysis and validation) involved in the development process. The horizontal axis represents the amount of adaptability of the system, that is its ability to cope with evolution still maintaining dependability. The standard development process carries out most of the development and validation activities before the system is running that is during development. The result is a running system that, at run time, is frozen with respect to evolution. Considering development processes that allow increasingly degrees of adaptability allows to move along the horizontal axis thus ideally tending to a development process that is entirely managed at run time. In the middle we can place development processes that allow larger and larger portions of the system to change at run time and that make use for validation purposes of artefacts that can be produced statically. In the following section we describe three instances of the Softure Development Process that have been proposed in the scope of the projects PLASTIC, CONNECT, and PFM respectively. Although completely different, and described at a different level of detail, these instances show how different dependability requirements can be considered and dynamically assessed. Note that PLASTIC and CONNECT, in particular, are two EU IP projects (STREP and FET respectively). Clearly, we cannot provide (and it is also out of the scope of this paper) the reader with neither a validation/comparison with respect to the state of the art nor a detailed treatment (e.g., assumptions and inherent limitations) of each single technique/method/tool developed within the specific project. The reader interested in these aspects can refer to [36] and [21] (and the on-line documentation therein). Moreover, we cannot describe in details all the models that, at different level and in different ways, are analyzed and manipulated to contribute to evaluate/estimate (some of) the different dependability attributes. Rather, our aim is to report our attempts towards different instantiations of the Softure development process.

4 Instantiating the Process Model: 3 Scenarios

In this section we describe the approach we have undertaken in recent projects to address the challenge of assessing dependability for adaptive software systems. We consider three different scenarios. We will mainly concentrate on the first one that concerns the ended IST PLASTIC [36] project. It can be considered as a specific instance of Softure as context-aware software for next generation networking environments. Another scenario comes from the preliminary results of the recently started FET CONNECT [21] project. The CONNECT goal is to enable continuous composition of networked systems in order to respond to the evolution of functionalities provided to and required from the networked environment. In the last scenario, we shortly describe the PFM framework developed as part of a project internal to our group. In particular, we describe the application of PFM to the management of the performance of the Siena publish/subscribe middleware [16, 19]. PFM allows the management of the system performance at run time based on monitoring and model-based performance evaluation [17].

Before diving into the presentation of the three projects, it must be noted that the three experienced approaches will be described with different level of detail since they have a different size and maturity, and they are completely different in nature with respect to kind of models, their usage degree at run time, and their purposes. For instance, in PLASTIC (part of) the models are created at design time and (possibly) evolved at run time basing on the results of the analysis and monitoring activities. In the more open scenario of CONNECT, models are created at run time, through the learning activities, and exploited at run time for generating connectors on the fly. Moreover, some of the described results, at present, might be considered either a little bit outdated, for the ended projects PLASTIC and PFM, or not enough mature, for the ongoing CONNECT project. For instance, the UML and the QoS profiles used within PLASTIC have both become obsolete and the more recent UML MARTE profile [35] can be found today. Again, it is out of the scope of this paper to embark on such a discussion.

4.1 The PLASTIC Project

The main goal of the PLASTIC project is the rapid and easy development/deployment of context-aware adaptive services for the next generation pervasive networking environment, such as Beyond 3rd Generation (B3G) networks [41]. B3G networks are an effective way to realize pervasive computing by offering broad connectivity through various network technologies pursuing the convergence of wireless telecommunication and IP networks (e.g., UMTS, WiFi and Bluetooth).

Ubiquitous networking empowered by B3G networks makes it possible for mobile users to access networked software services across heterogeneous infrastructures through resource-constrained devices characterized by their heterogeneity and limitedness. Software applications running over this kind of infrastructure must cope with resource scarcity and with the inherent faulty and heterogeneous nature of this environment. Indeed, to ensure that users meet their non-functional requirements by experiencing the best QoS according to their needs and specific contexts of use, services need to be context-aware, adaptable, and dependable.

This section describes our experience in this direction by describing the PLASTIC development process which integrates different engineering methods, tools and models for supporting a user-centric and comprehensive process (from design to deployment to validation). PLASTIC provides a set of tools[1] that are all based on the *PLASTIC Service Conceptual Model*[2] and support the service life cycle, from design to implementation to validation to execution. The conceptual model formalizes all the concepts needed for developing B3G service-oriented applications. To this end, the model proposes an elicitation of base abstractions that need to be accounted for developing applications for B3G networking infrastructures. Starting from the analysis of the characteristics of B3G networks, the relevant abstractions have been identified and refined according to the PLASTIC goals. Explicitly considering B3G networks, the *PLASTIC middleware* conveniently combines the heterogeneous wireless networks in reach, which for various reasons (e.g., cost effectiveness, distinct administration and infrastructureless ad hoc interaction) are not integrated at the network layer. With reference to Fig. 2, where we show the service oriented interaction pattern, the PLASTIC middleware [18] provides enhanced support for the publication, discovery and access of services over B3G. Hence, the PLASTIC middleware supports services for being aware of the networking environment and for adapting to its changes. The middleware is able to capture the various networks and observe their status, and abstract their properties in order to fully exploit the underlying network diversity without relying on any pre-established knowledge or

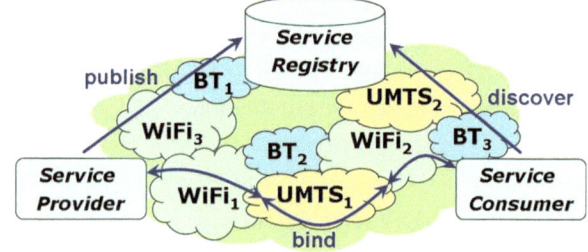

Fig. 2 Service oriented interaction pattern over B3G

---

[1] Available at http://gforge.inria.fr/projects/plastic-dvp/.

[2] The *Formal description of the PLASTIC conceptual model and of its relationship with the PLASTIC platform toolset* is available at http://www.ist-plastic.org/.

Fig. 3 Development
environment

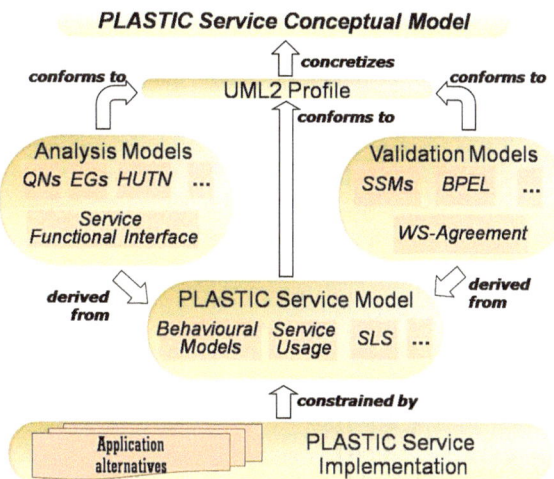

infrastructure. To this end, the middleware exploits at run time a B3G *network context model* that introduces (in particular) the notion of Network Infrastructural Path between the service provider and consumer. Specifically, a network infrastructural path is a combination of (possibly different) wireless networks together with their network-level services. For instance, referring to Fig. 2, a possible network infrastructural path is $WiFi_1 \Leftrightarrow UMTS_1 \Leftrightarrow WiFi_2$.

The overall approach is model driven, starting from the conceptual model till the execution service model used to monitor the service. With reference to Fig. 3, the PLASTIC conceptual model has been concretely implemented as a *UML2 profile* and, by means of the PLASTIC development environment tools, the functional behavior of the service and its non-functional characteristics can be modeled. Then, nonfunctional analysis and development activities are iteratively performed [10]. The analysis aims at computing QoS indices of the service at different levels of detail, from early design to implementation to publication, to support designers and programmers in the development of services that satisfy the specified QoSs, i.e., Service Level Specifications (SLSs). In PLASTIC, among QoS dimensions, we consider performance and reliability. The principal performance indices are *utilization* and *throughput* of (logical and physical) resources, as well as *response time* for a given task. The considered reliability measures are, instead, *probability of failure on demand* and *mean time to failure*. Discrete set of values—e.g., high, medium, low—are used to identify ranges. The obtained QoS indices are the base to guarantee the implementation of dependable services that satisfy the required/offered QoS. In particular, the SLS relies on information retrieved by the analysis of the quantitative models Queuing Networks (QNs—see the first chapter) and Execution Graphs (EGs) derived from the service model. The kind of QNs we sue in PLASTIC is "product form QN".

The analysis and validation activities rely on artifacts produced from the PLASTIC service model through different model transformations. For instance, the service model editor [7] and the Service Level Agreement (SLA) editor, that are part of the PLASTIC platform toolset, are integrated through a model-to-code transformation. Once the service model has been specified, a model-to-code transformation can be performed in order to translate the parts of the service model that are needed for specifying the agreement (e.g., involved parties, other services, operations, etc.) into a HUTN file (i.e., a human-usable textual notation for SLA) which the SLA editor is capable to import. The SLS attached to the published service and the SLA are formally specified by using the language SLAng [29].

After the service has been implemented, the PLASTIC validation framework enables the off-line, prior to the service publication, and on-line, after the service publication, validation of the services with respect to functional—through test models such as Symbolic State Machines (SSMs) or based on BPEL processes—and non-functional properties [13]. This means that through validation it is possible to assess whether the service exhibits the given SLS. On-line validation concerns the "checking" activities that are performed after service deployment such as SLA monitoring [37].

PLASTIC builds on Web Services (WS) and component-based technologies, and (as one of the main novelties) introduces the notion of *requested Service Level Specification* (SLS) and *offered SLS* to deal with the non-functional dimensions—i.e., QoS—that will be used to establish the SLA between the service consumer and the service provider. Services are offered by adaptable components and are deployed on heterogeneous resource-constrained mobile devices. Adaptable components are implemented by using CHAMELEON, a formal framework for adaptive Java applications [5, 6, 8, 31]. By exploiting CHAMELEON the PLASTIC services support two types of adaptation, namely *SLS-based adaptation* driven by the (requested/offered) SLS and *context-aware adaptation* driven by the characteristic of the (provider, network and consumer) execution context.

PLASTIC services are implemented by using the CHAMELEON *Programming Model* [5, 6, 8, 31] that, extending the Java language, permits developers to implement services in terms of *generic code*. Such a generic code, opportunely preprocessed, generates a set of different *application alternatives*, i.e., different standard Java components that represent different ways of implementing a provider/consumer application. Therefore, an adaptable software service might be implemented as and consumed by different application alternatives (i.e., different adaptations). Each alternative is characterized by (i) the resources it demands to be correctly executed (i.e., *Resource Demand*) and (ii) the so called *Code-embedded SLSs*. The latter are QoS indices retrieved by the non-functional analysis. They are specified by the developers at generic code level through annotations attached to methods and are then automatically "injected" into the application alternatives by CHAMELEON. Upon service publication, code-embedded SLSs are then combined with the SLSs specified by the service provider hence contributing to determine the final SLSs offered by the different alternatives.

Figure 4 shows how adaptive PLASTIC services are published, discovered and accessed by describing the steps involved within the PLASTIC Service-oriented Interaction Pattern for the provision and consumption of adaptive services.

The service provider publishes into the *PLASTIC Registry* the service description in terms of both functional specifications and associated offered SLSs (1). Specif-

Fig. 4 PLASTIC interaction
pattern

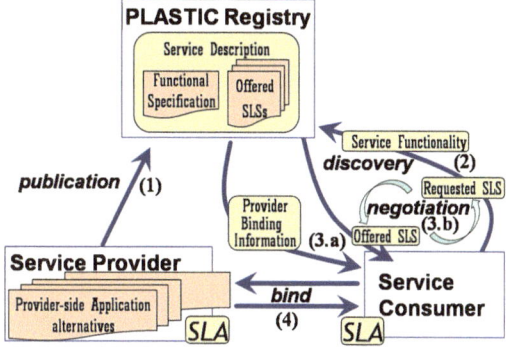

ically, a provider can publish a service with different SLSs, each one associated
to a different provider-side application alternative that represents a way of adapting the service. The service consumer queries the PLASTIC registry for a service
functionality, additionally specifying the requested SLS (2). The PLASTIC registry
searches for service descriptions that satisfy the consumer request. If suitable service descriptions are present in the service registry, the service consumer can choose
one of them on the base of their offered SLSs. After the service consumer accepts
an offered SLS, the registry returns the actual reference to the provider-side application alternative that implements the (adapted) service with the accepted SLS (3.a).
Thus, the SLA can be established and the service consumption can take place (4).
If no suitable published service is able to directly and fully satisfy the requested
SLS, negotiation is necessary (3.b). The negotiation phase starts by offering a set of
alternative SLSs. The consumer can accept one of the proposed SLSs, or perform
an "adjusted" request by reiterating the process till an SLA is possibly reached. In
Fig. 4 the box *SLA* labeling the provider and the consumer represents the agreement
reached by both of them.

Hereafter, we describe some of the (run time) models defined for an eHealth
application that has been developed by using the PLASTIC methodologies and
tools previously introduced. However, at the end of the section, we will briefly describe the CHAMELEON framework and show an excerpt of the CHAMELEON-based
generic code, derived through model-to-code transformations, for the resource-
aware adaptable components implementing the modeled eHealth service. A detailed description of the CHAMELEON framework can be found in [5, 6, 8, 31].

A PLASTIC eHealth Application. The main purpose of the eHealth application
is to attend persons, which live in countryside and widespread areas. In particular, it
aims at distributing effectively existing assistant systems to mobile and remote patients and doctors, improving quality of service and system availability while giving
those users even the benefits of disconnected mobile operations. The main capabilities of the application are depicted in Fig. 5.

In case of an emergency, the patient sends an alarm that can be forwarded
to available resources that are not included in customary eHealth service deploy-
ments, such as relatives to the patient, rural doctors and social workers (this is the
AlarmManagement use case in the figure). This behavior is permitted only once

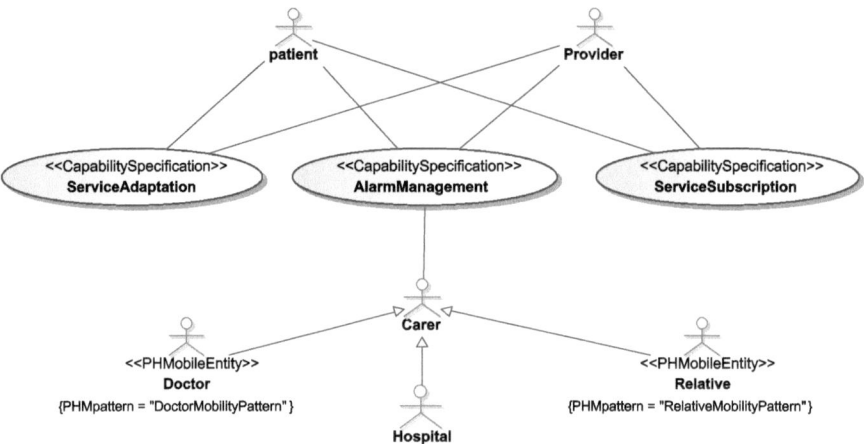

Fig. 5 eHealth use cases

Fig. 6 eHealth architecture

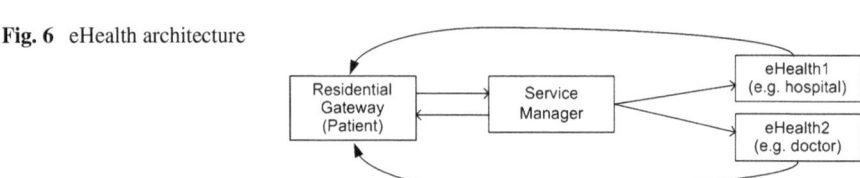

the patient has subscribed the service (`ServiceSubscription` use case). More-over, while using the service, the family supervisor context can change because of structural modifications, mobility, new supervisor is assigned to the customer etc. Structural modifications can occur also to the patient side that is new de-vices can be deployed and, hence, new device drivers are required and suitable (with respect to the new devices) versions of the application service must be de-ployed (`ServiceAdaptation` use case). The rest of the section focuses on the `AlarmManagement` use case only even though it provides the reader with all the required information to understand the application of the PLASTIC development process and its tool support.

The architecture of the eHealth application is depicted in Fig. 6. The patient is equipped with electronic devices and by means of a residential gateway it is in contact with specialists and relatives. In the `AlarmManagement` use case, the patient presses an alarm button and an alarm request is sent to the service manager through the residential gateway. The service manager attempts to notify `eHealth1` (in this case the hospital). If the request can be satisfied by the hospital an alarm notification is returned to the patient. Alternatively, the service manager tries the discovering of other registered eHealth services (e.g. a doctor or a relative) and sends them the alarm request taking into account a priority queue. An alarm notification is sent to the residential gateway by the reached eHealth service.

Following the PLASTIC development process, the specification of the eHealth application starts from the definition of the services that have to be aggregated or

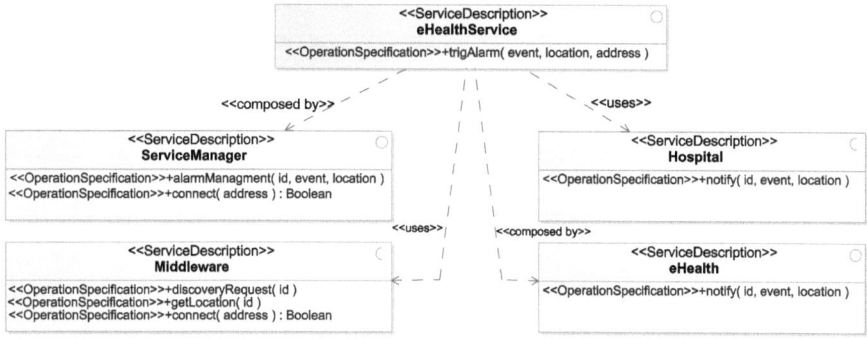

Fig. 7 Service description diagram

combined. For this purpose, the *service description diagram* in Fig. 7 is produced. In this specification, eHealthService is the front-end to many small services which can be PLASTIC services that still have to be developed (in this case referred by composed by stereotyped dependencies) or already existing services which are simply used by the other ones and referred in the model by means of uses stereotyped dependencies. For instance, eHealthService uses the Middleware intended to be an always available service that exports the methods of the PLASTIC middleware which supports the discovery, provisioning, and access of context-aware services over devices providing heterogeneous B3G networks access.

Once all services are defined, a number of *business process descriptions* have to be provided. In particular, for each capability of the larger services, a business process model has to be specified in order to describe the interactions among the involved smaller services. In Fig. 8 the trigAlarm and alarmManagement capabilities of the eHealthService and ServiceManager services, respectively are modeled. In particular, when the patient presses the alarm button, the trigAlarm operation of the eHealthService service is invoked. This opens a connection with the ServiceManager and invokes the alarmManagement operation (see Fig. 8.a). This operation is described in the right-hand side of the figure. According to the requirements summarized above, an alarm can be managed by the hospital (with a probability of 0.7 as specified by the non-functional annotation PAprob borrowed from the UML SPT Profile[3]). Alternatively, a relative or a doctor is notified (see the invoked notify operation of eHealth in the figure) after a discovery operation performed by exploiting the middleware facilities.

In general, a service can be implemented by one or more components and, in turn, a component can be used to implement one or more services. The PLASTIC approach proposes the use of the *service specification diagram* for defining the components implementing the "smaller" services. The diagram in Fig. 9 specifies the sample components that implement the eHealth service which will be de-

---

[3]http://www.omg.org/cgi-bin/doc?formal/2005-01-02.

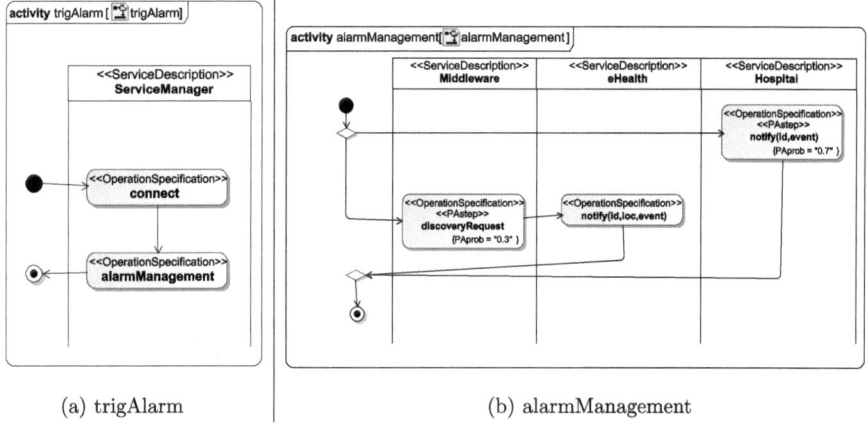

(a) trigAlarm   (b) alarmManagement

Fig. 8 Business process descriptions

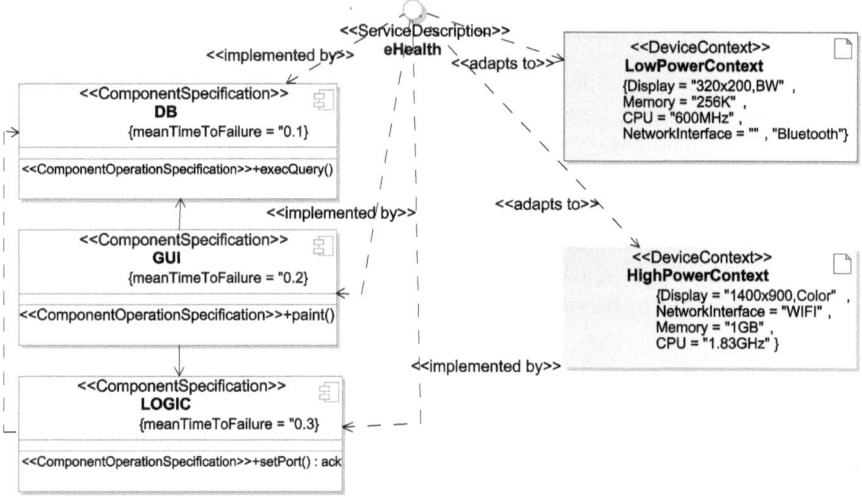

Fig. 9 Service specification diagram

ployed on the devices of the relatives and the doctors. The services installed on the residential gateway, in the service manager, and in the hospital are not taken into account here since they are not mobile and do not require context aware adaptations. According to Fig. 9, eHealth is implemented by three sample components: DB is devoted to the storing of data managed by the application; GUI offers the operations for creating windows, buttons, dialogs, menus and everything required for user interactions; LOGIC is a component that implements the logic of eHealth. The diagram contains also the description of the contexts in which the service will be able to adapt. In particular, eHealth can be deployed on two different contexts distinguished into LowPowerContext and HighPowerContext and described by

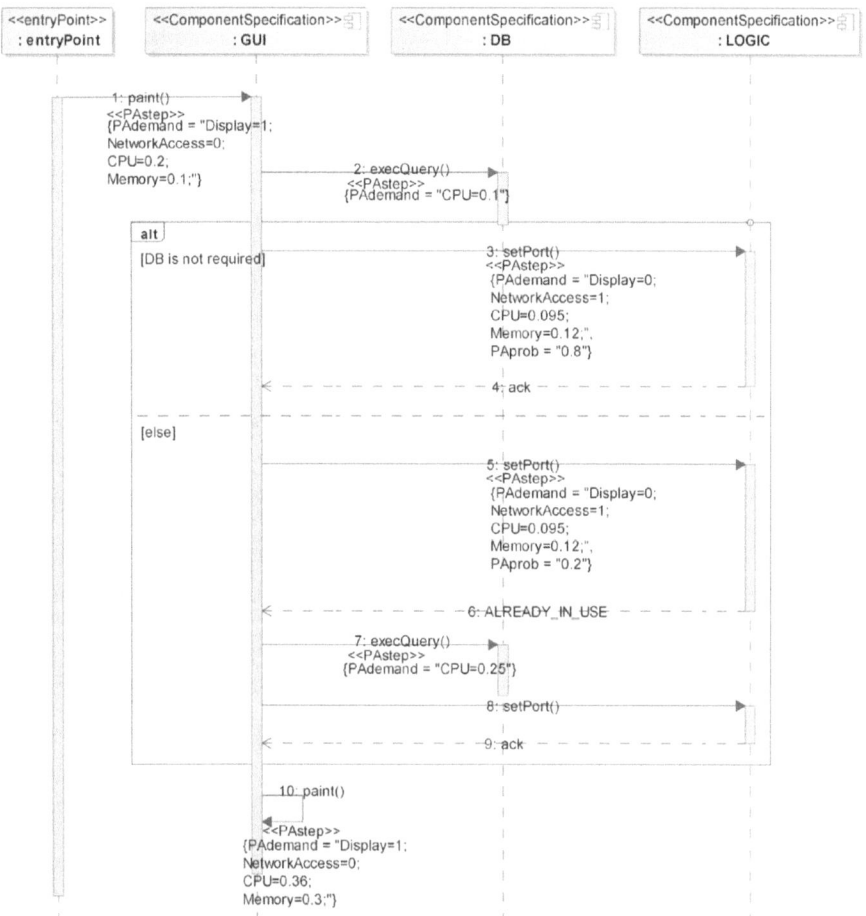

Fig. 10 Elementary service dynamics diagram

means of entries defining the device resources like CPU power, memory capacity, etc. In a service specification diagram, components can be annotated with QoS information like the `meanTimeToFailure` which is borrowed from [34] and which is an estimate of the mean time until a component's first failure. These information will be taken into account for non-functional analysis purposes.

Once the components implementing the `eHealth` service have been identified, their interactions can be specified. The *elementary service dynamics diagram* in Fig. 10 depicts the message exchanges that occur when the `notify` operation of the `eHealth` service is invoked to answer the patient that pressed the alarm button. The notification exploits the `execQuery()` operation to interact with the `DB` component, and the `setPort()` operation to open a connection with the patient. The model contains also non-functional annotations in order to enable performance analysis. In particular, taking into account the UML SPT profile, the message invo-

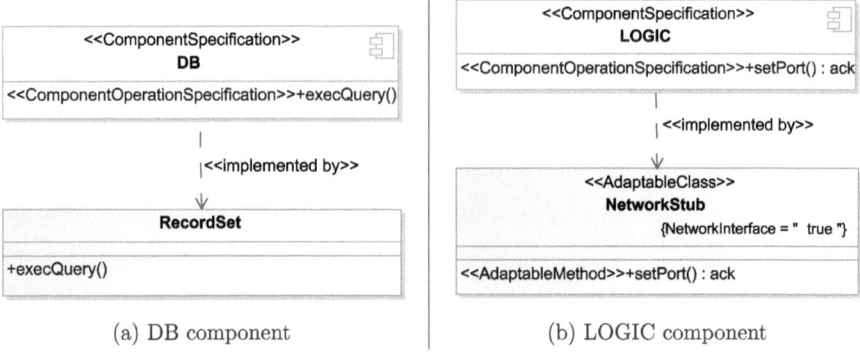

(a) DB component   (b) LOGIC component

Fig. 11 Component design diagrams

cations are PAStep stereotyped and tagged with additional information describing the resources required for their execution. For instance, the execution of the set-Port() operation can require more CPU in case more queries have to be performed on the data base.

In order to have a comprehensive description of eHealth, each component implementing the service need to be specified at a lower level of abstraction by means of *component design diagrams* like the ones in Fig. 11. In these diagrams, the classes implementing the DB and LOGIC components are modelled. As it will be clear later, the stereotype AdaptableClass is used to distinguish the classes which are adaptable according to specified resource annotations. For instance, the LOGIC component is implemented by means of the adaptable class NetworkStub, among others, which embodies a variability based on the resource NetworkInterface. The variability can be solved leading to the WIFI and Bluetooth alternatives with respect to the possible device contexts described in Fig. 9. Component implementations can also depend on non-adaptable classes (e.g. the class implementing the DB component in Fig. 11). This is the case of standard components that do not require resource adaptations.

To identify the physical mobile entities in the system we introduce some others modeling constructs like the «PHMobEntity» stereotype (see Doctor or Relative actor in the use case of Fig. 5). This stereotype has a tag value (PHMpattern) that points to the mobility pattern of the identified entity. Such mobility pattern is described by a *physical mobility pattern diagram* that is a *state diagram* where the states represent the system configurations (hardware plus software) the entity interacts with during his/its moves, while the arrows model the feasible moving among configurations. Each state is annotated with: (i) the name of the deployment diagram describing the configuration represented by the state (PHMobContextInstanceRef tag value), and (ii) the estimated total time the entity spends in the context during the observation interval (PHMobRestime).

In Fig. 12.a we report the mobility pattern for the doctor in the eHealth service. At home the doctor activates his device and the eHealth service starts its execution. During the working time, the doctor moves between the surgery and the houses of patients requiring assistance. The doctor service should be always available during the working time of the doctor and this implies an additional configuration that we model by means of the *transport* state.

The system configurations (or contexts) are described by deployment diagrams. One deployment diagram is associated to each different physical context. Nodes in the deployment are stereotyped with PHMobContextDescription having a tag value (ContextDescription) pointing to the description of the device/network characteristics represented by the node. In Fig. 12.b we report the configuration of the eHealth service for the doctor when s/he is in the surgery. The doctor runs the service (actually two components implementing the service) on his laptop and the available network connection is a WiFi network. The characteristics of the laptop and the provider server are described in the *HighPowerContext* description (see Fig. 9) while the network features are described in the NetworkContext description reported for simplicity in the deployment diagram itself.

The last phase of the development process focuses on the code derivation of the resource-aware adaptable components implementing the modeled eHealth service. Model-to-code transformations are used for this purpose. In particular, relying on the CHAMELEON programming model (see below), models are translated automatically into generic code skeletons (like the one in Listing 1) by means of a developed code generator based on the *Eclipse Java Emitter Template framework* (part of the EMF framework [15]). JSP-like templates define explicitly the code structure and get the data they need from the UML model of the specified service exported into EMF. With this generation engine, the generated code can be customized and then re-generated without losing already defined customizations.

With respect to service context-awareness and adaptability, a key role is played by the integration between analysis techniques (from which SLS is devised/refined) and the Model-to-code techniques. That is, the SLS (or an its part) drives the skeleton code generation. After the generation of the skeleton code has been done, the

```
1  adaptable public class NetworkStub {
2    ...
3    adaptable public void NetworkStub();
4    void setPort() {
5      */ Method definition */
6    }
7  }
8
9    alternative A1 adapts NetworkStub {
10     void setPort() {
11       */ Method definition that takes into account the WIFI resource*/
12     }
13   }
14
15   alternative A2 adapts NetworkStub {
16     void setPort() {
17       */ Method definition that takes into account the WIFI resource */
18     }
19   }
20 }
```

Listing 1 Fragment of the generated *NetworkStub* adaptable class

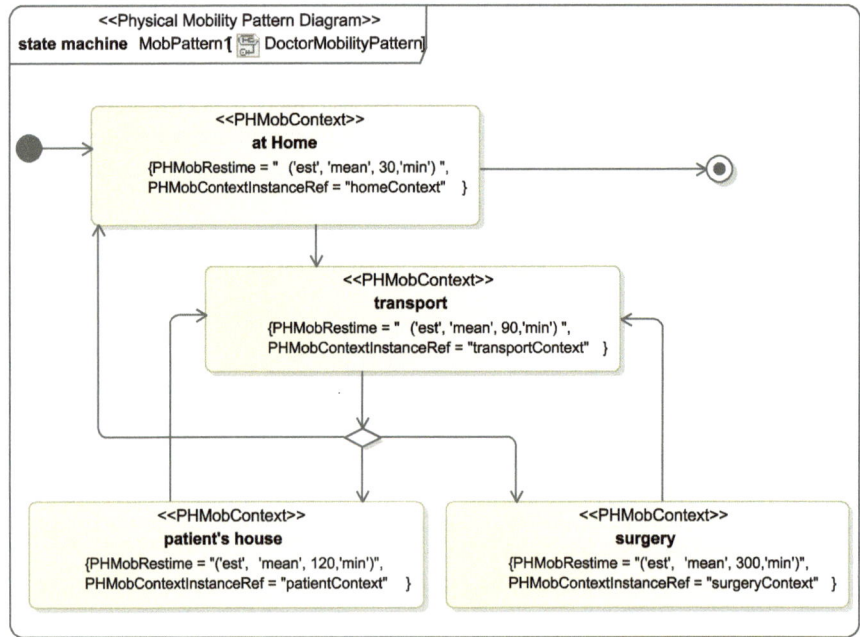

(a) Mobility Pattern

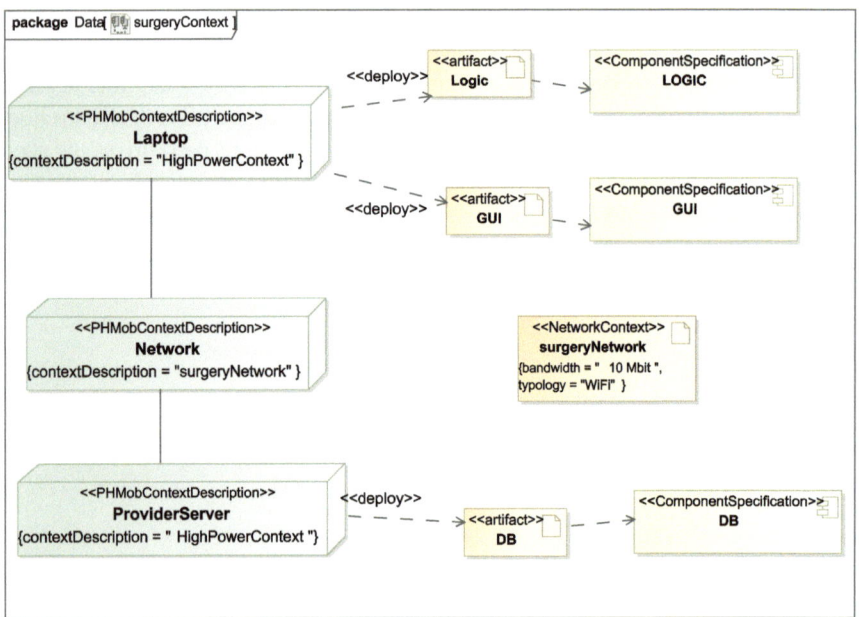

(b) Configuration

Fig. 12 Mobility pattern diagram

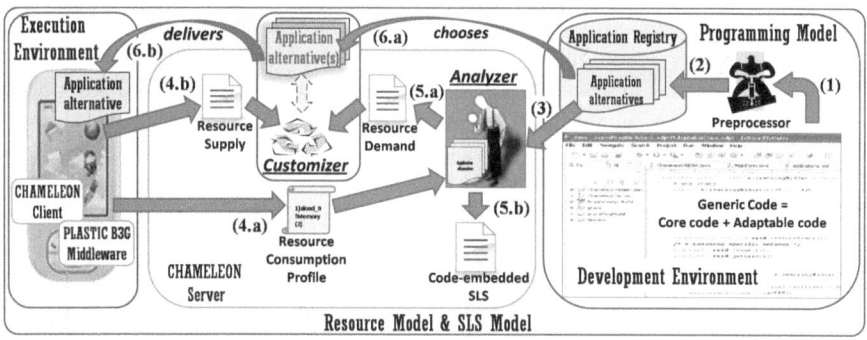

Fig. 13 CHAMELEON framework

specific service logic within the generic code has to be implemented still taking into account the SLS. This is done by using the CHAMELEON Development Environment (and hence the CHAMELEON Programming Model) we are going to present. Finally, the whole code is validated against the devised SLS and hence certified.

In the following we briefly describe the CHAMELEON framework and how it supports the implementation of PLASTIC adaptive services and their provision and consumption.

▶ **Programming Model**. Referring to right-hand side of Fig. 13, the *Development Environment* (DE) is based on a *Programming Model* that provides developers with a set of ad-hoc extensions to Java for easily specifying services code in a flexible and declarative way. As already mentioned, services code is a *generic* code that consists of two parts: the *core* and the *adaptable* code—see in Fig. 13 the screenshoot of our DE implemented as an Eclipse plugin [5]. The core code is the frozen portion of the application and represents its invariant semantics. The adaptable one represents the degree of variability that makes the code capable to adapt. The generic code is preprocessed by the CHAMELEON *Preprocessor* (1), also part of the DE, and a set of different standard Java application alternatives is automatically derived and stored into the *Application Registry* (2) (as part of the PLASTIC registry).

▶ **Resource and SLS Models**. The resource model is a formal model that allows the characterization of the resources needed to consume/provide a service and it is at the base of context-aware adaptation. The SLS model is a model that permits developers to attach non-functional information at generic code level through code-embedded SLSs and is used for SLS-based adaptation purposes.

▶ **Chameleon Server-Side**. Still referring to Fig. 13, the *Analyzer* (running on the CHAMELEON server) is an interpreter that, abstracting a standard JVM, is able to analyze the application alternatives (3) and derive their resource consumption (5.a) and the code-embedded SLSs (5.b). The analyzer is parametric with respect to the characteristics of the execution environment as described through the *Resource Consumptions Profile* sent by the device (4.a). The profile provides a characterization of the target execution environment, in terms of the impact that Java bytecode instructions have on the resources. Note that this impact depends on the execution environment since the same bytecode instruction may require different resources in different execution environments.

▶ **Chameleon Client-Side**. *PLASTIC-enabled device*s (see left-hand side of Fig. 13) are devices deploying and running the CHAMELEON *Client* component and the *PLASTIC B3G Middleware* [18] that together are able to retrieve contextual information. A PLASTIC-enabled device provides a declarative description of the execution context in terms of the resources it supplies (i.e., *Resource Supply*) and the resource consumption profile.

▶ **Customizer**. The resource demands (5.a) of the application alternatives together with the resource supply sent by the device (4.b) are used by the *Customizer* that is able to choose (6.a) and propose a set of "best" suited application alternatives, and deliver (6.b) consumer- and/or provider-side standard Java applications that (via the Over-The-Air (OTA) provisioning technique [1]) can be automatically deployed in the target devices for execution. The customizer bases on the notion of *compatibility* that is used to decide if an application alternative can run safely on the requesting device, i.e., if for every resource demanded by the alternative a "sufficient amount" is supplied by the execution environment.

4.2 The CONNECT Project

Our everyday activities are increasingly dependent upon the assistance of digital systems that pervade our living environment. However, the current ubiquity of digital systems is technology-dependent. The efficacy of integrating and composing networked systems is proportional to the level of interoperability of the systems' respective underlying technologies. This leads to a landscape of technological islands of networked systems, although interoperability bridges may possibly be deployed among them. Further, the fast pace at which technology evolves at all abstraction layers increasingly challenges the lifetime of networked systems in the digital environment.

The CONNECT project [21] aims at dropping the heterogeneity barriers that prevent networked systems from being eternal, thus enabling the continuous composition of networked systems to respond to the evolution of functionalities provided to and/or required from the networked environment, independently of the embedded software technologies. CONNECT specifically targets the dynamic synthesis of connectors via which networked systems communicate. The resulting *emergent connectors* (or CONNECTors) then compose and further adapt the interaction protocols run by the connected systems, which realize application- down to middleware-layer protocols.

The CONNECT synthesis process relies on a formal foundation for connectors, which allows learning, reasoning about and adapting the interaction behavior of networked systems. With respect to PLASTIC and PFM below (even though towards completely different goals), CONNECT operates a drastic shift by learning, reasoning about and synthesizing connector behavior *at run time*. Indeed, the use of

Fig. 14 CONNECTors

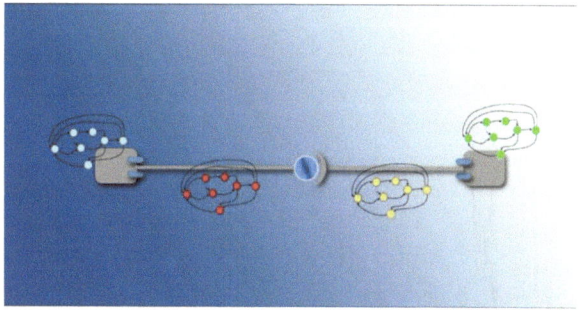

connector specifications pioneered by the software architecture research field has mainly been considered as a design-time concern, for which automated reasoning is now getting practical even if limitations remain. On the other hand, recent effort in the semantic Web domain brings ontology-based semantic knowledge and reasoning at run time but networked system solutions based thereupon are currently mainly focused on the functional behavior of networked systems, with few attempts to capture their interaction behavior as well as non-functional properties. After the first year, the approach we have planned to undertake within CONNECT aims at learning the interaction protocols (both application and middleware layer) behavior by observing the interactions of the networked systems and the corresponding models, i.e., extended LTSs (see Fig. 14), are derived and exploited at run time for generating connectors on the fly.

Towards this aim, CONNECT raises a set of unique challenges in the area of software systems engineering, from theoretical foundations to specify the interaction behavior of networked systems to run time methods and tools to turn specifications into running protocols, and vice versa. CONNECT addresses several key challenges: (i) interoperability that increasingly needs to be overcome by networked systems. This calls for a paradigm shift that goes beyond today's middleware solutions and effectively lies in the dynamic synthesis of emergent connectors. (ii) Theories for emergent connectors, (iii) dynamic connector behavior learning and (iv) synthesis, and (v) ensuring dependability of the overall synthesis process.

In the following we describes our early experience in the dynamic connector synthesis. With the aim of achieving eternal universal interoperability among heterogeneous networked systems, a key concept of CONNECT is synthesizing new interaction behaviors out of the ones implemented by the systems to be made interoperable, and further generating corresponding CONNECTors to bridge protocols. So far, we have devised a preliminary theory of *mediating connectors* (also called *mediators*).

The idea is to formally characterize mediators between mismatching protocols by rigorously defining, in particular, the necessary conditions that must hold for protocols to be mediated. These conditions will led to the definition of complex protocol matching and mapping relationships. The relationships represent two essential operations for the dynamic synthesis of mediating connectors to enable eternal networked systems. In fact, the matching relationship allows the rigorous characterization of the conditions that must hold for two heterogeneous protocols in order

Fig. 15 CONNECTor
synthesis overview

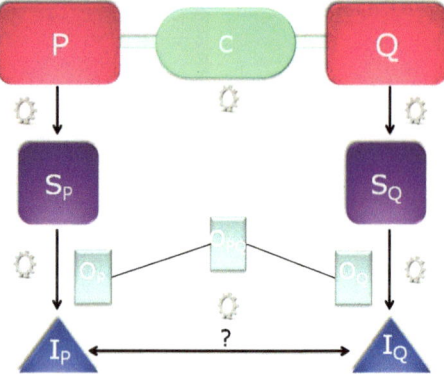

to interoperate through a mediator connector. Thus it allows one to state/check the
existence of a mediator for two heterogeneous protocols. The mapping relationship
allows the formal definition of the algorithm that should be performed in order to automatically synthesize the required mediator. Both relationships will be defined with
respect to a behavioral model of the networked systems' interaction protocol. Thus,
also in CONNECT, managing models at run time during the (synthesis) process is
a key aspect and models play a key role in synthesizing the connector behavior and
in validating that, through it, the desired system dependability is achieved.

Overview of the Automated CONNECTor Synthesis Approach. Starting from
two protocols, we want to check if their functionalities match, i.e., if the interacting
parties may coordinate and achieve their respective goals. If this is the case, then
we synthesize a mediator, otherwise they cannot communicate, at least based on our
methodology. Figure 15 depicts the overall idea.

The basic ingredients are: (i) the behavior of two protocols represented by LTSs
P and Q, (ii) two ontologies O_P and O_Q describing the meaning of P and Q
actions, and (iii) a mapping O_{PQ} between the two ontologies. Note that, when referring to protocol behavior, we mean the actions of a networked system that are
observable at the interface level, i.e., its input/output actions. We further consider
protocols P and Q that are minimal where we recall that every finite LTS has a
unique minimal representative. Based on the structural characteristics of the two
protocols, we build an abstraction for each of them, which we call structure. For P
and Q, the abstraction is identified in the figure by S_P and S_Q, respectively. Then,
using the ontology mapping function, we find the common language for the two
protocols (pairs of words with the same meaning). This leads us to highlight the
induced LTSs for both protocols (see I_P and I_Q), i.e., the structures where only
the words belonging to the common language are highlighted. Finally, we check if
the induced LTSs have a functional matching relation. In other words, we check if
part of the provided/required functionalities of the two protocols are similar, i.e.,
are equivalent according to a suitable functional matching relation that we briefly
describe below. If this is the case, then we synthesize a mediator, otherwise we cannot provide a mediator to let them communicate. Given two protocols P and Q, the
mediator C that we synthesize is such that when building the parallel composition

$P|Q|C$, the protocols P, Q are able to communicate to evolve to their final states. This is achievable by checking that the observable behaviors of P, Q are equivalent through a suitable notion of bisimilarity. The following briefly describes our protocol matching and mapping relationships. The former allows for checking whether there exists a mediator that makes two heterogeneous protocol interoperate. The latter allows for the definition of the algorithm that has to be performed in order to automatically synthesize the mediator.

CONNECT Matching Relationship. It defines necessary conditions that must hold in order for a set of networked systems to interoperate through a mediating CONNECTor. The matching condition is that they have complementary behaviors. Moreover, two functionalities are complementary if they can be abstracted by the same model under a suitable notion of behavioral equivalence that is driven by ontological information. If the functionalities of two networked systems match and, hence, the two networked systems perform complementary functionalities, then they can interoperate via a suitable mediating connector. In other words, if the matching relationship is satisfied, then there exists a mediating connector making the two networked systems interoperate. This mediating connector is abstracted by a mapping relationship. The synthesized mediator provides complementary interfaces to the two protocols, and manages exchange of information between the two (at the right synchronization point) driven by the mapping relationship.

4.3 The PFM Project

A desirable characteristic of software systems, in general, is the ability to continue to properly work even after damages and system misbehaviors are experienced. This ability should allow for repairing the system configuration and maintaining a certain level of quality of service (e.g., performance and availability). To this aim, a crucial role is played by the ability of the system to react and adapt automatically (i.e., without the intervention of a human administrator) and dynamically (i.e., without service interruption, or with a minimal one).

This section briefly discusses PFM, a framework to manage performance of software system at run time based on monitoring and model-based performance evaluation [17]. The approach makes use of performance models as abstractions of the managed application that, although specified at design time, are also available at run time when the system is operating. The framework monitors the performance of the application and, when a performance problem occurs, it decides the new application configuration on the basis of feedback provided by the on-line evaluation of performance models. The main characteristic of this approach is the way reconfiguration alternatives are generated. In fact, differently from other approaches, PFM does not rely on a fixed repository of predefined configurations, rather, starting from the data retrieved by the on-line monitoring of the performance models (that represents a snapshot of the current "performance state"), a number of new configuration alternatives are dynamically generated by applying the rules defined within the reconfiguration policy. Once such alternatives have been generated the on-line evaluation is performed by predicting which one of them is most suitable for resolving the problem occurred. In particular, the choice of the new system configuration might consider several factors, such as, for example, security and reliability of the application, and resources needed to implement the new configuration.

In this approach performance evaluation models are used to predict the system performance of the next system reconfiguration alternative. The performance models are "product form QNs". To this aim, each eligible system configuration is described by means of a predictive model instantiated with the actual values observed over the system until the moment of the performance alarm. The models are then evaluated and on the basis of the obtained results the framework decides the reconfiguration to perform over the software system. Therefore, the predictive models, representing the system alternatives, are evaluated at run time and this poses strong requirements on the models themselves. PMF has been experimented to manage the performance of the PFM publish/subscribe middleware [16, 19]. The experiment shows that the usage of predictive models improves the decision step. The system reconfigured according to the chosen alternative has better performance than the other alternatives generated during the reconfiguration process. The configuration alternatives we experimented all deal with structural changes of the PFM network topology in order to improve messages routing.

Figures 16(a) and 16(b) describe the processes and flow of the activities in an adaptation step of the PFM framework, respectively. In particular, with reference to Fig. 16(a), Fig. 16(b) outlines a reconfiguration loop exploding the Plan Changes step (see label 2). The application configuration is modelled by means of a performance model at the software architecture level (see label 1). During the monitoring the framework observes a performance problem and throws an alarm. After the analysis of the monitored data, the plan changes activity starts. Inputs of this activity are the performance model of the current running system configuration and the monitored data. Given the set of reconfiguration policies RP_i defined for the

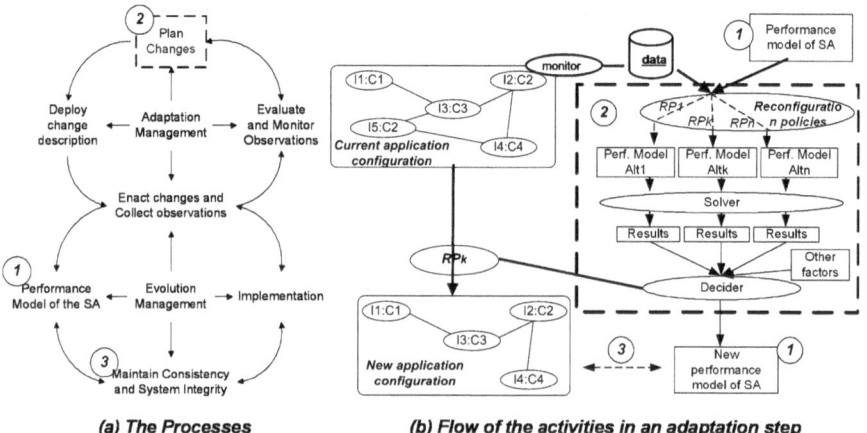

(a) The Processes   (b) Flow of the activities in an adaptation step

Fig. 16 Adaptation for performance

application, a set of suitable reconfiguration alternatives is generated. Each alternative is modelled by means of a performance model, created on-the-fly by modifying the current performance model. Each model is initialized with the monitored data, and then evaluated by using a solver tool. Finally, the evaluation results are compared, and the most rewarding configuration is selected and applied to the system. This step (step labeled with 3) maintains by construction the consistency among the (new) performance model and the system configuration.

5 Concluding Remarks

In this paper we have discussed our thesis on software in the future. Softure requires to rethink the whole software engineering process since it never stabilizes, but it is permanently under maintenance. Software evolution, which is traditionally practiced as an off-line activity, must often be accommodated at run time for Softure.

Run time models, languages and methodologies will play a key role in achieving adaptability and dependability for future software applications. In a broader software engineering perspective it is therefore mandatory to reconcile the static/compile time development approach to the dynamic/interpreter oriented one, thus making models and validation technique manageable lightweight tools for run time use. There are several challenges that are far to be solved in this domain.

We reported three experiences to adaptive software development and provision as different instances of the problem raised by Softure. These experiences represent our attempts towards the non trivial concrete instantiation of the Softure development process. They are not entirely innovative *per se* rather they are used in a completely new and non trivial fashion. The three experienced approaches are different in nature with respect to the usage degree of models at run time. In Fig. 17, we informally compare the three approaches by showing the tendency of models usage along the software life cycle. From compile to run time, the three diagrams show the percentage of the total number of models used by each approach. This dimension gives us a means to evaluate the underlying development processes with respect to the requirements dictated by Softure. The PFM, PLASTIC, and CONNECT development processes are *softure development processes* since they all allow for the construction of self-adaptive systems that manage models at run time in order to adapt to possible changes. In PFM, all the models are built at design-time, and those needed for performance prediction and dynamic reconfiguration are kept at run time. In PLASTIC, not all the models are built at design-time. Part of them plus new ones, generated during later phases, are kept at run time in order to perform context-aware and SLS-based adaptation. In CONNECT, only ontological information and the related models are available at design-time. By exploiting learning and synthesis techniques, all the needed models are automatically inferred and used at run time in order to achieve dynamic interoperability. It is worth noting that, due to a higher percentage of models managed at run time, in CONNECT the efficiency of the dynamic model-based analysis is more crucial.

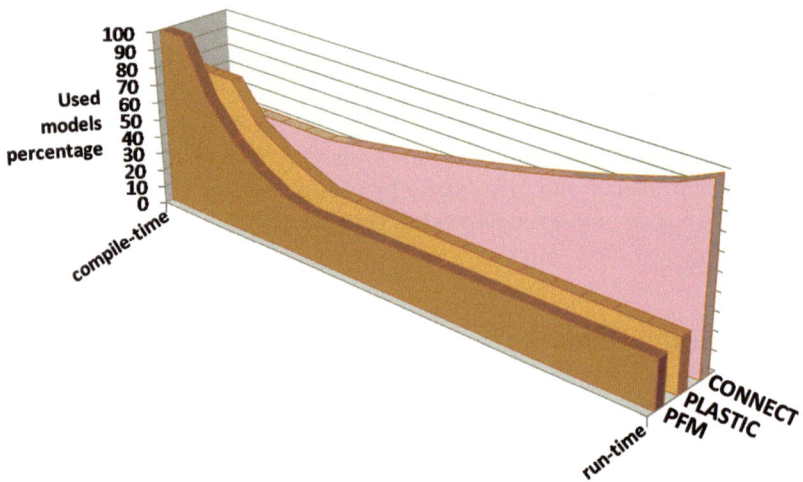

Fig. 17 Models@run.time degree

Summarizing our message is that in the Softure domain it is important to think and research *point to point* theories and techniques but it is mandatory to re-think the whole development process breaking the traditional division among development phases by moving some activities from design-time to deployment- and run time, hence asking for both more efficient verification and validation techniques and new modeling notations and tools. Furthermore, to support dynamic adaptation, the focus of software development should shift from a traditional and static approach where most of code is written from scratch to a more reuse-oriented and dynamic approach where the needed components or services are first discovered and then assembled together to form the system to be executed. This lead to develop support for an evolutionary development process made of continuous *discover-assemble-execute* iterations. Development methodologies and tools must account in a rigorous way of *quantitative* concerns, allowing programmers to deal with these concerns declaratively. Models must become simpler and lighter by exploiting compositionality and partial evaluation techniques. Innovative development processes should be defined to properly reflect these new concerns arising from software for ubiquitous computing.

References

[1] Over-The-Air (OTA). http://developers.sun.com/mobility/midp/articles/ota/
[2] Aldrich, J., Chambers, C., Notkin, D.: Architectural reasoning in archjava. In: ECOOP '02: Proceedings of the 16th European Conference on Object-Oriented Programming, pp. 334–367. Springer, London (2002)
[3] Aldrich, J., Chambers, C., Notkin, D.: Archjava: connecting software architecture to implementation. In: ICSE '02: Proceedings of the 24th International Conference on Software Engineering, pp. 187–197. ACM, New York (2002)

[4] Allen, R., Garlan, D.: A formal basis for architectural connection. ACM Trans. Softw. Eng. Methodol. **6**(3), 213–249 (1997)

[5] Autili, M., Benedetto, P.D., Inverardi, P.: CHAMELEON Project - SEA group. http://di.univaq.it/chameleon/

[6] Autili, M., Benedetto, P.D., Inverardi, P.: CHAMELEON Project - SEA group. http://sourceforge.net/projects/uda-chameleon/

[7] Autili, M., Berardinelli, L., Cortellessa, V., Di Marco, A., Di Ruscio, D., Inverardi, P., Tivoli, M.: A development process for self-adapting service oriented applications. In: Proc. of ICSOC, Vienna, Austria, Sept. 2007

[8] Autili, M., Benedetto, P.D., Inverardi, P.: Context-aware adaptive services: the plastic approach. In: Chechik, M., Wirsing, M. (eds.) FASE. Lecture Notes in Computer Science, vol. 5503, pp. 124–139. Springer, Berlin (2009)

[9] Baldauf, M., Dustdar, S., Rosenberg, F.: A survey on context-aware systems. Int. J. Ad Hoc Ubiq. Comput. **2**(4), 263–277 (2007)

[10] Balsamo, S., Di Marco, A., Inverardi, P., Simeoni, M.: Model-based performance prediction in software development: A survey. IEEE Trans. Softw. Eng. **30**(5), 295–310 (2004)

[11] Baresi, L., Heckel, R., Thone, S., Varro', D.: Style-based refinement of dynamic software architectures. In: WICSA '04: Proceedings of the Fourth Working IEEE/IFIP Conference on Software Architecture, p. 155. IEEE Computer Society, Washington (2004)

[12] Barthe, G.: MOBIUS, Securing the Next Generation of Java-Based Global Computers, ERCIM News (2005)

[13] Bertolino, A., Angelis, G.D., Di Marco, A., Inverardi, P., Sabetta, A., Tivoli, M.: A framework for analyzing and testing the performance of software services. In: In Proc. of the 3rd ISoLA, vol. 17. Springer, Berlin (2008)

[14] Bucchiarone, A., Pelliccione, P., Vattani, C., Runge, O.: Self-repairing systems modeling and verification using agg. In: WICSA/ECSA, pp. 181–190 (2009)

[15] Budinsky, F., Steinberg, D., Merks, E., Ellersick, R., Grose, T.J.: Eclipse Modeling Framework. Addison-Wesley, Reading (2003)

[16] Caporuscio, M., Carzaniga, A., Wolf, A.L.: Design and evaluation of a support service for mobile, wireless publish/subscribe applications. IEEE Trans. Softw. Eng. **29**(12), 1059–1071 (2003)

[17] Caporuscio, M., Di Marco, A., Inverardi, P.: Model-based system reconfiguration for dynamic performance management. J. Syst. Softw. **80**(4), 455–473 (2007). doi:10.1016/j.jss.2006.07.039

[18] Caporuscio, M., Raverdy, P.-G., Moungla, H., Issarny, V.: ubiSOAP: A service oriented middleware for seamless networking. In: Proc. of 6th ICSOC (2008)

[19] Carzaniga, A., Rosenblum, D.S., Wolf, A.L.: Design and evaluation of a wide-area event notification service. Foundations of Intrusion Tolerant Systems (2003). doi:10.1109/FITS.2003.1264940

[20] Cheng, B.H.C., de Lemos, R., Giese, H., Inverardi, P., Magee, J. (eds.): Software Engineering for Self-adaptive Systems [outcome of a Dagstuhl Seminar]. Lecture Notes in Computer Science, vol. 5525. Springer, Berlin (2009)

[21] CONNECT FET Project. Home page on line at: http://connect-forever.eu/

[22] Ehrig, H., Ermel, C., Runge, O., Bucchiarone, A., Pelliccione, P.: Formal analysis and verification of self-healing systems. In: FASE, pp. 139–153 (2010)

[23] Georgiadis, I., Magee, J., Kramer, J.: Self-organising software architectures for distributed systems. In: WOSS '02: Proceedings of the First Workshop on Self-healing Systems, pp. 33–38. ACM, New York (2002)

[24] Grassi, V., Mirandola, R., Sabetta, A.: A model-driven approach to performability analysis of dynamically reconfigurable component-based systems. In: WOSP, pp. 103–114 (2007)

[25] Hirsch, D., Inverardi, P., Montanari, U.: Graph grammars and constraint solving for software architecture styles. In: ISAW '98: Proceedings of the Third International Workshop on Software Architecture, pp. 69–72. ACM, New York (1998)

[26] Hirschfeld, R., Costanza, P., Nierstrasz, O.: Context-oriented programming. J. Object Technol. **7**(3), 125–151 (2008)

[27] IFIP WG 10.4 on Dependable Computing and Fault Tolerance: http://www.dependability. org/wg10.4/
[28] Inverardi, P., Tivoli, M.: The future of software: adaptation and dependability, pp. 1–31 (2009). doi:10.1007/978-3-540-95888-8_1
[29] Skene, J., Lamanna, D., Emmerich, W.: Precise service level agreements. In: Proc. of the 26th ICSE, Edinburgh, UK, pp. 179–188 (2004)
[30] Le Metayer, D.: Describing software architecture styles using graph grammars. IEEE Trans. Softw. Eng. **24**(7), 521–533 (1998)
[31] Autili, M., Di Benedetto, P., Inverardi, P., Tamburri, D.A.: Towards self-evolving context-aware services. In: Proc. of Context-aware Adaptation Mechanisms for Pervasive and Ubiquitous Services (CAMPUS), DisCoTec'08 vol. 11 (2008) http://eceasst.cs.tu-berlin.de/index.php/eceasst/issue/view/18
[32] Magee, J., Kramer, J.: Dynamic structure in software architectures. SIGSOFT Softw. Eng. Notes **21**(6), 3–14 (1996)
[33] Necula, G.C.: Proof-Carrying Code, pp. 106–119. ACM Press, New York (1997)
[34] OMG: UML Profile for Modeling Quality of Service and Fault Tolerance Characteristics and Mechanisms (2006) Version 1.0, formal/06-05-02
[35] OMG: UML Profile for Modeling and Analysis of Real-time and Embedded Systems (2009). http://www.omg.org/spec/MARTE/1.0/
[36] PLASTIC IST Project. Home page on line at: http://www.ist-plastic.org
[37] Raimondi, F., Skene, J., Emmerich, W.: Efficient online monitoring of web-service SLAs. In: Proc. of the 16th ACM SIGSOFT/FSE, Nov. 2008
[38] Schilit, B., Adams, N., Want, R.: Context-aware computing applications. In: IEEE Workshop on Mobile Computing Systems and Applications, Santa Cruz, CA, US (1994)
[39] Taentzer, G., Goedicke, M., Meyer, T.: Dynamic change management by distributed graph transformation: towards configurable distributed systems. In: TAGT'98: Selected papers from the 6th International Workshop on Theory and Application of Graph Transformations, pp. 179–193. Springer, London (2000)
[40] Hong, J.-Y., Suh, E.-H., Kim, S.-J.: Context-aware systems: A literature review and classification. Expert Syst. Appl. **36**(4), 8509–8522 (2009)
[41] Zahariadis, T., Doshi, B.: Applications and services for the B3G/4G era. IEEE Wirel. Commun. **11**(5) (2004)

M. Autili (✉)
Dipartimento di Informatica, Università degli Studi di L'Aquila, Coppito, Italy
e-mail: marco.autili@di.univaq.it

P. Inverardi
Dipartimento di Informatica, Università degli Studi di L'Aquila, Coppito, Italy
e-mail: paola.inverardi@di.univaq.it

M. Tivoli
Dipartimento di Informatica, Università degli Studi di L'Aquila, Coppito, Italy
e-mail: massimo.tivoli@di.univaq.it

On the Modeling and Management of Cloud Data Analytics

Claris Castillo, Asser Tantawi, Malgorzata Steinder, and Giovanni Pacifici

Abstract A new era is dawning where vast amount of data is subjected to intensive analysis in a cloud computing environment. Over the years, data about a myriad of things, ranging from user clicks to galaxies, have been accumulated, and continue to be collected, on storage media. The increasing availability of such data, along with the abundant supply of compute power and the urge to create useful knowledge, gave rise to a new data analytics paradigm in which data is subjected to intensive analysis, and additional data is created in the process. Meanwhile, a new cloud computing environment has emerged where seemingly limitless compute and storage resources are being provided to host computation and data for multiple users through virtualization technologies. Such a cloud environment is becoming the home for data analytics. Consequently, providing good performance at run-time to data analytics workload is an important issue for cloud management. In this paper, we provide an overview of the data analytics and cloud environment landscapes, and investigate the performance management issues related to running data analytics in the cloud. In particular, we focus on topics such as workload characterization, profiling analytics applications and their pattern of data usage, cloud resource allocation, placement of computation and data and their dynamic migration in the cloud, and performance prediction. In solving such management problems one relies on various run-time analytic models. We discuss approaches for modeling and optimizing the dynamic data analytics workload in the cloud environment. All along, we use the Map-Reduce paradigm as an illustration of data analytics.

Keywords Data analytics · Cloud computing · Map-Reduce · Hadoop · Data placement · Inventory modeling

1 Introduction

Data analytics refers to the process of inspecting, cleaning, transforming, and modeling data with the goal of highlighting useful information, suggesting conclusions,

D. Ardagna, L. Zhang (eds.), *Run-time Models for Self-managing Systems and Applications*, 153–174, Autonomic Systems, DOI 10.1007/978-3-0346-0433-8_7, © Springer Basel AG 2010

and supporting decision making [1]. Data analytic tools have been crucial to the success of science as well as business. For instance, in biological sciences, multiple data mining techniques have been developed and used to expedite the discovery of the human genome [2]. Business analytics, on the other hand, have been essential for companies to differentiate themselves from their competitors, by giving them deeper insight into market dynamics [3].

In the past, only large enterprises and the governments had the means to acquire, store, and process large volumes of data. This landscape is changing due to the following developments.

- **Data availability and pervasiveness**. To a large extent, the growth in data volume has been driven by the proliferation and pervasiveness of devices equipped with sensors, such as mobile phones and high resolution digital cameras which are continuously capturing and transferring high volumes of raw data across the Globe [4].
- **Reduction of storage cost**. The cost of storage has reduced dramatically in the last decade. Thus, making cost-effective for institutions and individuals to retain large volumes of data. Such realization has led more businesses to rely on data analytic techniques to differentiate themselves from their competitors; and to scientists to expand their data universe and gain better insight of complex phenomena.
- **Adoption of the *Cloud Computing* paradigm**. With the adoption of the *Cloud Computing* paradigm and its business model, i.e., charge model based on *actual* resource usage, users can achieve complex data analytic tasks on large data sets without incurring additional ownership and maintenance cost. This advance plays a pivotal role in the adoption and pervasiveness of data analytics today and in the future. In fact, few Internet *data-marts* offering Cloud-like services such as data hosting, data visualization and data analytics have successfully established themselves in the Cloud domain [5–8].
- **Emergence of new programming paradigms**. Crucial to the *democratization* of data analytics across the industry and research communities has been the emergence of new programming paradigms that enable the efficient processing of large data sets on clusters of commodity hardware, e.g., Map-Reduce [9] and Pig [10]. More importantly, the development of *open source* software frameworks— Hadoop [11]—to support these new programming models have promoted their further development and adoption.

As a result of these advances a new class of Internet services is evolving, data analytic clouds, which offer data storage, data management, compute resources and data analytic tools. A user gains access to these services by specifying a data analytic query in a high-level query language, which the platform parses, parallelizes and executes with a near real-time efficiency.

In this paper, we provide an overview of the data analytics landscape, and investigate the performance management issues related to running data analytics in the cloud. The nature of the applications providing data analytic services in terms of their resource needs is that they are highly dynamic and vary during run-time based on the data and the analytic operations. Moreover, the underlying cloud environment which provides the needed virtual resources is highly dynamic as it attempts to migrate and balance its vast physical resources among a large number of users. It is apparent, therefore, that run-time models are crucial in this data analytic cloud environment to provide the management functions needed for its efficient operation.

The paper is organized as follows. In Sect. 2, we consider large-scale technologies related to data computation and storage, then present the Map-Reduce paradigm as an example of data analytics. The performance management issues encountered in data analytic clouds are discussed in Sect. 3. Then, in Sect. 4, we consider a particular management problem, namely data placement, and propose promising modeling and optimization techniques that are borrowed from the field of multi-stage inventory control. Section 5 concludes the paper.

2 Data Analysis at a Large Scale

Data analytics is a process of inspecting, organizing, filtering, and transforming and modeling data with the objective of extracting useful information. Numerous techniques and tools exist to perform data analysis in the areas of statistical modeling, predictive analysis, data mining, business intelligence, text analysis, image recognition, among others. Recently, it has become necessary to analyze very large amount of data. This necessitates parallel processing of potentially distributed data sets.

A key component of distributed data analytics is a collection of parallel data analytic algorithms. The research on adapting the existing data analytic techniques to the parallel world is in fact ongoing. Our focus in this paper is on the second key component—a middleware platform that permits the execution of such parallel data analytics computations and on the management techniques it needs to provide.

2.1 Parallel DBMS

Several platforms for distributed data analysis have been proposed starting with parallel database in the 80s. Parallel databases work by partitioning the data among a set of instances in a shared-nothing architecture [12] and transforming an SQL query in a dataflow whose operators are parallelized among the instances. Parallel databases come with efficient means to store the data (such as a column store [13]) and highly efficient query optimization algorithms. However, they generally cannot deal with data stored in flat files on disk, and they require data to conform to a defined schema. We are also not familiar with any study proving the scalability of parallel DBMSs beyond hundreds of distributed nodes [14]. With this limitation, huge data sets may be processed only if powerful (and hence expensive) hardware is used.

2.2 Map-Reduce Framework

These issues are addressed by the Map-Reduce framework, which has been proposed as a way to analyze large data sets on a cluster of computers [9]. Map-Reduce
allows a programmer to specify two operators, *map*, which maps input key/value
pairs into an intermediate set of key value pairs and *reduce*, which merges intermediate values with the same key to produce a single result, as illustrated in Fig. 1.
Optionally, a job includes a combiner function that takes a key and a subset of
associated values and produces a single value that effectively represents (for the
purposes of producing the job output) the given subset of values. This function is
allowed to be interposed between the map and reduce functions, and can be useful
when it efficiently reduces the amount of data to be handled in later processing. The
Map-Reduce framework executes these operators in an embarrassingly parallel and
fault tolerant manner.

However, the Map-Reduce framework suffers from certain inefficiencies related
to distributed query processing and data management, which have been solved in
the parallel database systems, as discussed in [15]. A hybrid approach has been
investigated in [14].

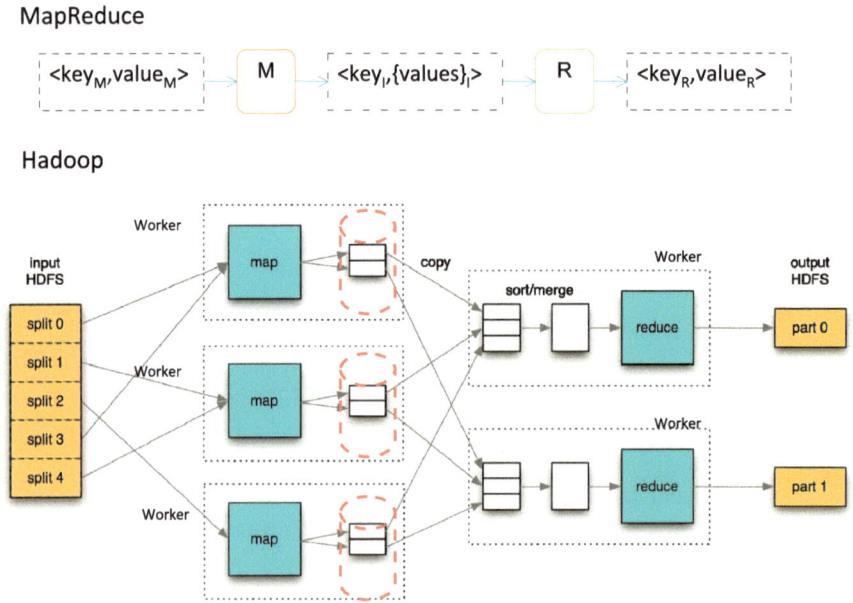

Fig. 1 The Map-Reduce programming model and Hadoop framework

2.2.1 Hadoop

Hadoop [11] is an open-source implementation of Map-Reduce framework. Its main components are the Map-Reduce engine and the Hadoop File System (HDFS).

HDFS is a distributed filesystem similar to the Google File System (GFS). It is designed to provide high streaming throughput to large, write-once-read-many-times files. It is designed to run on a collection of commodity machines, and is thus designed with fault tolerance in mind. A file is stored as a sequence of large blocks; the typical block size is 64 MB. Each block is replicated for fault tolerance; the default number of copies is three. The operation of writing a block is done synchronously on all the copies.

The Hadoop Map-Reduce engine is a Java-based platform that supports the Map-Reduce programming model [9]. A job's input is anything that implements a certain interface for producing job input records; Hadoop includes a framework that is commonly used to parse job input from an HDFS file. Similarly, a job's output can be written to anything that implements a certain interface for consuming job output records; Hadoop includes a framework that is commonly used to write job output into HDFS.

Recall that Map-Reduce is a parallel programming paradigm, therefore, its implementation is fully parallelized. The running of a job is organized into two stages of tasks; within each stage the tasks are independent. The first stage consists of *map tasks*, and the second consists of *reduce tasks*. The platform takes care of collecting all the values associated in map output with a given key and passing them to an invocation of the reduce function. This re-organization of the intermediate data (that is the data output by the map function, input to the reduce function) is an important part of what the platform does, and is split between the map tasks and the reduce tasks. The Hadoop Map-Reduce layer stores intermediate data in the local filesystems (not HDFS) of the machines running the map and reduce functions; this is an important part of that layer's design for fault tolerance. A job specifies how it is divided into tasks. The input is divided into chunks called *splits*; each map task processes one *input split*. The intermediate data is divided by a partition function on intermediate keys. A job specifies the number of partitions and the partition function. There is one reduce task per partition. The partition function maps a key into the partition number.

The main principle behind the Hadoop framework is that computations are done with as little data movement as possible. This is effectively achieved by the scheduler in the following manner: upon assigning a *map* task to a worker node, the scheduler favors a task whose *input split* is stored *closer* to the worker node, thereby allowing the scheduler to minimize transfer cost. To make this selection, the scheduler takes into account the network topology connecting the machines participating in the Hadoop cluster. For instance, let us assume that a Hadoop cluster is deployed in a data center connected using the conventional tree-hierarchical model [16]. For a given *map* task, an *input split* stored in the same machine hosting the worker node provides for the maximum data locality possible. This is in contrast to an *input split* stored in a different rack to the one hosting the worker node. In the latter case, the *input split* will have to be transferred through potentially over-subscribed or congested links [16].

2.3 Hive and Pig

A limitation of Map-Reduce paradigm is its limited expressiveness, i.e. only simple queries can be mapped to map and reduce computations. This limitation is resolved by higher level query interfaces on top of Map-Reduce, which allow more complicated tasks to be encoded.

Hive [17] allows the execution of simplified SQL queries on top of Map-Reduce. It transforms raw files from HDFS into tables in a row store according to a user-specified metadata. Each table is stored back to the HDFS in its own directory. The row store uses hash-based partitioning to distribute the data amongst subdirectories. Once data has been structured, SQL-like queries may be executed against it. Hive supports a simplified set of SQL operators that permit multiple operations such as data selection, joins and grouping. A query is compiled into a parse tree, which is later optimized and mapped into a sequence of Map-Reduce jobs.

Pig [10] differs from Hive in that it uses a procedural approach, i.e. it allows queries to be specified as sequences of steps rather than declarative computations. It also provides a richer data model that supports collections such as tuples, bags and maps, and allows nesting of data structures within each other. Data schema may be specified in the query—hence there is no rigid schema associated with the data. Operators support operations such as joining, grouping, filtering, and iterations; and, they may be nested. Like in Hive, the program is parsed and then mapped into a sequence of Map-Reduce jobs.

2.4 Dryad

While Hive and Pig use Map-Reduce as an underlying execution environment, a different approach is taken by Dryad/DryadLINQ [18]. Dryad is a general purpose execution engine for data-parallel applications. The computations are expressed as a dataflow graph, whose vertices are mapped to computers and cores in a distributed environment, and edges describe communication channels. Dryad supports multiple such channels including files, TCP, and shared memory. Its programming language, DryadLINQ [19], supports a broader set of operators than Map-Reduce. Since Dryad is designed with dataflow jobs in mind, it benefits from query optimization and pipelining techniques not present in Map-Reduce.

3 Performance Management

Resource management and scheduling of data intensive jobs have been extensively studied in the Grid (Data-Grid) and HPC [20–24] communities. Large scale data analysis in a cloud environment poses challenges that have not been addressed by the grid community and offers opportunities for better and simpler management that could not be explored before. These challenges and opportunities stem from the different structure of modern data analytic computations, the scale and constraints of the infrastructure where such jobs are executed, and from the changed management objective. In this section, we review the assumptions of large scale data analysis in a cloud environment as a resource management problem and discuss their impact on performance management priorities and approaches. We illustrate these issues using data analytic models presented in Sect. 2.

3.1 Fine-Grained and Embarrassingly Parallel Structure of Data Analytic Computations

Modern data analytic workloads usually involve a very large number of small computations executing in parallel. For example, a typical Map-Reduce job may consist of thousands of *map* and *reduce* tasks, usually a lot more than the number of compute nodes in the system. High levels of computation partitioning and a relatively small size of individual tasks are a design point of these platforms. This is in contrast to grid workloads which can be characterized as consisting of multiple (but still relatively few) long running tasks, possibly executing in parallel.

The structure of a Map-Reduce job is similar to that of a Bag-of-Tasks (BoT) application in HPC and Grid-like environments. That is, a *map phase* consists of a set of independent *map tasks* that can be scheduled independently in space and time. However, tasks belonging to a BoT application operate on data files and therefore they have a more coarse-grained view of resources. This is in contrast to map-reduce jobs where data is striped across all computers in a Map-Reduce cluster, and each individual *map* task operates on one individual *input split* of typically 64 megabytes. This makes Map-Reduce tasks independent of one another.

This embarrassingly parallel structure of modern data analytic computations has several implications on performance management.

3.1.1 Opportunity for Better Scheduling

The highly parallel nature of data analytic jobs combined with the built-in resiliency of the middleware platform that executes them opens the door for new scheduling knobs that could not be taken advantage of before.

First, the scheduler may consider killing and restarting a task in a different location. Killing a task only foregoes the work that the task has done without affecting other running tasks. Since tasks are small, the amount of wasted resource and the impact of overall system throughput are also small. Killing a running task and restarting it elsewhere or at a latter time is helpful if due to high variance among the execution times of tasks, due to large differences in compute node performance, or due to higher priority applications, the allocation of resources needs to be changed.

Second, since tasks run independently they can be scheduled as resources become available. Therefore, the number of machines or resources used by a job can vary over time. Such computation model fits very well with the intrinsic elasticity found in cloud environments.

Finally, multiple instances of an individual task can be executed simultaneously (speculatively) depending on the availability of resources. This allows for adaption to resource heterogeneity and poor reliability conditions as the performance perceived by a task may vary depending on the machine hosting its execution.

While the options of task kill and restart, and speculative scheduling offer potential great benefits from the perspective of speeding up individual jobs, they also have impact on the overall system goodput [25, 26]. The management system that takes advantage of them needs to model and optimize for these competing objectives.

3.1.2 Job Profiling

Understanding the characterization of data analytic workloads is crucial to performance management of jobs. Profiling aims to characterize job execution time and resource usage in various phases. This understanding may later be used by the scheduler to estimate job completion time and to minimize the overlapping of resource usage among tasks executing in parallel on the same physical node.

Profiling data-intensive jobs, however, is a challenging problem due to the fact that the performance signature of a job is generally a function of its input data set. Performance signature refers to the resource usage of the application during its execution and how this usage impacts its performance. More specifically, multiple instances of an application may stress different resources depending on the characteristics of the data being processed and therefore require different allocation of resources. For example, an application that analyses purchasing patterns in an online market place may require more resources to process transactions committed over the weekend versus transactions committed over the week. This may be due to a higher volume of transactions or because their characteristics require the execution of additional data mining algorithms. Furthermore, in a multi-stage data flow the resource usage of one phase highly depends on the data generated by other phases. For example, the disk I/O contention experienced by a *reduce* task during its *reduce shuffling* phase depends on the amount of intermediate data being shuffled and the rate at which this data is being generated and copied.

Another set of complications stems from the multi-stage nature of jobs. A typical data intensive computation goes through phases of reading the data, computing, and writing down the results. This structure is preserved in modern data analytic frameworks. Recall from Sect. 2 that the characterization of a Map-Reduce job can be subdivided into multiple stages [9]: the *map* stage is divided into the *mapping* and the *map shuffling* phase, and the *reduce* stage is divided into three phases of *copying, reduce shuffling*, and *reducing*. All these phases stress different resources at different times. For instance, the *copying* phase stresses the network when a *reduce* task starts, while the *reduce shuffling* phase stresses disk I/O at the completion of *map* tasks when the intermediate data does not fit into the main memory of the *reduce* task.

The embarrassingly parallel nature of modern data analytic tasks offers, however, new possibilities in this area of profiling, which could not be considered before.

First, a subset of a job may be executed in a sandbox environment. The sandbox executions allows the key resource usage and performance characteristics to be measured for a job before its entirety is executed in production. Sandbox measurements may then be used to assess job resource usage and performance in production.

Another approach recognizes that, while a job is in progress, the execution time of future *map* (*reduce*) tasks may be estimated from the execution time of the *map* (or *reduce*) tasks that have already completed [27].

Both these approaches, while promising, are associated with limitations and challenges. The effectiveness of sandbox profiling depends on the distribution of data and computation. In other words, the subset data selected has to be a representative of the overall input data set. The larger the data set used for profiling the higher quality job signature is obtained. On the other hand, the larger the data set, the more resources need to be spent on profiling. Furthermore, the usefulness of a profile developed in a sandbox environment in production depends on the similarity of the sandbox and production environments.

Online profiling has the advantage of not requiring a sandbox, but is only able to estimate the parameters of individual stages (i.e., a *map* stage and a *reduce* stage) while they are in progress, and hence cannot be used to estimate parameters of the entire job.

Another possible opportunity stems from the fact that as each job is sliced into a very large number of small tasks, its individual phases (data input, computation, data output) are divided accordingly. A typical *map* or *reduce* task is very short, and hence the phases it goes through are also very short. Recall that the objective of detailed resource usage profiling to enable co-scheduling of tasks with different resource requirements at any given time. This is clearly an essential strategy when tasks (and their individual phases) are long. In Map-Reduce framework, an entire task execution may fit into a measurement and control interval of a reasonably configured management system. Hence, there may be little benefit for the scheduler from detailed understanding of individual task phases; rather, average resource needs throughout task execution should suffice. The task scheduler is then responsible for selecting the right number and composition of tasks to be executed on a node. Fine grained resource allocation among tasks depending on their phase of execution is the responsibility of OS scheduling.

3.2 Large Scale, Commodity-Hardware Infrastructure

Large-scale commodity-hardware infrastructure has emerged as the most cost-effective way of providing computation as an utility. Furthermore, the adoption of commodity hardware allows for more affordable ways of tracking advances in new technologies, such as multicore processors. As a matter of fact, Cloud computing has embraced this approach in order to fully realize the vision of computation as a commodity.

Simply putting together a large amount of commodity hardware is not sufficient for enabling its use in an effective and efficient manner. The underlying reason behind this observation is that low-end compute resources exhibit important limitations that, if not addressed appropriately, can hinder their adoption. For example, failures are the norms in low-end compute devices such as disk and memory. Developing middleware and applications capable of handling failures gracefully is a key challenge in adopting commodity-based infrastructures. Network devices at affordable prices have bandwidths with a maximum limit of 1 Gbps. As explained later, network bottleneck is one of the main constraints in environments supporting data intensive applications. On a similar note, disk latency of low-end disks can hinder the ability of provisioning for time requirements to users submitting data analytic jobs. Important advances need to be made in the context of resource management in order to effectively use commodity-hardware infrastructures at a large scale, while providing reasonable quality of service to users.

3.2.1 Scheduling and Workload Performance Modeling Must Recognize that Frequent Failure Is the Norm

Managing workload performance in commodity-hardware infrastructure is a major challenge for the realization of data analytic clouds. One of the main reasons behind this is the unreliability of inexpensive hardware, which leads to high failure rates and potential ungraceful performance degradation on behalf of the applications.

Data storage is the central component of large-scale data analytics. The realization of large-scale commodity-hardware storage infrastructure, similar to the one built by Google [28], has shown that hardware replication is more cost effective in handling failures as compared to writing software that will handle those failures gracefully. However, the applicability of this principle to the development of technology for data analytic clouds is questionable, since power bills remain the same even when storage prices keep falling [29]. We argue that more cost-aware replication techniques need to be developed in order to build fault-tolerant infrastructures from commodity hardware.

Significant research work has been done in the context of job scheduling in unreliable distributed systems [30]. In general, these solutions provide job completion guarantees by taking into account resource reliability when assigning resources to jobs. This approach has worked well in computing environments such as Planetlab, wherein delivering best-effort performance is sufficient. However, its suitability is questionable for data analytic clouds wherein resource management decisions are likely to be driven by SLAs. We argue that resource management mechanisms in data analytic clouds will likely incorporate SLAs, application requirements and re-source reliability in a more tightly coupled manner.

Developing solutions to this problem is crucial, considering that the probability of a node failing in a shared-nothing cluster of machines built from unreliable com-modity hardware is increasing rapidly; and the problem is likely to get worse as the scale of these environments grow. Google, for example, has reported 1.2 failures per data analytic job in its current computing platform [9].

3.2.2 Dataflow Resilience Issues

A typical data analytic job consists of a data flow where each compute stage con-sumes intermediate data produced by the previous stage. For instance, as it was explained in Sect. 2, a Map-Reduce job consists of a dataflow with two stages: a *map* and a *reduce* stage. If the intermediate data generated between stages is not persisted, in order to recover from a failure that occurred in the nth compute stage all $n - 1$ previous stages have to be re-executed. Consequently, in the presence of failure the response time experienced by the user can increase significantly.

Recall from Sect. 2 that in Hadoop, intermediate data generated by *map* tasks is persisted to local disk only. Therefore, if a machine fails during the execution of a map-reduce tuple, all the intermediate data stored in the failing node has to be re-generated. In other words, all the *map* tasks executed in the failing node have to be re-executed. Following this observation, the highest recovery cost results from fail-ures occurring after the *map* phase has finished, since all the intermediate data has already been generated. In [31], the authors report up to 50% increase in makespan in the presence of a single failure after the *map* phase has completed. From the per-spective of the Cloud, this may represent violation of the SLA, or reduction of the good-put of the system, or both.

A naive solution to the problem of reliability for dataflows is to replicate inter-mediate data so that, in the presence of failure, a job can resume from a previous checkpoint [31]. This solution, however, may be expensive in terms of storage and network overhead specially since the size of datasets continues growing steadily. We believe that to accommodate for this, data analytic cloud will rely on cost-aware replication mechanisms which take into account the cost for replicating and regen-erating data in the system. So for example, under conditions of limited storage, it may be more reasonable to disable replication for jobs whose cpu requirements are low. We believe that much research opportunities stem from the need to develop cost-aware replication techniques for dataflows.

3.2.3 Scheduling and Resource Allocation Must Increase Data Locality of Tasks to Prevent Network Overload

As data sets grow steadily, one of the key challenges in developing *scalable* data analytic platforms is that of enabling data access to data analytic jobs. Without effective and efficient resource management mechanisms, a typical data analytic job may require transferring large volumes of data across the network. This would result in a degradation of performance as perceived, for example, by the completion time of the jobs and the throughput of the system [25]. We argue that a better integration of data movement with computation is needed for developing data analytic platforms capable of scaling to a large number of users and steadily growing data sets.

This challenge is further exacerbated by the current state of the network technology in data centers. For instance, it has been reported that in traditional data centers bandwidth over-subscriptions with factors higher than 1:5 are not uncommon [16]. This suggests that reduction in network traffic across different levels of a tree-topology should be taken into account when placing data and computation for data intensive jobs. More recently, several solutions have been proposed that seek to eliminate the source of network contention [16]. Although these solutions seem promising, there are still several issues that need to be addressed regarding I/O performance, some examples being memory and disk bandwidth and I/O interconnects [32]. Additionally, we argue that maximizing data locality, i.e., avoiding network-sharing among jobs as much as possible, allows for the development of more manageable systems.

The importance of this performance issue has been recognized by existing middleware for data analytic jobs, e.g., Dryad [25] and Hadoop [11]. Solutions that seek at achieving *full* data locality in conventional Hadoop clusters, i.e., clusters in which all *map* tasks process *input splits* stored locally, requires either impractical replication of *input splits* or sub-optimal system throughput.

Data replication has prevailed in Data-Grids as an effective mechanism to achieve data locality. In such systems, data is replicated and placed across multiple participating sites, so that the scheduler has more flexibility while placing computation close to the data. That is, once the data has been replicated and placed across the system, the problem of achieving data locality can be formulated as a computation placement problem with data transfer, compute, and storage constraints [33]. Following similar arguments to the one discussed earlier, we expect data analytic clouds to rely less on aggressive data replication to comply with the storage and network capacity and power requirements of the system.

Another approach for increasing data locality in Hadoop is to delay the assignment of *map* tasks to worker nodes, in order to increase the likelihood that a local *input* split is available upon start of execution [34]. However, this approach assumes that the placement of data and computation overlap to a great extent, i.e., HDFS and Map-Reduce cluster are hosted in the same set of machines. In data analytic clouds using Hadoop, this may not always hold since the configurations of both Map-Reduce cluster and HDFS cluster are defined independently. The Map-Reduce cluster depends on the number of resources that the user is willing to pay for, while the placement of the data in the HDFS cluster is determined when the data is generated and stored in the cloud (an event that may have occurred in the past).

3.2.4 Leveraging Low Latency Storage Technology

For the last four decades, disk storage has been the primary means of storing data in computer systems. During this period, the capacity of disks has increased more than 1000-fold but disk access rate has grown at much slower pace. In the Hadoop framework, the performance experienced by Map-Reduce jobs are limited by the disk access rate when reading and writing data. This hinders the ability of the Hadoop framework to support data analytic jobs with stringent time requirements.

To address the challenge of high disk latency new storage architectures have been proposed which rely on fast-access storage solutions such as Flash and Random Access Memory (RAM) to achieve the throughput and latency requirements of emerging Internet-scale services. The adoption of such storage scheme has the potential of speeding up data analytic jobs, and also of enabling the support for online and interactive data analytics in the cloud. For example, having storage levels with different read and write access rates allow us to differentiate among data analytic jobs with different time requirements. As a result, data analytic jobs requiring random access to global data objects would benefit from having data objects stored in a distributed RAM-based solution rather than in a distributed disk-based file system [35].

Several challenging research problems stem from the adoption of these developing technologies. For example, the development of efficient placement algorithms, which make cost-effective placement decisions taking into account cost per byte and latency requirements, will be crucial to the success of multi-storage solutions. One important problem in this context is that of promoting (demoting) data to a higher (lower) storage level with a faster (slower) access rate, depending on the requirement of the applications and the state of the system (e.g., utilization of the storage levels). There are many similarities that can be found between these problems and the ones usually found in the context of data caching. Nevertheless, we believe that certain unique aspects of the data analytic workloads, such as their predominant read-only pattern, offer a potential for novel research contributions.

3.3 Management Objective to Provide User-Level Performance Guarantees at Low Cost

Classical batch environments are driven by the need of the scientific community to harness the computing power of clusters of computers, while enabling sharing across institutions. Users interact with the grid by requesting some amount of resources (e.g., physical machines) to run their computation.

In a data analytic cloud, a user pays more for more resource usage. Hence a finer grained SLA definition is needed—a user should be able to select from a range of performance levels available to him for a particular job and pay a different price according to the selected level. The preferred SLA definition would be expressed in terms of the job performance rather than its resource allocation. The level of performance offered by the cloud for a particular price is a factor that users will use to select their provider.

At the same time, the cloud operator is motivated by profit and hence needs to provide access to services at a lowest cost possible. Besides reducing the cost of hardware, which is a factor whose implications were discussed in Sect. 3.2, the cloud operator needs to assure high level of automation in all aspects of management and achieve as high utilization of resources as possible. This implies an environment which is shared among many users.

3.3.1 Defining User-Level SLA and SLA Management Issues

Most existing batch schedulers optimize system throughput. The need to provide higher level guarantees has been recognized by the grid community and research has been done to enable QoS guarantee in batch schedulers [36]. However, these solutions have not been adopted due to their complexity and limited flexibility.

In the cloud environments, throughput is not a sufficient measure of system performance. One possible performance goal for a job execution in the cloud is its completion time. A user submitting a job should be able to choose from a range of possible completion times and pay accordingly to the chosen value. To support SLA definitions, the cloud management system would need a fairly accurate estimate of job resource needs and execution times. As we have considered in Sect. 3.1.2 such accurate job profiles may be very difficult to obtain making completion-time based goals infeasible in practice.

What SLA definitions are reasonable to support by the cloud is an open question. Goals defining the desired job progress rate or resource allocation are possible candidates, which do not require detailed profiles.

Clearly, supporting user-level performance goals will necessitate the development of appropriate performance models and resource allocation strategies.

3.3.2 Fine Grained Resource Sharing

In the world where cloud revenue is tightly coupled with the amount of workload processed by the cloud platform, even a small improvement to system throughput may be significant from the business perspective. The development of fine-grained level resource management techniques is crucial to enable efficient sharing of resources across multiple tasks, jobs, and users in a data analytic cloud.

In a grid environment, the scheduler operates on resources at a very coarse level; that is, it allocates resources, e.g., processors, for the *exclusive* use of the job for a given time window. This necessarily leads to resource waste as it is very difficult to find a schedule of jobs that utilizes all resources to capacity.

Resource virtualization is one technology that has proven successful at providing shared access to resources in a broad range of computing environments. Virtual machines usually provide dynamic means to isolate CPU and memory resources among multiple workloads. However, their effectiveness in environments supporting I/O intensive workloads has been challenged due to the high overhead and poor isolation of I/O operations [37]. Besides, virtual machines come with substantial overhead in terms of CPU and memory, which reduce the cost-effectiveness of the cloud. Hence, techniques that provide fine grained resource management within an OS instance need to be investigated in order to support data analytics in virtual environments.

Resource sharing and fine grained resource allocation have been broadly studied in the context of web workloads, and techniques such as load balancing, flow control [38], and dynamic application placement have been developed [39–41]. Typically they focus on managing one resource that is deemed a bottleneck of a particular system, such as network, for static web content [42], or CPU for application server workloads [38]. For data analytic jobs, it is not possible to define a bottleneck resource a priori. As explained in Sect. 2, a typical *map* task in a Hadoop framework proceeds through stages of reading split data from disk, computation, writing intermediate data to local disk, and sending intermediate data over the network. Depending on the job type or even data processed by individual tasks, the bottleneck resource may be either a disk, a CPU, or the network.

One property of data analytic computations that helps with fine grained resource management is their degree of parallelism. It is easier to pack lots of small computations on a set of resources than a small number of large ones – fine granularity scheduling makes it possible to accommodate tasks with unusually long execution times. It is possible to change job resource allocation almost any time during its execution and fine grained resource management mechanisms at OS level may be used to optimize utilization of all resources.

4 Modeling and Optimization

In order to address the afore-mentioned performance management issues, one usually resorts to analytical models which are solved to find optimal operating points. Traditionally, the field of computer modeling and analysis employs, for the most part, queueing models to evaluate the performance of computer systems and networks [43]. In fact, long before computers, queueing models had been developed in the field of operations research to model resource contention, be they tellers in a bank or machines in a manufacturing production line. The issue then was assessing the delay experienced by customers lining up in order to receive service from a server. The problems of interest varied from scheduling disciplines, server sizing, server utilization, to probabilistic queueing characteristics. Single station queues as well as tandem queues, and more advanced networks of queues were analyzed, in many cases through making simplifying assumptions about the arrival process of customers and the service process of the servers. With the introduction of computers with batch operating systems, time sharing systems, and computer networks, it was natural to use the already developed field of queueing modeling and analysis in order to study the performance of computers and networks. The analogy is striking. Batch jobs, user requests, database queries, and packets correspond to customers.

CPU, disks, and communications links correspond to servers. The focus is on resource utilization and delay characteristics. Now, given the topic at hand, namely the data analytics cloud, would queueing models continue to be useful in assessing performance in this new environment or is there a need for an alternative (or complementary) modeling methodology? To answer this question we need to consider the items of concern in the data analytics cloud and the performance questions and problems that need be answered and solved, respectively.

As we discussed before, there are mainly two items of concern in the data analytics paradigm: data and computation. Data is vast, spread out, dynamic, and managed by many entities. Computation varies in complexity from simple to mathematically involved. A computation may have several stages, forming a mesh of composite generic computations, and may be generating more data in the process. The traditional paradigm of making all data available before starting the computation, then storing resulting data is no longer valid. Rather, data may be streamed, computation units may work in parallel, buffering resulting data and triggering further computation units. In general, data and computation do not initially coexist in the same location. This arrangement resembles data that is flowing through computation nodes, being transformed and transported to subsequent nodes, until some final results are obtained. It is worth mentioning that this process may be continual, always working with newly available data. In any event, the focus seems to be on the data flow. Thus, typical questions are: Will a computation starve due to lack of available data to process? Will the local storage area be overwhelmed with data? When and how much data should be transported from one node to another? How long should data be kept in case a computation has to be redone due to a failure? Other questions are concerned with total execution time of a data analytics job and its prediction, the sequencing of stages within a job, and the multitude of workers executing tasks within a job.

Given this new data analytics paradigm and cloud environment, one finds a promising modeling area, again rooted in operation research, namely inventory modeling, and more generally supply chain modeling. First, we review inventory modeling in Sect. 4.1 and discuss the analogy with data analytics modeling in Sect. 4.2. Then, we consider the Map-Reduce paradigm as an example in Sect. 4.3.

4.1 Inventory Modeling

Inventory control is focused around the item. The main question there is: when and how many items to order? Obviously inventory modeling and analysis is a vast area and has been around for a long time, see for example [44]. Here, we provide a brief, high level summary of the relevant aspects. In particular, we are interested in production, multi-echelon, multi-indenture inventory systems [45, 46]. An inventory is a storage area for items. There are different types of items, each is characterized by storage requirements, demand characteristics, potential lifetime, and relevant costs.

In a multi-echelon inventory system, inventories are connected through a transportation network in a hierarchical fashion, and more generally as a mesh. In a multi-indenture inventory system, items form a hierarchy in such a way that as one moves down from a higher level to a lower level in the hierarchy, one finds items corresponding to systems, subsystems, and unit components. A production-inventory is characterized by exogenous arrivals of items, such as parts and raw materials, then as items move from one inventory to another they go through processing stages, altering their types, until a final product is stored in inventory locations where there is an exogenous demand for them. There are costs associated with purchasing, transporting, keeping, and processing items. There are capacities for various inventories, processing stages, and transportation channels. There are a lot of uncertainties surrounding demand, transportation, prices, and production. The problem is that given the various costs, capacities, and uncertainties, how to optimally control this complex inventory system. There has been a wealth of analytical work addressing such issues, building on linear and non linear optimization techniques, stochastic control techniques, game theory, risk analysis, and forecasting [47].

Particular to our discussion, multi-stage and more generally multi-echelon, pure-inventory and production-inventory problems have been considered extensively. One of the early work on finding the optimal inventory levels in a multi-echelon inventory system is [48], where a simplified computation of the optimal policy is provided. Queueing theoretic approaches have also been employed to model and analyze the inventory system, then a constrained optimization problem, which could be linear, nonlinear, integer or mixed, is solved, see for example [49]. Game theoretic approaches have also been used in order to model and contrast competitive and cooperative policies, while proving properties of Nash equilibria [50]. Typically, information about orders are known at different locations in the inventory network, though it has been established that sharing inventory status information leads to more efficient overall system operation [51].

4.2 Modeling Data Analytics

One of the pioneering work in using inventory modeling in distributed computer systems, addressing the problem of data pre-fetching from a file system, is [52]. Given a set of concurrent processes accessing streams of data from the file system with different rates, the problem is to find an optimal data pre-fetching mechanism across multiple levels in the data access path. The analogy to an inventory system is drawn whereby data corresponds to items, buffer space to inventories, data requests to item demand, data access time corresponds to lead time for the delay incurred when ordering items, and batched pre-fetching corresponds to the size of the order. The multi-level storage pre-fetching gives rise to a multi-echelon inventory system consisting, say, of a hierarchy of retailer storage, distribution centers, and warehouses. The authors demonstrate experimentally that solutions from inventory theory, when applied to this data pre-fetching problem, the overall performance of the system is improved.

Another example of stream data processing in a large-scale distributed system, though not explicitly linked to inventory control, is considered in [53]. The scenario is closely related to a realistic scenario in cloud data analytics in that the size of data is very large such that one cannot store all the data required by a computation in the node where the computation resides. Instead, data is streamed and intermediate data, that is generated by various computation entities in a composition of computations, is also streamed to subsequent stages of computation. In deciding on whether a stored data object should be replaced or kept, a retention value function is defined. Using such retention values, and given the pattern of data usage, a network-flow optimization problem is formulated and solved using known techniques. An extension to this optimization problem is considered where load balancing is also accomplished. Though not explicitly stated, the system could be modeled as a multi-stage production-inventory system, where data corresponds to items and buffers to inventories, computation corresponds to production, intermediate data corresponds to intermediate parts, results correspond to final products which are subjected to a demand corresponding to interactive requests launching such a collection of computations.

4.3 Modeling Map-Reduce Workflows

As discussed in Sect. 2, an example of data analytics is the Map-Reduce paradigm. There, important performance management issues are: the allocation of resources to multiple Map-Reduce jobs during the *map* and *reduce* phases of the computation and the decision on storage location (in the cloud) of results of tasks executing the various phases. See for example [54], where a job is defined as a pair of Map and Reduce phases, and a workflow as a series of stages of jobs. Several policies for resource allocation are presented and contrasted. Let us consider the particular problem of data storage between two sequential stages. In other words, the output of multiple *reduce* tasks of the job in the first stage is to be consumed, as input to multiple *map* tasks of the job in the second stage. As the output of each of the *reduce* tasks is generated and written to the distributed file system, it is most likely stored locally where the respective *reduce* task is located. One needs to decide on the optimal locations of the subsequent *map* tasks, since this will determine the data transfer operations that will have to be performed. These data transfer operations have a cost related to the amount of data to be transferred, the communication overhead, and the location of both the source (*reduce* task location) and destination (*map* task location), constrained by the storage capacities of the various locations. The complexity of the problem increases as one considers all the stages that make up a Map-Reduce workflow and the simultaneous execution of multiple Map-Reduce workflows.

A multi-stage production-inventory model of the multi-stage Map-Reduce problem is apparent. Exogenous items that are initially placed in some inventory locations correspond to the base data available to the first Map-Reduce stage. The sequence of production stages correspond to the stages of the Map-Reduce work-flow. Each production stage processes multiple items which may come from several inventories, in the same way that a Reduce task, say, would process data produced by multiple Map tasks in the same job. The number of items that are stored in an inventory location depends on the storage capacity of the particular inventory and the types and characteristics of the items. Demand corresponds to downstream production stages, and ultimately the demand for the final product, in the same way that the data request rate and its pattern of access depend on the Map and Reduce tasks and the desired location of the final output result of the Map-Reduce workflow. The various costs in this inventory system corresponds to delays, overheads, and utilities in the Map-Reduce system.

The authors are not aware of work in the literature which models Map-Reduce workflows, nor more general data analytics examples, as inventory systems. Further, the authors believe that many of the analytical modeling results, or extensions thereof, that have been obtained for inventory systems could be potentially applied in the management of data analytics clouds.

5 Conclusion

The availability of large amounts of data, combined with recently developed easy-to-use, large-scale computation and storage technologies, and the realization of the cloud computing environment led to the birth of the data analytic cloud. This new environment comes with several challenges in its performance management. Firstly, we presented a detailed overview of the landscape of this new environment, considering the cloud as well as the technologies associated with analyzing large amounts of data. In particular, we focused on the Map-Reduce paradigm as an illustrative example of data analytics. Secondly, we described a few of the most important issues related to the performance management of this new data analytic cloud environment. Then, we considered a particular performance management issue, namely data placement, and presented a particular approach for its modeling and analysis. This approach builds on the extensive work in the area of multistage production-inventory modeling.

As the data analytic cloud is still in its infancy, one needs to keep a close track of its evolution and development. New technologies in virtualization, storage, communication, computation models are constantly emerging. As a consequence, performance management issues and challenges may shift. Though, analytical models may prove robust as small changes take place, perhaps affecting model parameters and optimization constraints. The particular modeling approach proposed in this paper, though promising, calls for extensive investigation to prove or disprove its viability.

References

[1] Definition of Data Analytics, http://en.wikipedia.org/wiki/
[2] Perez-Iratxeta, C., Bork, P., Andrade, M.: Association of genes to genetically inherited diseases using data mining. Nat. Genet. **31**(3), 316–319 (2002)

[3] Davenport, T.H., Harris, J.G.: Competing on Analytics: The New Science of Winning. Harvard Business School Press, Boston (2007)
[4] IDC: The diverse and exploding digital universe. Technical report, IDC (2008). An Updated Forecast of Worldwide Information Growth Through 2011
[5] NASA Nebula, http://nebula.nasa.gov/
[6] IBM: ManyEyes, http://manyeyes.alphaworks.ibm.com/manyeyes/
[7] Swivel, http://www.swivel.com/
[8] Infochimps, http://infochimps.org
[9] Dean, J., Ghemawat, S.: MapReduce: simplified data processing on large clusters. In: Sixth Symposium on Operating System Design and Implementation (OSDI'04), San Francisco, CA, US, pp. 1–10 (2004)
[10] Olston, C., Benjamin, R., Srivastava, U., Kumar, R., Tomkins, A.: Pig Latin: a not-so-foreign language for data processing. In: Proceedings of the ACM SIGMOD International Conference, Auckland, New Zealand, June 2008
[11] Apache, Apache Hadoop, http://hadoop.apache.org/
[12] Fushimi, S., Kitsuregawa, M., Tanaka, H.: An overview of the system software of a parallel relational database machine. In: Proceedings of the 12th International Conference on Very Large Databases, pp. 209–219, Kyoto, Japan, August 1986
[13] Abadi, D.J.: Column-stores for wide and sparse data. In: Conference on Innovative Data Systems Research (2007)
[14] Abouzeid, A., Bajda-Pawlikowski, K., Abadi, D., Silberschatz, A., Rasin, A.: Hadoopdb: an architectural hybrid of mapreduce and DBMS technologies for analytical workloads. In: Proceedings of the International Conference on Very Large Data Bases, vol. 2, no. 1, pp. 922–933. VLDB Endowment (2009)
[15] Stonebraker, M., Abadi, D., Dewitt, D.J., Madden, S., Paulson, E., Pavlo, A., Rasin, A.: MapReduce and parallel DBMSs: Friends or foes? Commun. ACM **53**(1), 64–71 (2010)
[16] Greenberg, A., Hamilton, J.R., Jain, N., Kandula, S., Kim, C., Lahiri, P., Maltz, D.A., Patel, P., Sengupta, S.: Vl2: a scalable and flexible data center network. In: SIGCOMM '09: Proceedings of the ACM SIGCOMM 2009 Conference on Data Communication, pp. 51–62. ACM, New York (2009)
[17] Apache, Hive, http://wiki.apache.org/hadoop/Hive
[18] Isard, M., Budiu, M., Yu, Y., Birrell, A., Fetterly, D.: Dryad: distributed data-parallel programs from sequential building blocks. In: ACM European Conference on Computer Systems (Eurosys), pp. 198–207, March 2007
[19] Isard, M., Yu, Y.: Distributed data-parallel computing using a high-level programming language. In: SIGMOD, Providence, RA, July 2009
[20] Ranganathan, K., Foster, I.: Decoupling computation and data scheduling in distributed data-intensive applications. In: HPDC '02: Proceedings of the 11th IEEE International Symposium on High Performance Distributed Computing, p. 352. IEEE Computer Society, Washington (2002)
[21] Kosar, T., Livny, M.: Stork: making data placement a first class citizen in the grid. In: ICDCS '04: Proceedings of the 24th International Conference on Distributed Computing Systems (ICDCS'04), pp. 342–349. IEEE Computer Society, Washington (2004)
[22] Romosan, A., Rotem, D., Shoshani, A., Wright, D.: Co-scheduling of computation and data on computer clusters. In: SSDBM'2005: Proceedings of the 17th International Conference on Scientific and Statistical Database Management, pp. 103–112. Lawrence Berkeley Laboratory, Berkeley (2005)
[23] Mohamed, H.H., Epema, D.H.J.: An evaluation of the close-to-files processor and data co-allocation policy in multiclusters. In: CLUSTER '04: Proceedings of the 2004 IEEE International Conference on Cluster Computing, pp. 287–298. IEEE Computer Society, Washington (2004)
[24] Zhang, Z., Wang, C., Vazhkudai, S.S., Ma, X., Pike, G.G., Cobb, J.W., Mueller, F.: Optimizing center performance through coordinated data staging, scheduling and recovery. In: SC '07: Proceedings of the 2007 ACM/IEEE Conference on Supercomputing, pp. 1–11. ACM, New York (2007)

[25] Isard, M., Prabhakaran, V., Currey, J., Wieder, U., Talwar, K., Goldberg, A.: Quincy: fair scheduling for distributed computing clusters. In: SOSP '09: Proceedings of the ACM SIGOPS 22nd Symposium on Operating Systems Principles, pp. 261–276. ACM, New York (2009)

[26] Zaharia, M., Konwinksi, A., Joseph, A.D., Katz, R., Stoica, I.: Improving mapreduce performance in heterogeneous environments. In: USENIX Symposium on Operating Systems Design and Implementation, pp. 1–14, USENIX (2008)

[27] Polo, J., Carrera, D., Becerra, Y., Torres, J., Ayguade, E., Steinder, M., Whalley, I.: Performance-drive task co-scheduling for mapreduce environments. In: IEEE/IFIP Network Operations and Management Symposium (NOMS), Osaka, Japan, April 2010

[28] Ghemawat, S., Gobioff, H., Leung, S.-T.: The google file system. SIGOPS Oper. Syst. Rev. **37**(5), 29–43 (2003)

[29] Jacobs, A.: The pathologies of big data. Queue **7**(6), 10–19 (2009)

[30] Sonnek, J., Chandra, A., Weissman, J.: Adaptive reputation-based scheduling on unreliable distributed infrastructures. IEEE Trans. Parallel Distrib. Syst. **18**(11), 1551–1564 (2007)

[31] Ko, S.Y., Hoque, I., Cho, B., Gupta, I.: On avaialability of intermediate data in cloud ccomputations. In: 12th Workshop on Hop Topics in Operating Systems (Usenix'09), pp. 1–10, San Diego, CA, US, June 2009

[32] Dean, J.: 2009 Large-scale distributed systems at google: Current systems and future directions. Keynote at ACM SIGOPS International Workshop on Large Scale Distributed Systems and Middleware (LADIS). http://www.cs.cornell.edu/projects/ladis2009/program.htm#keynote3

[33] Dasgupta, G., Dasgupta, K., Viswanathan, B.: Data-WISE: efficient management of data-intensive workflows in scheduled grid environments. In: IEEE/IFIP Network Operations and Management Symposium, April 2008

[34] Zaharia, M., Borthakur, D., Sen Sarma, J., Elmeleegy, K., Shenker, S., Stoica, I.: Job scheduling for multi-user mapreduce clusters. Technical Report UCB/EECS-2009-55, EECS Department, University of California, Berkeley (2009). http://www.eecs.berkeley.edu/Pubs/TechRpts/2009/EECS-2009-55.html

[35] Lin, J., Bahety, A., Konda, S., Mahindrakar, S.: Low latency, high-throughput access to static global resources within the Hadoop framework. Technical Report HCIL-2009-01, College of Information Studies and Department of Computer Science, University of Maryland, June 2009. http://hcil.cs.umd.edu/trs/2009-01/2009-01.pdf

[36] Castillo, C., Rouskas, G.N., Harfoush, K.: Efficient resource management using advance reservations for heterogeneous grids. In: Proceedings of the IEEE International Parallel and Distributed Processing Symposium (IPDPS), Miami, Florida, April 2008

[37] Wang, G., Ng, T.S.E.: The impact of virtualization on network performance of amazon EC2 data center. In: IEEE Conference on Computer Communications (INFOCOM), pp. 1–9, March 2010

[38] Pacifici, G., Spreitzer, M., Tantawi, A., Youssef, A.: Performance management for cluster-based web services. IEEE J. Sel. Areas Commun. **23**(12) (2005)

[39] Ardagna, D., Trubian, M., Zhang, L.: SLA based profit optimization in multi-tier web application systems. In: Int'l Conf. Service Oriented Computing, New York, NY, pp. 173–182 (2004)

[40] Tang, C., Steinder, M., Spreitzer, M., Pacifici, G.: A scalable application placement controller for enterprise data centers. In: WWW Conference, Banff, Alberta, Canada (2007)

[41] Urgaonkar, B., Shenoy, P., Roscoe, T.: Resource overbooking and application profiling in shared hosting platforms. In: Proc. Fifth Symposium on Operating Systems Design and Implementation, Boston, MA, Dec. 2002

[42] Abdelzaher, T.F., Bhatti, N.: Web content adaptation to improve server overload behavior. In: WWW '99: Proceedings of the Eighth International Conference on World Wide Web, pp. 1563–1577. Elsevier/North-Holland, New York (1999)

[43] Squillante, M.: Stochastic analysis of multiserver autonomic systems. Autonomic Systems, this issue (2011)

[44] Zipkin, P.H.: Foundations of Inventory Management. McGraw-Hill, New York (2000)

[45] Hax, A.C., Candea, D.: Production and Inventory Management. Prentice-Hall, Englewood Cliffs (1984)

[46] Sherbrooke, C.C.: Optimal Inventory Modeling of Systems: Multi-echelon Techniques. Kluwer, Norwell (2004)

[47] Simchi-Levi, D., Wu, S.D., Shen, Z.-J.M.: Handbook of Quantitative Supply Chain Analysis: Modeling in the E-business Era. Kluwer, Norwell (2004)

[48] Clark, A.J., Scarf, H.: Optimal policies for a multi-echelon inventory problem. Manag. Sci. **6**(4), 474–490 (1960)

[49] Liu, L., Liu, X., Yao, D.D.: Analysis and optimization of a multistage inventory-queue system. Manag. Sci. **50**(3), 365–380 (2004)

[50] Cachon, G.P., Zipkin, P.H.: Competitive and cooperative inventory policies in a two-stage supply chain. Manag. Sci. **45**(7), 936–953 (1999)

[51] Cachon, G.P., Fisher, M.: Supply chain inventory management and the value of shared information. Manag. Sci. **46**(8), 1032–1048 (2000)

[52] Zhang, Z., Kulkarni, A., Ma, X., Zhou, Y.: Memory resource allocation for file system prefetching: from a supply chain management perspective. In: Proceedings of the 4th ACM European Conference on Computer Systems, pp. 75–88. ACM, New York (2009)

[53] Hildrum, K., Douglis, F., Wolf, J.L., Yu, P.S., Fleischer, L., Katta, A.: Storage optimization for large-scale distributed stream-processing systems. IEEE Trans. Storage **3**(4), 1–28 (2008)

[54] Sandholm, T., Lai, K.: Mapreduce optimization using regulated dynamic prioritization. In: SIGMETRICS '09: Proceedings of the Eleventh International Joint Conference on Measurement and Modeling of Computer Systems, pp. 299–310. ACM, New York (2009)

C. Castillo (✉)
IBM T.J. Watson Research Center, P.O. Box 704, Yorktown Heights, NY 10598, USA
e-mail: claris@us.ibm.com

A. Tantawi
IBM T.J. Watson Research Center, P.O. Box 704, Yorktown Heights, NY 10598, USA
e-mail: tantawi@us.ibm.com

M. Steinder
IBM T.J. Watson Research Center, P.O. Box 704, Yorktown Heights, NY 10598, USA
e-mail: steinder@us.ibm.com

G. Pacifici
IBM T.J. Watson Research Center, P.O. Box 704, Yorktown Heights, NY 10598, USA
e-mail: giovanni@us.ibm.com